U.S. Policy Toward South Asia

U.S. Policy Toward South Asia

Shivaji Ganguly

Westview Press
BOULDER, SAN FRANCISCO, & OXFORD

Westview Special Studies on South and Southeast Asia

This Westview softcover edition is printed on acid-free paper and bound in library-quality, coated covers that carry the highest rating of the National Association of State Textbook Administrators, in consultation with the Association of American Publishers and the Book Manufacturers' Institute.

Published in 1990 in the United States of America by Westview Press, Inc., 5500 Central Avenue, Boulder, Colorado 80301, and in the United Kingdom by Westview Press, Inc., 36 Lonsdale Road, Summertown, Oxford OX2 7EW

Library of Congress Cataloging-in-Publication Data
Ganguly, Shivaji.
  U.S. policy toward South Asia / Shivaji Ganguly.
    p. cm.—(Westview special studies on South and
Southeast Asia)
  ISBN 0-8133-7960-1
  1. South Asia—Foreign relations—United States. 2. United
States—Foreign relations—South Asia. 3. United States—Foreign
relations—1945–   . I. Title. II. Series.
DS341.3.U6G36 1990
327.73054—dc20   90-30277
                                                                  CIP

Printed and bound in the United States of America

The paper used in this publication meets the requirements
of the American National Standard for Permanence of Paper
for Printed Library Materials Z39.48-1984.

10   9   8   7   6   5   4   3   2   1

Contents

Foreword

The nations of South Asia contain a fifth of the human race. They include one state (India) that is certainly the world's largest democracy and one other (Pakistan) that has been an intermittent ally of the U.S. since 1953. For over thirty-five years Washington's policy has shifted uneasily from benign (some would call it malign) neglect of this region to intense involvement in its economic, political, and military affairs. Further, the U.S. has often been torn between India and Pakistan, seeing in the former certain ideological and moral values and in the latter certain strategic and military advantages. The situation seems to be permanent: we are not much closer in 1988 to a resolution of these ambiguities than we were in the early 50s, when the U.S. first became deeply engaged in the region.

This book, by a leading Indian scholar, fills an important gap in our understanding of the reasons for America's sporadic—yet fateful—involvement in and policy toward South Asia. Dr. Ganguly has asked not only what American policy has been and why certain policies have been followed, but how those policies came to be chosen and implemented. He conclusively demonstrates that the process of policymaking is significant in its own right when it approaches a distant region that has not been crucial to vital American interests. Dr. Ganguly raises important new questions about the American policymaking process and complements—and in some cases supplants—the existing literature on the subject. In doing so, he has contributed a work that will be of immense value both to scholars interested in how policy is made and to policymakers themselves. Most of the latter are ahistorical, their collective institutional memories stretch back no further than their own recent careers. Dr. Ganguly shows us decisively that the contradictions so evident in recent American policy toward South Asia—grappling with the threat of external powers to the region while trying to balance strategic interests in India and Pakistan and still pursuing policies concerning regional economic and political development, non-proliferation, and human rights—flow not only from the complexity of the task but from the process by which these policies are made.

Stephen P. Cohen
University of Illinois at Urbana

Preface

The literature on U.S. foreign policy is dominated by relations with the Soviet Union and Western Europe. American relations with Africa, Southeast Asia, Latin America, and South Asia are relatively neglected and episodic in nature (e.g., studies of traumatic events such as the Korean and Vietnamese wars). This absence of interest is especially marked in the case of South Asia. Yet American decisions have profoundly affected the lives of most South Asians, the societies of regional states, and their external policies. It has often been noted that this influence relationship is disproportionately one-sided: American decisions affect South Asians far more than South Asian decisions can ever affect Americans.

The purpose of this study is to systematically examine the sources and patterns of American responses toward events in South Asia over a period of time, through an examination of four major regional events: three wars and a non-conflict crisis-situation. In doing this we hope to make a contribution not only to what is substantively known about U.S. policy toward South Asia but to the broader literature on foreign policy formation.

This study is thus not a narrative of events but a comparative analysis of the foreign policy of a major global power. Our four case studies involved three different American administrations and include: (1) the Sino-Indian War of 1962 (Kennedy), (2) the food crisis in India of 1965-67 (Johnson), (3) the Indo-Pakistan War of 1965 (Johnson), and (4) the Indo-Pakistan War of 1971 (Nixon). Of these four case studies, only the second is non-conflictual in character.

These case studies constitute the heart of this book, although they will be preceded by a discussion of the conceptual problems surrounding foreign policy analysis (Chapter 1) and a brief survey of America's involvement in South Asia (Chapter 2). They follow a standard format. Each begins with an overview of the issue area. They then describe the U.S. approach to the situation, delineate U.S. patterns of response in terms of levels of involvement, examine the systemic and institutional variables in the policy process, and try to explicate the role conception of those involved in making the decision. A concluding chapter summarizes recent developments in the Carter and Reagan administrations and integrates our findings.

In examining the U.S. response to these issue areas this study assumes that a true understanding of the foreign policy process requires a dual approach: we focus on both the decisional setting and the features of the relevant issue areas that generated a particular American response.

The task of this study is thus both explanatory and exploratory. It tries to combine an examination of individual decisions and actions (or the analysis of a particular situation and event) with that of certain explanatory concepts derived from the relevant literature on foreign policy decisionmaking. Our analysis also proceeds on two different but interrelated levels—the U.S. foreign policy process and the structure of the U.S.-South Asian interaction continuum. Generally, we first seek to locate the sources of a specific policy decision and follow with an analysis of its significance with reference to the U.S. South Asian policy process.

Asking the right kinds of questions is basic to all scholarly inquiry, but questions without an analytical framework seldom suggest themselves. In analyzing U.S. policy and process in response to the four select issue areas, we have used in this study a simplified analytical framework; our concern will be with both the rationale behind each decision and the environment within which each foreign policy action took place. By examining the rationale and organizing our analysis around a particular decision, we have made an attempt to assess the significance of the relevant environment in the U.S. foreign policy process.

Several operational steps were involved in the preparation of each case study in this book. First, we identified the decisionmakers and the decisionmaking sequence (initial conditions, decision, and post-decisional actions). Second, we delineated the pertinent elements of the operational environment. Third, we analyzed the various relevant policy documents, public speeches and policy statements, written evidence, joint communiques, and U.N. documents. Fourth, we made use of certain quantitative data (such as volume of aid, trade, and arms sales). Finally, we tried to identify the effect of political pressure as evidenced by a sudden reversal in an existing pattern of relationships, after the application of a visible unilateral action (stoppage of economic and/or arms aid, or a verbal warning regarding the consequences of unacceptable behavior).

Much of this book is based upon interviews with participants in these events. I have also drawn upon published scholarly works, memoirs of ex-diplomats and Presidents, published works of important persons in public life, newspapers and periodicals, and official publications. Special attention has been given to recently opened archival material.

This project was essentially completed while I was the recipient of a Ford Foundation post-doctoral fellowship administered by the Program in Arms Control, Disarmament, and International Security (ACDIS) at the University of Illinois. I have benefitted from my association with many professional friends in India and the United States. I owe special thanks to Professor Stephen P. Cohen of the Department of Political Science at Illinois, who is one of the founders of ACDIS. I greatly valued the many group discussions organized by ACDIS and the stimulating intellectual company of Professor Edward Kolodziej and the late Professor Arthur Chilton (former ACDIS co-directors). ACDIS also provided me with timely secretarial assistance and funds to travel to Washington, D.C., for interviews. I also owe thanks to the Indian Council of World Affairs, New Delhi, for having granted me eleven months extraordinary leave so that I might complete this volume. I also owe a debt to Kanti Bajpai of M.S. University of Baroda, Amit Gupta of the University of Illinois, and Kavita Khory of Mount Holyoke College for their considerate assistance in the preparation of the final manuscript, and to Mary Anderson and Judy Jones of ACDIS for their administrative and editorial acumen.

This study could not have been undertaken or completed without the encouragement and understanding of my wife, Swati. My task was always enlivened by the delightful company of my daughter, Mila. Finally, it is to the memory of my father, Mr. Priyanath Ganguly, that this book is dedicated.

Shivaji Ganguly
Urbana and New Delhi

1

U.S. Foreign Policy:
An Analytical Perspective

International relations as a field does not lend itself to any great degree of precision. It is not only beset by contending theoretical perspectives but there are the obvious difficulties in getting access to technical data (e.g., on a particular weapons system or arms transfer) or to information on the short run plans of different countries.[1] Even more important, both practitioners and analysts are susceptible to misperceptions and distorted judgments of reality.[2]

These cautions apply whether one is studying one or another general aspect of international politics or the foreign policy of a particular country. Yet, there are ways to meet the challenge of achieving a systematic understanding of the apparently chaotic arena of politics. The task not only calls for the investigation of some (and not all) aspects of the changing reality of international "situations," or the collection, collation, and organization of relevant data through the filtering process of checking and consulting with different sources; it is also necessary to pose pertinent analytical questions within a meaningful frame of reference.[3] In this way we can identify patterns in the foreign policy process of a given country, patterns based upon a careful interpretation of relevant historical, political, socio-economic, organizational and behavioral data.

The literature that has grown up around the subject of American foreign policy since World War II has been mixed, both in terms of its adherence to systematic analytical criteria and its subject matter. Most of it has dwelt on America's role as a global power, with particular reference to relations with the Soviet Union, Europe, East Asia and the Middle East. By contrast, systematic studies on U.S. policy towards the states of Africa, South Asia and Latin America have been few and far between.

South Asian Policy: The Literature

The important studies of America's South Asian policy fall into four different (if overlapping) groups. The first consist of studies which are general in scope.[4] The second group deals with a particular facet of U.S. policy, often emphasizing the impact of military alliances or the strategic implications of the interplay between the great powers and the South Asian subsystem.[5] Although these studies are immensely useful they barely touch upon the different elements of the policy process.[6] This is understandable given the rigidity of the nation-as-actor approach of such studies.

The third group of studies relates specifically to economic assistance as a part of constructive U.S. efforts to sustain the ongoing developmental process in South Asia.[7] Of these, Wolf is the most theoretically oriented and goes at length into the wider ramifications of the problem of U.S. aid—which includes military assistance.

In marked contrast, a fourth group of studies analyzes U.S. policy toward South Asia from the standpoint of specific policies and the process that created them. This is a recent research trend.[8]

Notwithstanding the existence of these studies, there have been few integrated analyses which systematically relate the process of U.S. decision-making with the resultant pattern of South Asia policy. Of the few such efforts, the Rudolph's collection, *The Coordination of Complexity in South Asia* is worth noting.[9] Written for the Commission on the Organization of the Government for the Conduct of Foreign Policy (the "Murphy Commission") its basic purpose was to offer policy recommendations. It tries to combine theoretical analysis with detailed case studies of particular events and policy-settings.

Despite references to the wider context of the formulation and implementation of America's South Asia policy, the Rudolphs and associates covered little new ground, primarily focussing attention on the problems of policy management with a view to producing remedial organizational measures.

To summarize, most of the work in this area is either too general in scope or too narrowly focused to permit a systematic understanding of the sources and patterns of the U.S. approach to a regional system such as South Asia. Although many of the above studies are extremely perceptive and are basic to an understanding of a major power's relations with a distant geographical region, they do not give sufficient attention to the possibility of studying decision-making and its consequences within a systematic frame of reference. Our purpose is to do so.

Foreign Policy as Orientation and Adaptation

The primary purpose of this book is to examine the salient features of the foreign policy process from the stage of initiation to the point of action. Specifically, we shall explain the sources and pattern of orientation of U.S. foreign policy toward South Asia. By orientation we mean the external behavior of a country in terms of its level of involvement regarding various issue areas pertaining to the relevant external environment.[10] We shall also relate orientation to the modes of response and the specific approach involved in a particular policy decision.

Foreign policy orientations are never the function of a one-shot policy decision. Instead, orientations emerge through a "series of cumulative decisions" made over a period of time in order to adjust perceived goals, interests and values to the reality of the internal and external settings.[11] Orientation in this sense may be conceived as recurrent trends in the external behavior of a particular state.

Recurrent trends need not imply a single predominant tendency in the policy orientation of a state in regard to various issue areas. Though it is usual to identify orientation in terms of a single dimension (for instance, high or low level of involvement, passive non-interference or active intervention), viewed in a wider perspective the foreign policy of a country may exhibit all of these contradictory tendencies. In fact, foreign policy orientation is often the "mix" of several overlapping tendencies: non-interference, close cooperation, intervention and disengagement.[12]

Any improvement in our understanding of a country's foreign policies is dependent on our ability to state meaningful generalizations about its responses in different issue areas.[13] But even this will not permit us to conceptualize U.S. policy orientations in terms of basic functions. The task calls for an identification of the central functions of the structures underlying policy.

In identifying such central functions, we shall make U.S. foreign policy actions—related to select issue areas—as our unit of analysis. This approach is based on the assumption that all foreign policy activities of a nation are purposeful and goal-directed. In other words, foreign policy is supposed to do (or not do) "certain things" as "intended" by institutionally designated policymakers.[14] The assumption should not be construed to mean that the external behavior of a nation will necessarily be optimal or, say, a direct response to the immediate external situation. An appropriate way of handling this problem is to see foreign policy as a component of a continuous process whereby governments seek to bring about or oppose changes in the external environment. Thus, various foreign policy actions cumulatively constitute what has been aptly described as "adaptive behavior."[15]

The adaptive perspective on external behavior can be quite suggestive in conceptualizing foreign policy orientation in terms of its basic function. But there is one basic weakness in this formulation: its assignment of societal preservation as the principal determinant of external behavior.[16] While the criterion of societal survival sometimes determines the foreign policy action of certain states—particularly a small state's behavior (such as Israel), it hardly provides an adequate frame of reference for the behavior of a major power such as the U.S. in regard to a distant region like South Asia.

From an adaptive perspective, our task calls for an examination of the following interrelated dimensions of external behavior. First, what are the basic functions of the structures cited earlier (diplomatic, strategic, economic, humanitarian, etc.) in America's South Asia policy? What long-term goals has the U.S. sought to achieve in the regional environment? Have they been purely regional (i.e. South Asian) or also related to extra-regional considerations (i.e. internal organizational concerns) or priorities in other areas? Second, how has the U.S. behaved and reacted to changes in South Asia? Is the behavior *promotive*, in the sense of directly or indirectly underwriting changes in the external environment? Or is it indicative of a *preservative* policy designed to restore or maintain the existing level of regional balance of forces? Or is it a combination of both tendencies—e.g. a policy that permits economic and developmental changes in the context of political and military stability? From a different angle, is it merely the reflection of *acquiescent* behavior (implying thereby that it is a direct function of the policies of other nations in the region)? Or, has the U.S. shown an absolute unconcern, i.e., *intransigent* behavior, regarding the same region?[17]

When responding to different issue areas nations seek to adapt to or modify their international environment. But in reality they often pursue goals which pose operational constraints. What is more, formulation of these goals are sometimes influenced by distorted perceptions of the environment. Thus, the ability to respond effectively to the foreign environment is in part a function of the internal policy-making mechanism of a state.[18] This brings us to another goal of the present study: to demonstrate the extent to which the interplay between internal inputs and external stimuli influence American involvement in South Asia in the context of America's conception of its regional role and interests.[19]

What of the domestic sources of internal inputs within the decision-making process? Here, our inquiry is limited primarily to the interaction within the formal foreign policy-making system— comprising the White House, the bureaucracy, and sometimes Congress. In other words, we are concerned with the decision-making activities of the Executive Branch as endorsed, interdicted or refashioned by the Congress that have shaped U.S. response to situations in South Asia.[20]

In confining this study to the constitutionally designated foreign policy-making system, we are not denying the relevance of public opinion and interest groups. However, South Asian problems have remained so marginal to U.S. foreign policy that they have seldom generated any serious wider interest, with the possible exception of regional nuclear proliferation, and, more recently, the Soviet occupation of Afghanistan.

Other Approaches to Foreign Policy Analysis

It has been suggested that *what* a nation does is in no insignificant way a result of how it *decides* about its course of action.[21] The obvious implication of this suggestion is that a nation's external behavior is generated through its foreign policy-making process. To put it differently, in a given context America's South Asia policy is not only a direct function of its response to the salient external environment, but is also a function of the pattern of interaction that takes place between the executive branch and the Congress, the White House and relevant bureaucracies (e.g. Department of State, Department of Defense, AID, CIA, etc.), or between different designated policymakers within the policy-making system. Thus, to the extent that foreign policy is necessarily the result of a particular process of decision-making, the form of response may be profoundly conditioned by the way decisions are made. The conclusion is therefore quite inescapable that the observed external behavior of a nation cannot be explained merely in terms of a centrally controlled rational choice on the part of an abstraction called the state.[22]

There are two other commonly used approaches to the analysis of policy-making, the organizational process and bureaucratic politics models. The organizational process model is largely derived from the writings of Simon, Lindblom, and Cyert and March.[23] Unlike the rational choice model which starts with the assumption of a unitary actor and uses policy choice as its focus of analysis, the organizational process model views policy as an output produced by interaction between different role occupants. Hence the decision-making process is analyzed with reference to sequential goal preferences, the problem of control and coordination, and the stipulated ground rules for decision (standard operating procedures) within the organization. But considering the complexity of the task it is hardly surprising that the resultant decision is conceived in terms of "satisficing" rather than maximizing the solution. In contrast to the unqualified rationality stipulated by the rational choice model, the organizational process model is characterized by "bounded rationality" or "incrementalism."[24]

This model has some obvious inadequacies. It has been demonstrated that the fate of a foreign policy issue is shaped by the perceived organizational interests of the role occupants.[25] In an important study, Destler contends that organizational type solutions are mere "covers" for the conflicting political issues.[26] Hence the obvious implication for the organizational process model is that the alternative choices preferred by each organization or bureau are indicative of their interest in controlling the situation rather than providing a comprehensive choice suggested by the rational actor model.[27] Evidently this is more in the form of a damage limitations mechanism. Still, it is not off the mark to suggest that organizational process analysis tends to reflect the rational choice bias. In fact, organizational reforms have been introduced from time to time with a view to making it possible to produce a maximizing and not merely satisfying solution.

In a sense, the bureaucratic politics model is an advanced variant of the organizational process model. The bureaucratic politics model takes a political view of the making of decisions. It tends to assume that foreign policy decisions are outcomes of a bureaucratic political process characterized by different kinds of bargaining and coercive maneuvers on the part of various role occupants—hierarchically placed in the government—who are assumed to be in conflict over a wide range of national, organizational and personal issues. In contrast to the rational choice model, it sees no unitary actor but rather many role occupants who make decisions not by one-shot rational choices, but by "the pulling and hauling that is politics."[28] The basic focus of its analysis is government action that results from compromise through bargaining along regularized action channels. It is therefore hardly surprising that policy action generated by the bureaucratic political process would be incremental and comprehensive.

In recent years the bureaucratic politics paradigm has become one of the most fashionable approaches to the study of foreign policy decision-making. However, Robert Rothstein has rightly pointed out that in applying standard propositions about informal bureaucratic behavior to the arena of foreign policy-making our attention is bound to be turned away from some other issues essential for investigation.[29] It should be noted that irrespective of the divergent motivations or preferences of the role occupants, in responding to specific foreign policy issue areas they do not interact among themselves without reference to the latter. Issue areas have their own direct influence on the dynamics of the decisionmakers' response.

Two other perspectives should also be considered here. First, instead of viewing foreign policy action as a consensus resulting from political bargaining, it can be demonstrated that it is a function of psychological pressure generated by the need for group conformity.[30] It has been cogently documented elsewhere how pressure for group conformity tends to reverse or tone down dissident voices or ideas, as in the case of U.S. military involvement in Vietnam.[31]

The second perspective is based on the assumption that to the extent that the U.S. President enjoys constitutionally sanctioned inherent power and final responsibility in foreign and defense affairs, the saliency of bureaucratic politics in foreign policy may be limited. It is worth recalling that notwithstanding the reservations of the bureaucracy, not only did Nixon and Kissinger proceed with the dramatic Sino-U.S. rapprochement or the SALT agreement with Moscow, but they also sent a U.S. naval task force to the Bay of Bengal to intervene in the 1971 Bangladesh War between India and Pakistan.[32]

Such events indicate a lack of balance in the bureaucratic politics model. While students of this approach concentrate on the struggle among bureaucrats—who also constitute Presidential advisors—they do not focus on the nature of the relationship between the President and these bureaucrats. It is quite conceivable that what has been described as policy action produced through bureaucratic conflict is in reality a reinforcement exercise in support of Presidential preferences on certain issue areas. And whenever there are continuing differences between the President and "bureaucratic politicians" on certain issues, the course of action preferred by the former usually tends to prevail. But again, the relative autonomy and power enjoyed by the bureaucrats will vary with each administration. Students of bureaucratic politics have tended to confer, according to Perlmutter, "disproportionate" power to "members of the court" (a euphemism for the Presidential advisory entourage—that includes White House personal staff and senior officials of the State Department, Department of Defense, etc.), and thereby overlook the "court master"—the President—as the "real source."[33] This unequal relationship is symbolic of Presidential predominance in foreign and defense affairs. Unless we realize this, any attempt to look for an unqualified connection between U.S. foreign policy and bureaucratic politics will produce an incomplete understanding of the entire policy process.

Our view is that the extent to which bureaucrats are able to formulate policies is largely a function of Presidential attention. The court master involves himself in those issue areas which he decides to be important. What is described as bureaucratic conflict is often in fact a contest for Presidential attention. Conversely, it can be stated that the extent to which the bureaucracy enjoys autonomy is determined by the nature and urgency of the issue areas, and the varying degree of control resorted to by the Chief Executive (indicative of the different Presidential styles, or preferences in regard to the creation and use of a special advisory staff). However, in recent times with the expansion of foreign policy bureaucracies, in particular the Department of State—with its regional and functional bureaus advocating different interests and priorities—the President has tended to go around them, thereby taking a more active role in policy innovations and providing coherence in U.S. foreign policy.[34]

Where does the Congress stand in this process? The answer is brief and simple. Most scholars on U.S. foreign policy agree that Congressional involvement in the foreign policy process suffers from severe limitations, and that on the whole, Congress has accepted Presidential leadership in this area.[35] Excepting those decisions which involve the use of force or economic and arms aid, Congressional intercession has until recently been very rare. The influence of Congress on foreign policy has been primarily one of legitimizing (through bipartisan support) or amending certain aspects of the policy that have been decided by the executive branch in response to an external situation. But there has also been a basic divergence in the foreign policy approaches of the executive branch and the Congress. On various occasions, as in the case of the Vietnam War or the Cambodian invasion, these differences have been marked by serious Congressional criticism of the substance of U.S. foreign policy. In many ways this is indicative of the fact that while the executive has more often been identified with a policy of ambitious globalism, Congress has recently been associated with a rather restricted conception of U.S. diplomatic interests.

Role Conception

Our discussion to this point has assessed the importance and variety of sources of external state behavior. However, one other aspect should be considered: the extent to which the U.S. national role conception both on the global and regional levels has a bearing on U.S. foreign policy.[36]

Though "role" has been variously defined, we conceive of it as a set of norms or directives of action. A national role conception may be viewed as comprising those functions and tasks to which a particular nation is predisposed or has committed itself in relation to varying international situations or contexts. Role conception thus characterizes the external behavior of a nation in the light of certain recurrent observable patterns of response to varying external issues. It is thus possible to state a nation's role conception by referring to its external behavior in different issue areas over a period of time within the context of statements made by relevant policymakers.

The notion of role conception has several important implications. First, it mirrors specifically recognizable external behavior, though it does not preclude differing behavior in different circumstances. This suggests that role conception should be viewed as a part of the frame of reference for the relevant foreign policy action of a state.

Second, to the extent that a nation is actively involved in the wide range of global affairs, its role conception is likely to become more structured. From this perspective, it is possible to delineate the kind of discrete role or the level of activity that is expected from U.S. policy toward South Asia, e.g., whether as underwriter of regional peace and stability, as balancer, or as a dependable alliance partner or promoter of viable economic systems, etc. It should be noted that foreign policy action in different contexts is hardly the function of a single national role conception. In fact, it is likely to vary from nation to nation and in different sets of issue areas or situations.[37]

Third, we must not overemphasize the analytical power of role conception. For one thing, it is neither an independent variable that invariably determines the foreign policy of a nation nor is it merely a function of external stimuli.[38] This is not to understate its significance, but to put the concept in proper perspective. In making decisions most policymakers tend to define the expected role of their own countries with reference to specific issue areas. This expected role may be linked to domestic imperatives—historical experience, shared values of society or the country's socio-economic and political structures—as well as its perception of external circumstances. But again, in responding to external situations, nations seldom act in conformity with one single role conception. Instead, as we shall see below, they may act in a given situation under the influence of several conflicting role conceptions.

An Integrated Perspective

The sources of foreign policy can be studied from various vantage points. While these approaches each have their own merits, none alone can explain a complex phenomenon like external behavior. Like the proverbial six blind men and the elephant, they try to comprehend foreign policy in terms of their specialized point of contact.

Our view is that the foreign policy of a country—from the state of formulation to the point of action/response—is a function of a complex, sequential interactive process. Thus, it is like all human behavior. A nation's external behavior is not only the product of the decision-making process that generated it, but is also determined by a given set of formulated goals based on a perceived national role conception (if not an "operational code" of conduct)--within the limits imposed by existing capabilities.[39] A foreign policy designed to achieve these goals tends to elicit a reaction from the external environment which in turn constitutes (along with other elements) the basis of a future policy. Hence, foreign policy should be viewed more as an action-reaction chain rather than a one-dimensional process divided into different parts and made up of independent and dependent variables. True, it is convenient to focus on the separate parts for the purpose of investigation, but we must be careful not to overemphasize their causal significance.

In examining the pattern and sources of U.S. policy in South Asia we will make an attempt to approach the problem from an integrated analytical perspective We will explain both the "hows" and the "whys" of U.S. policy toward South Asia. In an important sense, however, these two lines of inquiry are symbiotically related. If viewed separately, they relate to two different segments of interstate relations. Thus, if the answers to the "hows" call for an analysis of the pattern of U.S. policy responses and actions in the context of transaction flow between the U.S. and South Asia, those of the "whys" require an examination of the process by which individuals make foreign policy decisions with reference to external issues. To concentrate our inquiry on one approach to the exclusion of the other would be wrong. Our integrated analytical perspective is based on the assumption of essential complementarity between these two approaches—modes of decisions and resultant pattern of actions—subsumed under the broad rubric of the foreign policy process.

Starting with this assumption of interdependency, we will describe the basic characteristics of America's South Asia policy with reference to the following interrelated questions. First, how does the U.S.—as a major power—respond to a specific South Asian situation/issue area at a given point of time? Second, what are the key elements in decision-making that influence the nature of the consequent response? Third, is the policy process marked by an element of continuity based on a stable set of long range regional goals or an overall national role conception relating to the region? Or, is the policy process sporadic and hence characterized by short run *ad hoc* calculations and choices? Or, is there an element of ambivalence (or contradiction) in the policy process created by the pressure of immediate issues or situations in the region, and pulls generated by, say, other regional priorities or global or extra-regional considerations?

An Additional Task

This is also the study of a superpower's external behavior in relation to a geographically distant external environment, in this case, South Asia. Hence, an objective of this study is to highlight the pattern of a superpower's involvement in this region. It is worth noting that this region has not often been considered relevant to America's central strategic interest—the state or level of stability of the triangular relationship between the U.S., the U.S.S.R., Europe, Japan and China. Consequently, most of the states of this region—

including the major ones such as India and Pakistan—have generally been viewed more as the objects rather than as the subjects of international relations.[40]

We do not wish to overstress this point, but it should be recalled that in the 1950s the U.S. military commitment to Pakistan and its economic aid to India were both the result of Cold War calculations. America's basic rationale was not only to counter Soviet or Chinese political influence in this region but to construct a viable structure of regional stability and thereby inhibit the growth of externally supported (or internal) communist movements. The marginality of South Asia in America's foreign policy was evident in other ways, also as the traditional Eurocentric bias of the international system influenced the direction of U.S. foreign policy even in the post-colonial era.

While the derivative nature of American interests in the region is self-evident, it is simplistic to explain the entire range of U.S. involvement in South Asia from this perspective. In a certain sense, almost every region has a derived relevance from time to time. Since the enunciation of the containment doctrine in 1947 the U.S. has moved from country to country (whether in Africa, Asia, Europe, or Latin America) in response to apparently threatening situations—some of which had a direct bearing on the superpower relationship. However, any study of a superpower based only on its management of globally relevant strategic situations highlights only one dimension of its role conception. We noted earlier that role conception as a concept is multifaceted. Its forms and contents are determined by different relationships, and thus vary from context to context. Our contention is that the process of involvement, once initiated with reference to central strategic interests, can subsequently generate its own justification for continuation in terms of regional requirements.[41]

To sum up, though South Asia (unlike Europe, the Middle East, Southeast Asia and East Asia) has attracted comparatively little American attention, the U.S. has not remained unconcerned about the problems of peace, stability, and the development of a region where other major powers (the U.S.S.R and China) are intimately involved. In light of this apparent paradox, a systematic study of American policy in South Asia also permits a better understanding of the kind of responses and reactions that such a state exhibits in relation to different policy issues, periodically posed by a so-called low priority external setting.

Our case studies attempt to test five arguments or propositions suggested by the literature. The first is quite basic, even elemental: is the foreign policy orientation of a superpower such as the U.S., in dealing with a relatively marginal region, purposive and directed, or does it tend to be random and sporadic? Second, to what degree, especially during a crisis situation, is American foreign policy adaptive—and therefore inherently ambivalent—because of the need to balance global, regional and bilateral relationships? Third, the literature suggests the importance of "national role" in the shaping of foreign policy. To what degree, therefore, has American foreign policy towards South Asia been the function of a multi-causal process determined by the interaction between systemic and institutional variables in the context of such a perceived national role? Fourth, modern American foreign policy is obviously dominated by the Presidential. To what degree has this institution similarly dominated in connection with a region that historically has not been central to Presidential concerns? Conversely, since Congressional participation in decision-making is required only when sizeable assets are transferred from the U.S., has Congress in fact played a minor role in U.S. policy towards South Asia at other times?

These propositions are necessarily tentative, and we will further explore their accuracy and utility in each case study. We offer another caveat as well. While it is true that understanding the foreign policy orientation of a major nation in relation to a specific external environment calls for an investigation of the relative importance of the systemic and the institutional sources of foreign policy action, the task also makes it necessary to examine the nature of its earlier contacts or the kinds of images that the latter tend to produce in regard to the environment. It is perhaps not an overstatement to suggest that foreign policy is not infrequently the prisoner of its past; America's South Asia policy of the 1960s or 1970s is no exception in this respect. We thus preface our case studies with a brief survey of America's involvement in South Asia.

Notes

1. The intensity of the debates between perspectives reached its height during the 1960s, when each of the contending schools of thought was trying to assert its superiority over the other. See the essays in Klaus Knorr and James N. Rosenau (eds.), *Contending Approaches to International Politics* (Princeton: Princeton University Press, 1969). More recently, the "scientific" school of foreign policy analysis has been in a state of retrenchment and consolidation. For a collection of research papers utilizing quantitative and related methodologies see Charles F. Hermann, Charles W. Kegley, Jr., and James N. Rosenau (eds.), *New Directions in the Study of Foreign Policy* (Boston: Allen and Unwin, 1987).

2. There is a substantial body of literature on this problem. See among others Robert Jervis, *Perception and Misperception in International Relations* (Princeton: Princeton University Press, 1976), Joseph De Rivera, *The Psychological Dimensions of Foreign Policy* (Columbus, Ohio: Merrill, 1968), and Herbert C. Kelman (ed.), *International Behavior: A Socio-Psychological Analysis* (New York: Holt, Rinehart and Winston, 1965), especially the papers in Part I.

3. Eugene J. Meehan, *The Theory and Method of Political Analysis* (Homewood, Illinois: Dorsey, 1965), Ch. 4.

4. For a recent collection containing chapters on several dimensions of America's regional policy as well as Indian and Pakistani strategies by American, Indian, and Pakistani authors see Stephen P. Cohen, ed., *The Security of South Asia* (Urbana: University of Illinois Press, 1987 and New Delhi: Vistaar, 1988). For earlier studies see William J. Barnds, *India, Pakistan, and the Great Powers* (New York: Praeger, 1972), Norman D. Palmer, *South Asia and United States Policy* (New York: Houghton Mifflin, 1966) and Palmer, *The United States and India: The Dimensions of Influence* (New York: Praeger, 1984).

5. See M.S. Venkataramani and H.C. Arya, "America's Military Alliance With Pakistan: The Evolution and Course of an Uneasy Partnership," *International Studies*, July-Oct. 1966 and Baldev Raj Nayar, "Treat India Seriously," *Foreign Policy*, Spring, 1975. A number of retired or active U.S. policymakers have also contributed to the literature: Chester Bowles was former Ambassador to India and Undersecretary of State, Phillips Talbot was former Assistant Secretary of State and Ambassador to Greece, Thomas Thornton was a member of the Policy Planning Staff, Department of State and served on the NSC staff; and William Barnds was with the CIA before he joined the staff of several Congressional committees.

6. Bowles is something of an exception in that he does deal with how differences emerge between the U.S. Mission abroad and State Department officials in Washington.

7. See P.T. Bauer, *United States Aid and Indian Economic Development* (New York: American Enterprise Association, 1959) John P. Lewis, *Quiet Crisis in India* (Bombay: Asia Publishers, 1963) and Charles Wolf

Foreign Aid: Theory and Practice in Southern Asia (New Jersey: Princeton University Press, 1960).

8. See Dan Haendel, *The Process of Priority Formulation: U.S. Foreign Policy in the Indo-Pakistani War of 1971* (Boulder: Westview, 1977), Sumit Ganguly, *The Origins of War in South Asia* (Boulder: Westview, 1986), and the *Commission on the Organization of the Government for the Conduct of Foreign Policy*, June 1975 (in seven volumes), Appendixes, Vol. 7 (Washington, D.C.: U.S. Government Printing Office), Appendix V, pp. 106-287. (Hereafter *Organization of the Government.*)

9. *Ibid.*

10. Issue area is considered as a situation in which the values and interests of the concerned actors are involved in such as way that the former tend to activate the roles and responses of the latter in certain patterns. For a systematic treatment of the concept, see James N. Rosenau (ed.), *Domestic Sources of Foreign Policy* (New York: Free Press, 1967), pp. 11-50.

11. K. J. Holsti, *International Politics: A Framework for Analysis* (Englewood Cliffs, N.J.: Prentice Hall, 1972), pp. 102-103.

12. It should be noted that even in the case of U.S. "isolationism" during the inter-war period, while the U.S. decided not to remain in the League of Nations, it sought to steer clear of entangling alliances and stay neutral in other people's quarrels; nevertheless U.S. policy-makers made their own bid for world peace by participating in a succession of disarmament conferences (Washington Treaty of 1922, Geneva Naval Conference of 1927, and London Naval Conference of 1935-36), or actively advocating the outlawing of aggressive war (Briand-Kellogg Pact, 1928). What is more, despite the enactment of the Neutrality Acts of the 1930s, the U.S. was not inhibited from providing arms to Britain in the early stage of the second World War, first on a "cash and carry" basis and later on a "Lend Lease Agreement".

13. Derived from *Organization of Government*, Vol. 7, Appendix V.

14. Stuart J. Thorson, "Adaptation and Foreign Policy Theory," in Patrick J. McGowan (ed.), *Sage International Yearbook of Foreign Policy Studies*, Vol. II (Beverly Hills: Sage, 1974), pp. 125-126.

15. James N. Rosenau, "Comparing Foreign Policies: Why, What, How," in James N. Rosenau (ed.), *Comparing Foreign Policies: Theories, Findings and Methods* (New York: John Wiley and Sons, 1974), pp. 4-7. For a perceptive treatment also see James N. Rosenau, "Foreign Policy as Adaptive Behavior: Some Preliminary Notes for a Theoretical Model," *Comparative Politics* 2 (April 1970), pp. 365-389.

16. Some scholars have contended that nations as "entities must adapt to their environment to survive." James N. Rosenau, *The Adaptation of National Societies: A Theory of Political System Behavior and Transformation* (New York: McCaleb-Seiber, 1970), p. 2. For a critical treatment of this aspect, see Stuart J. Thorson, "National Political Adaptation in a World Environment," in James N. Rosenau (ed.), *Comparing Foreign Policies*, pp. 123-138.

17. This and the following categories are derived (but modified) from Rosenau's four-fold scheme of external behavior (See Rosenau, *Adaptation*, f.n. 17, pp. 3-25.)

18. In addition, it is inconceivable that the policy-making process is initiated without reference to the particular nation's "adaptive capability" as also understood in terms of its natural, material, human and institutional resources available over a period of time. For a brief treatment of this aspect of "adaptive capability," see John P. Lovell, *Foreign Policy in Perspective: Strategy, Adaptation, Decision-making* (New York: Holt, Rinehart and Winston, 1970), pp. 146-155.

19. Although unlike the Middle East or Southeast Asia, South Asia never became an important agenda of international politics, it has shown certain unique characteristics as a regional subsystem. In fact, it has been one of the few regions in the world where the three major world powers have been quite intimately involved in regional conflicts (between India and Pakistan), economic aid and large arms transfers.

20. These activities not only relate to security issues involving the maintenance of balance in the target environment, influencing events therein or strengthening the U.S. international bargaining position. They also refer to military or economic aid programs, or general transactions pertaining to that region.

21. See James N. Rosenau's introductory comments on foreign policy action, in James N. Rosenau (ed.), *International Politics and Foreign Policy* (New York: The Free Press, Rev. Ed., 1969) p. 169.

22. For a balanced treatment on the limits of rational analysis, see John D. Steinbruner, *The Cybernetic Theory of Decision: New Dimension of Political Analysis* (Princeton: Princeton University Press, 1974). Graham T. Allison has pointed out how rational assumptions are used to support historical interpretation: *Essence of Decision: Explaining the Cuban Missile Crisis* Boston: Little Brown, 1971).

23. Herbert A. Simon, *Administrative Behavior*, 2nd Ed. (New York: Macmillan, 1957); Charles E. Lindblom, *The Policy-Making Process* (Englewood Cliffs, N.J: Prentice-Hall, 1968); R. M. Cyert and J. G. March, *A Behavioral Theory of the Firm* (Englewood Cliffs: Prentice-Hall, 1963).

24. See Simon, *Administrative Behavior*, p.xxiv and chapters IV and V on 'satisficing,' maximizing, and bounded rationality, and Lindblom, *The Policy Making Process* on incrementalism.

25. Morton Halperin, "Why Bureaucrats Play Games," *Foreign Policy*, Spring 1971, pp. 72, 74, 88-89.

26. I. M. Destler, Presidents, *Bureaucrats and Foreign Policy: The Politics of Organization Reforms* (Princeton: Princeton University Press, 1972), pp. 46-51.

27. Lincoln P. Bloomfield, *The Foreign Policy Process: Making Theory Relevant* (Beverly Hills: Sage, 1974), p. 22.

28. *Essence of Decision: Explaining the Cuban Missile Crisis* (Boston: Little Brown, 1971). Subsequently he jointly developed with Morton H.

Halperin the bureaucratic politics paradigm. (See "Bureaucratic politics: A Paradigm and some policy implications," in R. Ullman and Raymond Tanter (eds.), *Theory and Practice in International Relations* (Princeton: Princeton University Press, 1972), pp. 40-79.

29. Robert L. Rothstein, *Planning, Prediction and Policymaking in Foreign Affairs* (Boston: Little Brown, 1972), p. 205.

30. There are some scholars who believe that this consensus is rooted in the "goals" and "needs" of "ruling class" (sometimes described as the foreign policy "establishment") which makes U.S. foreign policy. See Gabriel Kolko, *The Roots of American Foreign Policy: An Analysis of Power and Purposes* (Boston: Beacon Press, 1969).

31. Irving L. Janis, *Victims of Group Think: A Psychological Study of Foreign Policy Decisions and Fiascos* (Boston: Houghton Mifflin, 1973).

32. See Marvin Kalb and Bernard Kalb, *Kissinger* (New York: Dell, 1975), pp. 120-141 and 248-304. The various meetings of the National Security Council's Washington Special Action Group (WSAG) on this crisis indicate how officials from the State regional bureau down to ambassador were advised to act according to Nixon's assessment of the situation that India should be held solely responsible for the outbreak of the war. Any dissenting voice within or outside WSAG was silenced by Kissinger by reminding him about Presidential preferences. For details, see Jack Anderson, *The Anderson Papers* (N.Y.: Ballantine Books, 1974) pp. 253-315.

33. Amos Perlmutter, "The Presidential Political Center and Foreign Policy: A Critique of the Revisionist and Bureaucratic Political Orientations," *World Politics*, Vol. 27, No. 1, 1975, p. 90.

34. *Organization of the Government*, Appendix V, pp. 106-287.

35. See Robert A. Dahl, *Congress and Foreign Policy* (New York: W.W. Norton, 1964) and James A. Robinson, *Congress and Foreign Policy Making* (Homewood, Ill.: Dorsey Press, 1967) and Francis Wilcox, *Congress, the Executive, and Foreign Policy* (New York: Harper, 1971).

36. Holsti found 16 different types of national roles in his study of 61 countries based on content and analysis of speeches by top policymakers. Holsti, pp. 296-302.

37. Kautilya, the ancient Indian practitioner of politics, conceptualized six different possible categories of policies for handling interstate relations: peace (binding through pledges), war (offensive operation), indifference (apparently marking time), strengthening one's position (for attack), subordinate ally or vassal (when devoid of strength) , and duplicity (engaged simultaneously in war and peace), see "Artha, the second end" in Wm. T. de Bary (ed.), *Sources of Indian Tradition* (New York: Columbia University Press, 1958), pp. 253-254. Morton Kaplan's work tends to stress the external setting, whereby the type of international system and its ground rules influence the external behavior of states. But even Kaplan points out how state action is also conditioned by the nature of the institutional setting. *System and Process in International Politics* (New York: John Wiley, 1957), pp. 39, 54.

38. This is a cognitive aid which policymakers frequently make use of in analyzing the supposed intentions or the behavioral characteristics of other states in particular and the state of international relations in general. It relates to the policymakers' beliefs and premises that have a bearing on the decision-making process. For a balanced treatment, see Alexander L. George, "The Operational Code: A neglected approach to the study of political leaders and decisionmaking," *International Studies Quarterly*, Vol. 13 (June 1969), pp. 190-222.

39. On the need for decision-making as well as national role and national interest approaches in relation to South Asia specifically, see Barnds, pp. ix-x.

40. A distinction used by Baldev Raj Nayar. See "Treat India Seriously," and *American Geopolitics and India* (New Delhi: Manohar, 1976).

41. Two studies on U.S. foreign policy are based on a similar analytical approach. See Alexander L. George and Richard Smoke, *Deterrence in American Foreign Policy: Theory and Practice* (New York: Columbia University Press, 1974); Morton Berkowitz, P.G. Bock and Vincent J. Fuccillo, *The Politics of American Foreign Policy: The Social Context of Decision* (Englewood Cliffs, N.J.: Prentice-Hall, 1977).

2

South Asia and U.S. Foreign Policy

South Asia constitutes a subsystem of powers with two major nations that are actually within South Asia, and three others, China, the U.S. and the USSR, that are extra-regional.[1] It also contains several states with minimal military power: Nepal, Bhutan, Sri Lanka, Bangladesh, and Afghanistan. By virtue of their global status, the U.S. and the USSR have been quite intimately involved in South Asia—a setting marked until recently by political instability, a relative diffusion of power and retarded economic development. It is these latter characteristics which may have prompted the two superpowers to fill the apparent power vacuum and to refashion it in order to strengthen their respective global and regional policies.

The central dilemma of U.S. policy in South Asia since 1947 has been to deal with the competing claims of the two principal states of this region, India and Pakistan. In a sense, the persistent ambivalence of America's South Asia policy is a result of the regional contest between these two states. But from the perspective of most American policymakers, this contest is not the issue: even though the strategic significance of South Asia is not comparable to that of Europe, the Middle East or East Asia, these policymakers have held certain preferences as to the direction of Indian and Pakistani external behavior.

Of these two Subcontinental states, if India was often an unimportant factor in U.S. perception of the global strategic equation, Pakistan was an inconsequential factor unless militarily aligned with the U.S.[2] The initial U.S. involvement in South Asia (i.e. after World War II) was barely influenced by the regional developments. What did shape the U.S. role was the shrinking British empire (which for many years enforced stability and order in this part of the world) and the rapid decline of the KMT regime in China. Subsequent U.S. military links to South Asia (Pakistan in particular), an offshoot of its concern vis-a-vis the Soviet Union, inadvertently accentuated the level of animosity between India and Pakistan. U.S. involvement not only annoyed India but also brought the Soviet Union (and later China) into the Subcontinent and made the region an arena of Cold War politics.

America's South Asian Connection

In many ways, U.S. involvement in India started during World War II. Before this, both official and unofficial contacts with India were minimal. While the U.S. maintained a few consular offices in India to look after commercial interests, it relied largely on British Foreign Office communications for information on the Indian political situation. As for unofficial Indian connections, initial American interest was limited to a few commercial transactions (part of the so-called East India trade), missionary activities of various Christian groups, and intellectual appreciation (especially that of the New England transcendentalists) of India's cultural resources. Also, renowned Indians such as Swami Vivekananda, Rabindranath Tagore and Sarojini Naidu visited the U.S., which familiarized India to a small but attentive portion of America. Before Pearl Harbor, India had been considered a "lamentable example" of British imperialism, but was perceived as an "exclusive British responsibility."[3] The U.S. really became involved in South Asia after its entry into World War II. British India served at that time as a spring-board for allied military operations against the Japanese in China and Southeast Asia. India's proximity to Japanese-occupied Southeast Asia and blockaded China constituted its strategic significance—especially because of its pivotal geographical position between the Asian and European war zones.

The U.S. was also interested in India's independent status.[4] The establishment of an interim nationalist government in India, as a prelude to the final transfer of power to two separate states, India and Pakistan, aroused U.S. interest about India's "self-government."[5] The U.S. government not only followed with "deep interest" Indian preference for an "independent policy" designed "to avoid involvement" with any particular grouping, but also recognized India's desire for friendly relations with the U.S.[6] Significantly, Americans were also aware of Indian concern about "infiltration" of its political setting by external "totalitarian influences," an allusion to Soviet supported communist movements or clandestine operations.[7] One important facet of the developments at this time was that India was trying to impress upon the State Department how India could be built up as a "strong bastion" for the free world against the threat of Soviet communist expansionism.[8]

Though interested in the emergence of an integrated India, the U.S. continued to have certain reservations about the Muslim demand for political and economic autonomy. However, once self-rule was granted to the two separate countries (India and Pakistan), it was averse to any action that might jeopardize the objective of "avoiding further balkanization of India."[9] In taking this position, the U.S. was in fact following British policy.[10] While the U.S. sought to encourage closer cooperation if not "loose federation" between India and Pakistan, it did not want to bypass Britain on Subcontinental issues. For its part, Britain was unwilling to seek U.S. advice on "common problems" in South Asia. Faced with this sensitivity, the only way the U.S. could avoid its predicament was "to stay out of Commonwealth problems."[11] An added consideration was how to preempt possible intra-alliance dissension over problems relating to an unchartered area. Yet, the U.S. was not willing to overlook India because of its priorities in Europe.[12]

In light of subsequent developments in Indo-U.S. relations, it is paradoxical that it was the Indian government that sought economic, political and military support from the U.S. The Indian government not only tried to draw U.S. attention to the Soviet "diplomatic offensive" against the U.S. but also expressed serious concern about Soviet intentions towards the disputed Kashmir, especially if it "becomes the center of real conflict and chaos gets deeper."[13] Clearly, India also resented what it saw as Britain's double standard toward South Asia. While the British government took for granted India's "friendliness and goodwill," it "woo[ed] Pakistan."[14]

This attitude toward Pakistan was due primarily to the comparative pliability of the Pakistan government, which continued to retain the services of a sizeable number of British civil and military personnel. In contrast, relatively few British personnel remained in Indian government service, especially at high levels. Additionally, India's size and potential, and the stability of its leadership—the product of a drawn out anti-colonial struggle—made it resistant to British maneuvering. Nonetheless, a closer Indo-U.S. relationship would have been anathema to the British government.[15]

Washington realized that Britain would not easily accept a more conspicuous U.S. role in South Asia, and opted for a low profile policy during the years immediately following the British recession. Partly to avoid complications with Britain, but more importantly because of the possible USSR threat in Europe (as well as in Turkey and Iran), the U.S. government seems to have decided to follow Whitehall's advice regarding South Asia. Therefore, during the period from 1947 to 1956 (the year of the Suez crisis) the direction of America's South Asian policy was heavily influenced by the British.[16]

After its independence, India attempted to secure bomber aircraft from the U.S. The deal was blocked by the State Department, despite the initial favorable response of Louis Johnson, the Secretary of Defense. According to one account, Whitehall's influence on the State Department prevented the sale.[17] While the fiasco of this sale might have displeased New Delhi, it was the U.S. stand on the Kashmir issue that actually caused Indian disillusionment with Washington. India brought the Kashmir question to the UN in early 1948, with a complaint against Pakistan.[18] To New Delhi's surprise, the U.S. sided with Britain and equated India with Pakistan in the dispute.[19] India was "surprised and distressed" that the "reference" it made was not properly taken into consideration.[20] America's inability to appreciate India's stand on the Kashmir question was a major source of dissension between New Delhi and Washington, and continued to complicate their relationship until the mid-60s. Presumably, what bothered New Delhi was that neither the legal strength of India's case nor U.S. concern about Soviet intentions in the Subcontinent were thought adequate reasons for the U.S. to take a more sympathetic stand.[21]

In spite of early favorable U.S. impressions of India, Indo-U.S. relations were marked occasionally by disagreements other than Kashmir. On one occasion, John Foster Dulles (then a member of the U.S. delegation to the U.N.) stated that "in India, Soviet communism exercises a strong influence through the interim Hindu government."[22] There was no basis for such an allegation. The Indian government was then concerned about Soviet tirades against it and was seeking U.S. sympathy and support. Dulles' remark was made in reaction to Indian attempts in the UN (which coincided with those of the Soviet Union) to liberalize the Trusteeship agreements. But, Dulles' allegation was to serve as an instant rationale for the extension of the U.S. military alliance system to Pakistan a few years later.[23]

On the whole, during 1947-1952, Cold War considerations were not a major element in America's South Asia policy. Equating

India and Pakistan on the Kashmir question, refusing to sell bomber aircraft to New Delhi, and Dulles' remarks regarding the alleged pro-Soviet stance of the Indian government—all were indications of the search for a role in South Asia based on consensus within the U.S. administration.[24] The search was complicated because the U.S. was prepared to follow the regional policy of its alliance partner (Britain), while seeking to explore the extension of its responsibility as a major world power to a region that was new to it. Before exploring further the extension of its influence to South Asia, it is necessary to summarize the key American perceptions and interests that evolved in the years immediately following the British withdrawal.

U.S. Perceptions of South Asia

South Asia has usually been regarded as only marginally important to the United States.[25] In the major U.S. security decisions of the day—stability of the international system, maintenance of nuclear balance or the problem of war and peace— South Asia was not considered a "determining" factor, for several reasons.[26] First, it was "not vital strategically"; it did not offer any "major resources" essential to American industry.[27] Second, the low level of economic and political interaction could not generate a positive image of South Asia in the American mind. American impressions, particularly of India, remained largely confined to stereotypes, both favorable and unfavorable. A former U.S. ambassador to India noted that the "Kiplingesque impression" of India—as a land of "cobras, Maharajahs, monkeys and famines"— persists even in the minds of many top U.S. government officials.[28]

Finally, the U.S. was slow to comprehend the full effects of the change brought about by British withdrawal from South Asia. In American perceptions, the area remained a preserve of British interests. Reflecting on this, a former Indian diplomat noted that neither America nor the Soviet Union nor China considered the transfer of power in this area to be of "any consequence in global politics until 1952."[29] Thus, U.S. interests in the region were for many years interpreted as philanthropic rather than commercial or strategic. From this perspective, South Asia (particularly India) has been seen by the U.S. as an impoverished region struggling bravely but futilely to govern itself through democratic institutions, which for humanitarian reasons Americans have felt obliged to assist. In a perceptive study of American images of China and India, an

American scholar concluded in the late 1950s that his nation's image of China was far more positive than that of India.[30]

This evaluation was significant because it was made during the ongoing Sino-American confrontation in East Asia. Though every government interviewee denied that personal views about India had a bearing on his or her participation in policy decisions, Isaacs found it difficult to accept the contention that negative views about India did not influence the process. Incidentally, this has been a widely accepted view among many articulate Indians, who tend to believe that America's South Asia policy has been based on certain instincts and prejudices of its foreign policymakers.[31]

Some responsible Americans have found the "psychological dimension" to be key in Indo-U.S. divergences.[32] One observer of South Asian affairs has viewed these divergences as one of "ups and downs" generated by mutual misunderstanding.[33] Reflecting on the same problem, former U.S. Secretary of State Henry Kissinger once contended that there was a kind of unreality about the Indo-U.S. relationship, largely created by an American "romantic conception" (especially in academia) about India on the one hand, and "excessive Indian expectation" toward the United States on the other.[34] In contrast, an "old India hand" and former Assistant Secretary of State Phillips Talbot submitted that U.S. interaction with India has followed the uneasy course of a "roller-coaster," stemming from different conceptions and objectives with reference to their wider interests.[35] Kissinger's mentor, former President Nixon, believed that there were no basic conflicts of interest between the U.S. and India, but thought it was "sentimentality" to assume that just because India and the U.S. were democracies their foreign policies must be identical.[36]

These conflicting images constitute the basic perspective of the U.S. on its role in South Asia. While some observers tended to advocate U.S. "detachment" from conflicts in South Asia, others, like former Defense Secretary McNamara, asserted South Asia's status as a "vital strategic area" and called for a structure of "security and stability" with U.S. support.[37] More recently, former Secretary of State Kissinger (in contrast to his earlier assessment) conceded to India "a special role of leadership" in South Asia and world affairs.[38] But again, it is not definitively known whether this was a symbolic or substantive concession to India's growing status. Incidentally, during his confirmation hearings Kissinger had recognized that "India is one of the major forces" in the Third World, whose stability and development were indispensable to the structure of South Asian peace and stability.[39] To American observers of foreign policy, the emergence of communist China underscored the importance of India's democratic experiment. India had been perceived as a democratic model for socio-economic and political development through persuasion, in contrast to the regimented controls and a certain degree of force that characterized the Chinese approach. To some Americans this contrasting approach was interpreted as a struggle between two different Asian political systems, clearly underlining South Asia's importance to the U.S.

Thus, Senator John F. Kennedy called for urgent U.S. participation in this contest to help India in its role as a "counter" to communist China.[40] He declared that "no thoughtful citizen" could ignore the U.S. "stake in the survival of free government in India," because "India stood as the only effective competitor to China."[41]

Reflecting on his country's South Asia policy, a former U.S. ambassador to India observed that "American interest" in India is that the latter shall retain its sovereignty, and that the majority of the Indian peoples "faith" in "democracy's ability to give them a better and fuller life be sustained and fortified."[42] Senator John Sherman Cooper (Kentucky), another former U.S. ambassador to India, attached considerable importance to free India's successful development. He believed that "a watchful Asia" will compare the results in India and China, to see whether economic betterment of the teeming millions is achieved most effectively through India's "voluntary methods" or through China's mechanism of "coercion."[43]

There has been a strong American viewpoint that emphasized the identity of U.S. and Indian foreign policy interests because of their commitments to democratic values, basic human rights, and willingness to cooperate on important bilateral or international issues. Yet, it would be unrealistic to suggest that just because India and the U.S. were democracies, they were expected to agree on every issue. In the State Department's language, while "differences of opinion" between India and the U.S. were considered inevitable, it was also believed that the two countries would continue to agree on "basic principles."[44] For the U.S., perhaps, it would have been an ideal relationship if both India and itself had similar views of world affairs. In the absence of that, while the U.S. sought to adjust Indo-U.S. differences, its fundamental interest was in the continuity and existence of India's freedom and democracy. To that end the U.S. was prepared to support India's efforts as far as possible. By contrast, Pakistan was seen only as a military ally, providing a listening post and bases for U.S. defense preparedness against the Soviet bloc.[45]

From this inventory of American assumptions about South Asia, it is evident that, in general, they are neither a consistent nor uniform index of the nature of the U.S. perception of this regional subsystem. In fact, American perception of its role in South Asia since the British withdrawal has been characterized by ambiguity and uncertainty.[46] This is not something peculiar to American views of South Asia, since it is not unusual to perceive a region or country in unqualified terms or by a single set of criteria. Depending on varying contexts, regions or countries are often perceived in singular terms, and thus may be seen as strategically important or inconsequential, economically significant or economically burdensome, and so forth.

U.S. Interests

What are American perceptions of U.S. interests in South Asia? A map of these perceptions can be derived both from U.S. policy statements regarding the region and trends in America's regional relations.

First, as we have pointed out, South Asia is seen as an area of marginal strategic importance.[47] Nonetheless, because of regional instability, the process of social, economic and political change, and the shifts in global power relationships, the U.S. cannot actually ignore the region. Thus, weighing the regional distribution of its global commitments, the U.S. has perceived its interests in South Asia as one of "achieving the maximum security" of this region with a "minimum of U.S. commitment."[48] Second, in terms of economic growth, South Asia is regarded as one of the poorest regions of the world. While America has been generally concerned about South Asia on humanitarian grounds, it has been equally interested in the development of "human and material resources" of this region from the standpoint of encouraging viable self-generating economies.[49] Thus, U.S. economic aid to South Asia, which constitutes the "most visible and largest aspect" of its "involvement," and its encouragement of developmental self-reliance (especially in agriculture) in India and Pakistan, are indicative of a substantial U.S. interest.[50]

Third, the U.S. has perceived among its regional strategic interests the construction of regional peace and stability—based on the independence and security of the countries of this region—that would not only permit resolution of intra-regional conflicts without external intervention, but also would ensure a balance of "activities" of the major external powers involved in South Asia.[51] It would appear that the U.S. has seen its interests in a certain balance of forces within South Asia that would prevent this region from becoming an arena of great powers' conflict. While it is difficult to get a direct U.S. official policy statement regarding preference for a Subcontinental balance of power, one can make this inference from the obvious consequence of the initial U.S. decision, notwithstanding the Cold War consideration, to render arms aid to Pakistan.[52] In any case, in pursuance of its strategic interests, while the U.S. has tried to bolster the general defense capability of this region against a hypothetical or real external communist threat, it has been equally concerned about maintaining its balanced bilateral relations with the major South Asian states.

Needless to say, various elements of American perception of both its regional interests and South Asia's strategic significance have not remained completely static. While American presence in South Asia has been marked by reduced activity when contrasted to its earlier higher level of involvement between 1954-63, basic elements of interest perception have not undergone any fundamental change. In fact, some of the elements that we specified above provide a broad reference frame for comprehending U.S. policy challenges or tasks, its decision-making dilemma, and its priorities for the South Asian environment.

There is no need to overstress the cumulative effects of the Kiplingesque stereotypes on America's perceived interests in South Asia, and their bearing on U.S. South Asia policy-making. What is important is that Harold Isaacs' reference to typical U.S. impressions of Indians (Hindus) as being dreamers and hypocrites, and Pakistanis (Muslims) as being good people and good fighters, merely illustrates the information gap between the U.S. and South Asia.[53] They do not constitute basic determinants of the U.S. perception of its role in South Asia. While typical impressions might have partially distorted the policy process, it is reasonable to assume that U.S. South Asian policy decisions have been made in terms of more tangible interests.

Growing Involvement

U.S. involvement in the region deepened as a result of the competition with the Soviet Union, despite its limited relevance to vital American interests. The Eisenhower-Dulles period saw attempts to extend the scope of Truman's policy of containment in Asia through a series of interlocking, multilateral defense arrangements, based on a coordinated alliance strategy to combat possible communist seizure of power in aligned Asian countries. Due attention was also given to economic development, hopefully ensuring economic and political stability, and reducing the chances of internal communist takeover. But, if the rationale behind U.S. involvement in Asia was provided by the containment doctrine as initially developed in Europe (in response to a hypothetical USSR threat), its immediate need was underlined by the more specific contexts of the American experience in Korea and the ongoing national liberation war against the French in Indochina.

By 1953, when the U.S. decided to render arms aid to Pakistan and inducted the latter into a military alliance system, a long series of developments elsewhere in Asia had produced a yawning gulf between New Delhi and Washington. First, there was India's independent position on the Korean question. This was marked by India's mediatory efforts to defuse the crisis. What appeared paradoxical to the U.S. was that initially India had endorsed the UN collective action against North Korea, but later took a more balanced position after the 38th Parallel was crossed by UN forces (provoking Chinese intervention).

Second, India had reservations about the Japanese Peace Treaty (1951) based on a plan formulated by John Foster Dulles. Later, India was to boycott the San Francisco conference where the treaty was signed. Third, New Delhi viewed increased U.S. presence in Asia after the Korean War as an inevitable process of extending the Cold War arena to Asia. By 1953, however, most of the Asian conflicts seemed to have subsided, at least for the time being. The Soviet Union had been contained in Europe and West Asia. Only in Indochina were the Vietnamese communists slowly but successfully gaining ground against French colonial rule through a war of national liberation. Though the U.S. was not overtly involved in this conflict, it was providing material assistance to French forces. The climax of this conflict would come later with the fall of Dien Bien Phu in mid-1954.

Fourth, around this time India began to demonstrate an independent foreign policy—not subservient to Western interests as alleged earlier by Moscow and Peking. Thus, the stage was set for increasingly friendly relations between India and the Soviet Union and China. With the death of Stalin (March 1953), the Soviets quickly moved to befriend India and other non-aligned countries. Under Khrushchev the Soviet Union decided to provide substantial economic aid to India, and also (in contrast to the U.S.) endorsed the Indian position on Kashmir. China had doubts about India's intentions, despite India's prompt recognition of the communist regime and advocacy of China's admission to the UN The forcible exercise of Chinese suzerainty over Tibet in 1950 led to some sharp exchanges, but India avoided further controversy by accepting the Chinese position. Later India mediated between China and the West during the Korean War. India's efforts to befriend Peking finally paid off with the conclusion of an agreement on Tibet in 1954. The high point in this relationship was reached at the first Afro-Asian Conference (1955) in Bandung, where India introduced China to the Afro-Asian group of nations.

Finally, there were other developments. McCarthyism, the Republican Presidential victory, Dulles' blunt criticism of India's non-alignment, Indian condemnation of U.S. H-bomb tests, the ban on the flight (in U.S. planes) of French paratroopers over India, and the U.S. opposition to the Indian stand on Kashmir—all contributed to policy divergence between India and the U.S.[54] The relatively cordial Indo-U.S. relationship that existed in the early years of the Truman administration had disappeared. In particular, India was especially disturbed by the U.S. announcement of military aid to Pakistan in the Spring of 1954, followed by a mutual security pact. The U.S. decision, according to Nehru, brought the Cold War "to the gates of the Subcontinent."[55] The different views on handling the communist nations were indicative of the growing rift between New Delhi and Washington. Whatever the rationale behind the U.S. decision to enter into a military pact with Pakistan, it caused the Indo-U.S. relationship to hit its lowest point.

The Pakistan Relationship

In many ways, the visit of the first Pakistani Premier, Liaquat Ali Khan, to the United States in May 1950 set the pace for the evolving process of U.S. military involvement in Pakistan. For Liaquat Ali Khan, this was a "voyage of discovery," an exploratory mission in search of an arrangement that could ensure Pakistan's status and security vis-a-vis India. Viewed differently, it implied the first major U.S. exposure to the developing external orientations of Pakistan—a newly independent South Asian political entity carved out of India after Britain's withdrawal. Prior to the Liaquat visit, there was little American awareness even about Pakistan's existence.

Having earlier failed to mobilize the Commonwealth opinion in full support of the Pakistani position on Kashmir,[56] or to generate any anti-Indian sentiments on a pan-Islamic platform in the Arab world,[57] Pakistan looked for moral and material sustenance elsewhere. While making an indirect plea for a Pakistani side role in the emerging U.S. containment strategy in Asia, Liaquat Ali Khan was apparently seeking arms, economic help and technical assistance from the U.S. administration. He pointed out that Pakistan was no passive onlooker to Asian developments, and expressed concern regarding developments taking place in China and threatening to engulf other parts of Asia. In some of his speeches, Liaquat had assured the U.S. administration and the American people that neither "threat" nor "material or ideological allurement" could divert Pakistan from its democratic path. It was the Islamic way of life, Liaquat Ali Khan pointed out, that gave unity, strength and vitality to Pakistan as a nation.[58] The whole exercise seemed designed to demonstrate Pakistan's dependability as an interacting partner.

The Pakistani Prime Minster's visit evoked quite favorable reactions in the American news media. Liaquat's visit enabled the U.S. administration to better appreciate Pakistan's external orientation in general and its security problems in particular; however, it did not result in any U.S. offer for investment or arms transfer, aside from the Point Four program. But then, without mutually compulsive contextual reasons or adequate preparations, a single visit of this sort seldom brings about a fundamental restructuring of the existing pattern of interaction between two countries. Evidently, the Truman administration had some reservations about an implicitly suggested U.S.-Pakistan arrangement. It sought to pursue a policy of "complete neutrality" regarding issues such as arms transfers in the South Asian region, as long as the differences between India and Pakistan were not sorted out.[59] In fact, even earlier, when the then Pakistan Defense Secretary Iskander Mirza came to Washington (July 1949) on a mission specifically to procure arms, the matter was vetoed by the U.S. administration.[60]

Even the Pakistani government had not as yet decided how far it could go in working out an arms transfer arrangement with the U.S. In theory, Pakistan professed non-alignment in its external relations during these early years.[61] Importantly, although in certain broad features Pakistan's external outlook appeared similar to that of India, its relationship with the U.S. was considered less problematic. Indeed, on many of the raging issues of the day, such as the Korean question and the Japanese peace treaty, Pakistan's position was much closer to that of the U.S. than of India.[62]

There was "little experience of past clashes" to constrain the mutual Pakistan-U.S. move to set up "closer ties."[63] It is hardly surprising that though an arms deal between the two countries could not be effected until the advent of the Eisenhower Presidency, it was declared by the U.S. administration as early as 1951:

> We do, however, have a great incentive to help Pakistan, for the reason that Pakistan is very cooperative with us and the Western countries. Pakistan has a very forthright attitude with respect to the basic issues. Pakistan did not send troops to Korea, but Pakistan has in other ways demonstrated her willingness to participate with us.[64]

The idea of a U.S.-Pakistan military tie came up for serious consideration in Washington the same year. Roughly at that time, while some experts in America were interested in suitable sites for air force bases in Pakistan, others considered the possibility that its army could provide manpower in other parts of Asia. Against this, Pakistani army general Ayub Khan wrestled with the idea of securing Pakistan's military supplies from the U.S. However, the likelihood of a military relationship between the two countries during the Truman administration does not need to be overstressed. It would be sufficient to say that there were some manifestations, however vague, in this direction. Indeed there was a general feeling that extension of arms to Pakistan could well secure its friendship and also bolster up its opposition to the Communist nations.

By the time of Liaquat Ali Khan's death in 1951, events both inside and outside Pakistan apparently paved the way toward the formation of a military alliance between the United States and Pakistan. Internally, Pakistan was sliding toward a state of political confusion. The Pakistani civil bureaucracy and the army emerged as the dominant elements in Pakistan's political system. These groups tended to believe that external military support was the most expedient route not only for achieving security (actually implying status) vis-a-vis India, but also for its own much needed political stability.[65] Externally, developments in West and Southeast Asia further hastened the process of U.S.-Pakistan convergence regarding a military alliance.

In the search for military allies in Southern Asia, American strategic thinking was conditioned largely by British perceptions of regional security issues.[66] According to participant as well as nonparticipant observers of the scene, the American decision to forge closer military links with Pakistan may be traced to the geostrategic thesis and the course of policy actions as articulated in the writings of Sir Olaf Caroe, a former member of the Indian Civil Service (later Governor of the North-West Frontier Province—now part of Pakistan).[67] When Britain left the Subcontinent, there was concern regarding the pattern of regional developments in West Asia in the context of the Soviet threat. Before 1947, this area, containing major oil reserves of the world, was managed by Britain through the Indian Army and the Royal Navy. The British thought that the absence of a single political authority on the Indian Subcontinent called for appropriate actions to counter possible Soviet moves toward the Gulf oilfields.[68]

Reflecting on this problem, Caroe contended that since the need for oil was expected to increase in the coming years there was need for an anti-communist alliance system that might ensure the West's access to the Gulf. In view of the British withdrawal from the area and India's policy of non-alignment, Caroe envisaged a crucial role for Pakistan to ensure stability in West and Southern Asia. In his strategic map, Pakistan was the key to the defense of Southwestern Asia. He said: "A conscious policy for receiving the immense resources around the Persian Gulf and for establishing a group of welfare states to combat communism in Southwestern Asia might indeed be inspired by Pakistan." Caroe's scheme for the defense of the Gulf region envisaged a pact between local powers (comprising the ring of Muslim states of Southwestern Asia, from Turkey to Arabia and Pakistan), underwritten by a concert of Commonwealth and Atlantic powers.[69]

India's role in this regional scheme was conceived only in terms of its membership in the Commonwealth. Further, India was expected to sort out its differences with Pakistan before its help could be acceptable in a region where "Pakistan stands in the first line."[70] Geopolitical reasons aside, India seems to have been considered less attractive as a partner on philosophical grounds. Some western observers believed that Pakistan's alliance with the West resulted from its natural affinity with the latter. It could also be adduced to "a certain positive quality" of the Muslim mind, opposed to the "complexity" and negativism of the Hindu mind—which puts stress on concepts such as non-alignment, non-violence, non-cooperation, etc.[71] There was also a view that Islam tended to "harmonize" quite well with Puritanism as expressed in the maxim, "Fear God: back your friends: keep your powder dry!" which reflected Pakistan's "general outlook."[72]

Although Caroe's book had come to the attention of the U.S. State Department, a U.S. sponsored defense pact in this area was not yet envisaged. But with the appointment of Brigadier General Henry A. Byroade as Assistant Secretary of State for the Near East, South Asia, and Africa in December 1951, the Defense Department was asked to proceed with the matter. Also, after the assassination of Pakistan's first Prime Minister Liaquat Ali Khan, a group of officials (led by General Ayub Khan and Defense Secretary Iskander Mirza with the support of Governor-General Ghulam Mohammad) attempted to persuade the U.S. to form a military alliance with Pakistan. In this endeavor they were assisted by key State and Defense Department officials.[73] In requesting U.S. military aid and a defense commitment, Pakistan made use of the Olaf Caroe thesis—although to balance India's preponderance in the Subcontinent.[74]

By early 1952, presumably exasperated with India's non-alignment policy, its unacceptable role in Korea and at the Japanese peace treaty conference, and its advocacy of Chinese admission to the U.N., Washington had come to the conclusion that Pakistan and Turkey, and not India, had the ability to counter a communist sweep.[75] The ground for the U.S.-Pakistan military pacts was prepared through negotiations, first in Washington and later in Karachi.[76] It is possible that Pakistan and the U.S. could have successfully concluded the military pacts during the last months of the Truman administration; yet due to the objections of Chester Bowles and George Kennan, and the "uncertainties" of other U.S. officials (including Secretary of State Dean Acheson), and since the term of the Truman administration was coming to an end, the defense scheme was deferred to the next administration.[77]

There is no need to go into the details leading to the subsequent establishment of the U.S. military connection with Pakistan. The story of the U.S.-Pakistan Mutual Defense agreement of May 1954, and Pakistan's entry into SEATO and CENTO has been dealt with by Selig S. Harrison and others.[78] What needs to be underlined, however, is that contrary to commonly held notions, the U.S. sponsored arrangements in Southern Asia were not specifically the brainchild of John Foster Dulles. Dulles had provided the ideological rationale and long range purpose behind these security schemes. In early 1953 after his fact-finding mission to 11 West and South Asian countries (including Egypt, Iraq, Turkey, Iran, Pakistan and India), Secretary of State Dulles produced a "Report on the Near East." In this report, he advanced the idea of a defense arrangement for what he called the "Northern

Tier" states, including Pakistan, Iran and Turkey. He perceived greater security concerns among states contiguous to the Soviet Union, and wanted them to work out an interlocking defense arrangement underwritten by the U.S. to counter any possible Soviet threat to this region.[79] The area comprising the "Northern tier" states had additional geostrategic importance. Its geographical propinquity with one of the most sensitive parts of the Soviet Union—the Central Asian Republics—made it a major security concern for the Soviet government. Pakistan's highly trained professional army and its adherence to Islamic ideology (which was often contrary to communist doctrine), underlined its potential utility as an alliance partner. The U.S. considered that Pakistan would provide much needed base facilities for the U.S. to operate effectively against any hypothetical Soviet attack.[80]

Aside from regional security implications, the U.S.-Pakistan military alliance also fostered the link between the civil-military establishments of the two countries. Incidentally, if the American connection had any bearing on Pakistani military organizations, professional thought and training, it also generated some "self-delusion" among the Pakistan military that it had mastered Pakistani politics.[81] It is doubtful whether the military really did master politics in Pakistan. It is quite conceivable that one of the reasons behind the Pakistani decision to opt for the U.S. military connection might have been the urgency of achieving domestic political stability in the context of heightened Indo-Pak tensions, by underwriting the key instrument of stability in Pakistan—the army. However, it would be sufficient to say that the perception of a need for a Pakistani military connection with the U.S. was essentially prompted by a perceived threat from India (if not a desire for achieving power parity with the latter), though domestic political considerations may have also played a crucial role in the making of this decision.[82]

In any event, the U.S.-Pakistan link and the establishment of an electronic surveillance installation near Peshawar[83] introduced an understandable bias in U.S. policy regarding certain issues involving India and Pakistan (Kashmir in particular). Indeed, to the extent that the State and Defense Departments stressed the importance of the U.S. air base at Peshawar, Pakistan's capacity to influence U.S. policy increased. In a sense the origin of the lopsided U.S. policy toward Pakistan and India may be traced to this facet of U.S.-Pakistan relations. Thus, irrespective of the state of Pakistani-Chinese, Sino-Soviet, U.S.-Soviet, Sino-Indian, or

Indo-U.S. relations, "military parity" between Pakistan and India became a "self-sufficient" goal of America's South Asia policy.[84]

For Pakistani leaders, the military assistance program came as a windfall that would enhance Pakistan's capability not so much against hypothetical communist expansionism as against its perceived enemy, India. Perceptive observers did not miss the paradoxical assumptions behind U.S. military assistance to Pakistan. One analyst noted that Pakistan was "more inclined to build her military strength as a bargaining factor" to deal with India on the Kashmir question than as a defense against other countries—including the Soviet Union. This was an admission privately expressed at that time in Pakistan.[85] In the U.S. there were only a few dissenting voices against rendering military assistance to Pakistan. Prominent Americans like Chester Bowles, Eleanor Roosevelt, Senator Fulbright, Congressman Emmanual Celler, Lewis Mumford and Dorothy Norman were opposed to the proposed military aid. To most Americans, however, the contemplated defense arrangement seemed to be quite in conformity with the basic goals of the U.S. containment strategy as worked out since the enunciation of the Truman Doctrine. "Military aid for Pakistan," *The New York Times* commented, "would be a good policy."[86] Earlier, the *Times* military correspondent, Hanson Baldwin, had asserted that U.S. military assistance "could mean the beginning of a viable Middle East defense and a new and more direct and vigorous approach to all the problems of the Indian Subcontinent and of Southeastern Asia."[87] But more importantly, on Capitol Hill and among Americans in general there was strong bipartisan support for the U.S. move to provide military aid to the Pakistanis.[88]

Global Benefits and Regional Costs

In negotiating the defense arrangement with Pakistan, the U.S. administration had been initially hesitant because of its likely impact on Indo-U.S. and Indo-Pakistani relations. Indeed, it was not unaware of Pakistan's obsession with India. While informal talks had been going on between the U.S. and Pakistan since 1951, and U.S. officials were generally convinced of the need to induct Pakistan into an anti-USSR military alliance, there was (American) apprehension that such action might not only accentuate strained Indo-Pakistani relations, but might well generate violent reactions in India and thereby affect relations between India and the U.S. The

Eisenhower administration sought to maintain friendly relationships
with the region as a whole and not just one nation.[89] It was also felt
that such action in the context of a defense arrangement might impel
the Afghans to move closer to the Soviet Union.[90]

There are reasons to believe that U.S. policymakers
seriously debated where "global benefits" would be greater than
"regional costs," in bringing Pakistan within the Western alliance
system. The signing of a military pact between Pakistan and the
U.S. might have been further delayed but for Soviet success in
breaking the U.S. thermonuclear monopoly in September 1953.
Also, there was evidence thereafter to suggest that the Soviet Union
had acquired the capability to launch direct nuclear strikes against the
U.S. mainland with long range bomber aircraft.[91] Confronted with
the grim prospect of a direct nuclear threat, U.S. policymakers
seemed to have been stampeded into a decision to secure military
base facilities on the Soviet periphery. With India's refusal, the
only country available to complete the much needed chain of
containment around Moscow in South Asia was Pakistan—with its
two separate wings adjacent to both West Asia and Southeast Asia.
The strategic importance of Pakistan presumably more than
compensated for possible damages incurred through India's
(hopefully) short-run displeasure.

Hindsight suggests that in sponsoring the military pacts in
Asia, the U.S. might have been afflicted with what might be called
irrational telescopic psychology, which tends to perceive immediate
military gains in terms of U.S. strategic insurance. Thus risks to
long range regional peace were viewed by the U.S. as acceptable. It
is ironic that despite the known motives behind Pakistan's urge for
concluding an arms deal with the U.S., the American government
did not fully comprehend the ramifications for South Asia. In
retrospect, it would appear that Washington neglected the possibility
of deeper Soviet involvement in the region and of closer Indo-Soviet
ties to counter the U.S.-Pakistan alliance. This lack of foresight is
understandable, considering that in early 1954 the Soviet Union was
still politically distant from South Asia (despite its geographical
proximity). Yet, there were some Americans who anticipated
regional developments. Chester Bowles had cautioned Dulles that
such a deal would present the Soviet Union with tempting choices.
He believed that the Soviet Union would not only offer arms aid to
India, but would also provide substantial economic aid to underwrite
India's Five Year Plan.[92] Subsequent events were to prove him
correct. Needless to say, the proposed defense scheme did not
achieve peace and stability in West and South Asia. It not only

complicated U.S. policy toward South Asia but may have provoked the Soviet Union into a more assertive foreign policy in the area.

Within two months of the Soviet thermonuclear explosion, Pakistan's Governor-general Ghulam Mohammed and Foreign Minister Zafrullah Khan met with President Eisenhower and Secretary of State Dulles in Washington in November 1953 to work out a mutually beneficial military arrangement. It was, however, only after a series of denials regarding the likelihood of an impending military deal,[93] and the conclusion of a Turco-Pakistan Pact, that the Pakistan-U.S. Mutual Defense Agreement was finally signed. In conformity with the Dullesian concept of the Northern Tier and Pakistan's need for strengthening its defense, Pakistan was literally guided by the U.S. administration to conclude a pact with Turkey for closer defense and politico-economic cooperation, on April 2, 1954, and then to sign a mutual defense agreement with the U.S. on May 19, 1954.[94] The Turco-Pakistan Pact, establishing the structure of regional cooperation, was a prerequisite for the supply of U.S. military hardware and training to the Pakistani armed forces. But surprisingly, having decided to opt for a policy of alignment, the Pakistan government was still not certain whether it should make a formal announcement regarding its abandonment of the policy of non-involvement in the Cold War contest. In fact, in a domestic press note issued on the day of the signing, the Pakistani government asserted that the U.S.-Pakistan agreement neither set up a military alliance nor called for any military base facilities in Pakistan for the U.S.[95]

On September 8, 1954 Pakistan joined the South East Asian Treaty Organization (SEATO) and thereby became a formal alliance partner in a U.S. sponsored military alliance system. It should be noted, however, that unlike its commitments to NATO members, this commitment did not oblige the United States to consider an attack on Pakistan as an attack on itself. Besides, the U.S. limited its commitment. Despite Pakistani opposition, the United States was able to get a reservation incorporated into the Treaty (Article IV, paragraph I), that its obligation was relevant only for cases of communist aggression.[96] These reservations suggest that the U.S. was concerned about reducing the adverse effects of the arrangement on Pakistan's non-communist neighbors.

By fall 1955, the Turco-Pakistan Treaty of Friendship and Cooperation had grown into what has been described as the Baghdad Pact (later CENTO). In view of the geographical distance between the two countries, other West Asian states were considered as members. Turkey entered into a defense alliance with Iraq on

February 24, 1955. Later Great Britain (April 15, 1955), Pakistan
(September 23, 1955), and Iran (November 3, 1955) joined the
alliance by depositing (in accordance with Article Five) the
instruments of accession with the Iraqi Ministry of Foreign
Affairs.[97] After joining the Baghdad Pact, Pakistan seemed to have
emerged as the most aligned of the U.S. allies in Asia.

    Pakistan's expectations for those pacts were not fulfilled.
First, the principal sponsor of the pact, the U.S., refused to become
a full member because of the likely impact on Israel. Second, the
Baghdad Pact was jolted in 1958 when a coup in Iraq led it to
withdraw (the name of the organization was then changed to the
Central Treaty Organization (CENTO). Third, despite Pakistani and
Iranian insistence, a NATO-type central command structure was
never instituted under a U.S. commander. Even from the
perspective of the U.S. interests, the Western-sponsored defense
arrangements did not solve but only complicated the task of building
a viable structure of regional security. For instance, it angered the
forces of Arab nationalism that considered the Western alliance-
building efforts an intrusion in the affairs of their world. In
addition, it spurred the Soviet Union to exploit Arab antagonism
toward the West with a view to erode Western influence in this
strategic belt. Apart from this, some of the nationalist Arab regimes
that opted for the policy of non-alignment, such as Egypt under
Nasser, demonstrated their solidarity with non-aligned India. These
same forces came into conflict with Pakistan because of the latter's
role in the formation of the Western alliance network in West Asia.

    Despite these adverse results, the Eisenhower administration
persisted. It was not publicly clear at that point whether the U.S.
was deriving tangible benefits out of its military ties with Pakistan.
The answer was, however, provided by the downing of a U.S.
intelligence gathering plane over the Soviet Union in May 1960. It
appears that the ill-fated U-2 had taken off from Peshawar (West
Pakistan) where the U.S. had a communications base. It is not
inconceivable that since the mid-1950s Pakistan had extended base
facilities to the U.S. Aside from anything else, the U-2 incident
makes it "spectacularly explicit" why the Pakistan government had
"unshakable bargaining power" in Washington and had been able to
get from the U.S. significant quantities of highly sophisticated
weapons.[98] In exchange for military assistance to Pakistan, the
U.S. was able to obtain facilities for gathering information not only
about the state of Soviet military preparations but also the specific
nature and exact location of potential targets within the Soviet
Union—e.g. military and industrial objectives.[99]

Thus, to the extent that the U.S. had to depend on Pakistan, even if for limited strategic reasons, the U.S. administration had to consolidate and further strengthen its military ties with Pakistan, notwithstanding the adverse impact on Indo-U.S. relationships. When the army came to power in Pakistan in 1958, the coup caused some initial discomfiture to the U.S. administration; however, it was not altogether an unwelcome development, especially to those U.S. officials who valued closer military ties with Pakistan.

One of the major steps in the development of regional security arrangements in West Asia was the extension (in November 1955) of direct U.S. protection to the territorial integrity and independence of the "Northern Tier" states (Pakistan, Iran, Iraq and Turkey).[100] Approving this declared policy of the Eisenhower administration, the U.S. Congress authorized (on March 9, 1957) the President to provide economic and military assistance to nations in the Middle East. More importantly, it expressed U.S. willingness to assist any nation in the region that sought help against "armed aggression from any country controlled by international communism."[101]

The U.S.-Pakistan Mutual Security Agreement of 1959 was in part the outcome of American efforts to underwrite the West Asian regional security system. But a more impelling reason behind this agreement was the understanding reached earlier at the Baghdad Pact Council meeting in London (July 1958) following the overthrow of the pro-West Iraqi regime on July 14, 1958. One important aspect of this meeting was that the U.S. made a bid to fill the gap caused by Iraq's withdrawal. It agreed to undertake almost the same obligations, those of a full member of the Baghdad Pact, by signing the Declaration of the Conference.

It was in conformity with the London Declaration that Washington concluded identical bilateral defense agreements with Pakistan, Iran and Turkey on March 5, 1959. Under the relevant operative clause (Article I) of this agreement, the American administration firmly committed itself to assist Pakistan in accordance with its own constitutional processes. The clause provided for "such appropriate action, including the use of armed forces" by the U.S. as may be mutually agreed upon and "as is envisaged by the Joint Resolution to Promote Peace and Stability in the Middle East."[102] Since this article made no direct reference to aggression by communist states, its scope was rather broadly interpreted by some Pakistani spokesmen. They suggested that because the U.S. defense commitment to Pakistan was operative against aggression from any quarter, communist or non-communist, the latter could depend on U.S. assistance in the event of a threat from India.[103] Needless to say, they had missed the significance of the qualifying phrase of the above article, "as is envisaged in the Joint Resolution" (of the U.S. Congress, March 9, 1957) which, as stated earlier, called for direct U.S. action in response to any armed aggression from a country controlled by international communism.

In considering Pakistan's misreading of its security agreement (1959) with the United States, the Indian government approached the Eisenhower administration for clarification. It was "specifically assured" by the U.S. that the latest agreement could not be used against India.[104] However, India could not afford to take chances with its security by depending on U.S. assurances or Pakistan's good intentions. From the outset, i.e. the time of Pakistan's decision to obtain U.S. military assistance, India's leaders were apprehensive that military aid might be used against them. Furthermore, Delhi feared an upset in the existing ratio of military forces between the two countries. In response to this predicament, the Indian government sought to avoid any step that could trigger an arms race in the Subcontinent. Yet, because India felt impelled to maintain a certain degree of military preparedness and to moderately increase its defense spending, Pakistan's arms deal with the U.S. seemed to have started a visible arms race in the Subcontinent, even if on a moderate scale.[105]

India and External Powers

U.S. support and aid for Pakistan not only caused India's displeasure but drew the Soviet Union and China into the Subcontinent. U.S. military aid to Pakistan produced considerable anxiety in India about its security, notwithstanding President Eisenhower's assurance to Nehru that the U.S.-Pakistan alliance "is not directed in any way against India."[106] This assurance hardly convinced India of Pakistan's peaceful intentions. On the contrary, India contended that the pact had introduced a new element in the Kashmir question, and hardened its posture on the issue, declaring that Kashmir's accession to India was legally final and complete.[107]

The continuing tension in Indo-U.S. relations was followed by a remarkable improvement in Indo-Soviet relations. The Soviets befriended India through economic aid and timely diplomatic support of the Indian stand on Kashmir whenever it came up before the United Nations. In contrast to the relative indifference of Stalin, the new Soviet leaders (Khrushchev and Bulganin) publicly endorsed Kashmir's accession to India during their visit to India in late 1955.

Aside from this clear enunciation of a pro-Indian position on Kashmir, the Soviet leaders not only promised to provide further economic aid to India, but also agreed to share the USSR's experience in industry and the development of nuclear energy for peaceful purposes. Before leaving for home, the Soviet leaders had given away as a gift, ten million dollars worth of farming machinery for a state agricultural farm in Rajasthan. In some ways however, the process of Indo-Soviet rapprochement had started as early as December 1953 with the conclusion of a five-year trade agreement between the two countries. When the Soviet Union formally agreed to help India build up a steel mill at Bhilai in early 1955, it clearly indicated a more substantive development of a new Soviet policy toward India. The subsequent reciprocal state visits by Indian Prime Minister Nehru to the Soviet Union (mid-1955) and Soviet leaders Khrushchev and Bulganin to India (November-December 1955), demonstrated the growing understanding and goodwill between the two countries.[108]

The Soviets, essentially as a result of the Cold War, were compelled to befriend India as a response to U.S. military involvement in Asia, particularly in Pakistan. Following their visit to India, Khrushchev and Bulganin, (then on a state visit to Afghanistan) supported the right of self-determination of the Pakhtuns in Pakistan's North West Frontier Province (NWFP).[109] This was obviously a diplomatic signal regarding their displeasure with Pakistan's membership in the U.S. sponsored military alliance system.

In some ways, the development of closer Indo-Soviet links followed the Afro-Asian conference at Bandung in April 1955. This conference not only marked China's entry into a non-communist forum, but symbolized the common aspirations for freedom and independence of the Afro-Asian nations. Significantly, at Bandung Chinese Premier Chou En-lai sought to mediate between both aligned and non-aligned Afro-Asian nations. This was in conflict with general Soviet antipathy toward the aligned Asian states.

Hindsight would suggest that the Soviet diplomatic offensive in Southern Asia was also indicative of its attempts to deny Communist China a monopoly on close relations with non-communist Asian entities. In fact, China had started developing friendly ties with India following the Nehru-Chou declaration of the Five Principles of peaceful coexistence in 1954. It launched the era of *Hindi-Chini Bhai Bhai* (Indians and Chinese are brothers). But paradoxically, even though SEATO was clearly directed against China, it did not inhibit the latter from appreciating the basic rationale behind Pakistan's membership in that alliance.[110]

It would appear from the subsequent revelations in the Sino-Soviet polemical debates of the sixties that Peking was quite disenchanted with the role played by the Soviet Union in South Asia in the mid-fifties. The gradual erosion of Soviet economic aid to China after 1956 contrasted with the Soviet decision to provide sizeable economic assistance to New Delhi. China reacted adversely to a Soviet aid policy that gave higher priority to a non-aligned India than to a Socialist alliance partner. In the U.S., this Soviet initiative was viewed with a certain degree of resentment. There were some who considered Nehru and Tito as "aides and allies of communist imperialism in fact and in effect, if not in diplomatic verbiage."[111]

Yet, the political complexity of South Asia generated its own demands. The injection of superpower politics into the region did not lead to a convergence of the lines of conflict at global and regional levels. It is this divergence which produced a degree of ambivalence in the American posture toward this region. The U.S. not only appreciated the need for a viable structure of stability in South Asia, but also recognized the urgency of economic and political development. The military-economic relationship with Pakistan and the subsequent launching of a program of economic aid to underwrite India's economic development served as the basic format of America's South Asia policy

By 1956, Indo-U.S. relations began to improve. New Delhi and Washington cooperated closely with each other in the UN during the Suez crisis of July 1956. The strong American criticism of the Anglo-French invasion of Egypt was favorably received in New Delhi. On the whole, in spite of India's cautious reaction to Soviet intervention in Hungary, the year 1956 was marked by an improved understanding between India and the U.S. In December 1956, Nehru made his second official trip to the U.S., one that was considered successful, marking the beginning of the third phase of U.S. South Asia policy. This phase was considered as one of mutual friendship and balanced appreciation of the respective foreign policies of the two countries.[112] The high point was reached in the Kennedy administration, when the U.S. became more closely involved in India, and the process culminated in U.S. arms transfers (sales and grants) to India in 1962 in the wake of the Sino-Indian War.

Even at the lowest point of their relationship, neither India nor the U.S. was prepared for a complete break. If India was keen to maintain a normal level of interaction with the U.S.—whether to obtain economic aid or to ensure balanced relations with the major world powers—the latter was interested in India's stability and development. In spite of their differences, the U.S. continued its economic aid to India, and the latter was not reluctant to accept it.

An increasing amount of U.S. economic aid began to flow into India at about the time when India launched its second five year plan (1956-61).[113] There are reasons to believe, however, that the substantial injection of Soviet aid dating from the mid-fifties led to a U.S. reassessment regarding its own aid to India.[114] During Eisenhower's first term the U.S. was not favorably disposed toward economic aid; during his second term, the U.S. started massive aid programs. Henceforth economic aid constituted a basic element in U.S. policy toward India. Obviously, it was perceived as a major countervailing instrument for matching competing Soviet influence in New Delhi and elsewhere in the Third World.[115]

The U.S. response was also heavily influenced by the acute foreign exchange crisis that faced India in 1957-58. The Cooper-Kennedy resolution, passed in the Senate at the end of 1959, stipulated a U.S. commitment to help India fulfill its development task. By August 1958, a World Bank consortium for India and Pakistan was established to help India through a coordinated approach by donor countries.[116] An added consideration behind U.S. aid was the ideological significance of India's economic development in contrast to that of China. There was apprehension in the U.S. that if the Indians "cave in," then China's performance—though "really quite mediocre"—would appear as the "wave of the "future" in the Third World.[117]

Apart from calculated discretion on the part of New Delhi and Washington (or mutual appreciation of their economic relationship), fortuitous circumstances led to an improvement of Indo-U.S. relations. First, by the end of the Eisenhower administration the "Camp David spirit" signalled that Cold War tensions had lessened between the U.S. and the Soviet Union. Second, by the end of 1959, a Sino-Indian confrontation was developing because of a revolt in Tibet and related border questions. Third, there were signs of growing Sino-Soviet divergence after 1960. While the cumulative effect of these developments was to foster closer Indo-U.S. rapport, it also marked the emergence of India as an area of agreement of parallel interests between Moscow and Washington—because of their common concern with China.[118]

Eisenhower's enthusiastic reception on his visit to India in December 1959 was symbolic of a new mood of Indo-U.S.

cordiality that gathered momentum with the Kennedy administration. When Kennedy assumed the Presidency, for the first time someone in the White House was personally interested in and concerned about the success of India's democratic experiment. Earlier, in various speeches in the Senate, he had urged greater attention be given to India and had advocated improved Indo-U.S. relations.

It would be oversimplistic to suggest that this change by itself could have ensured closer Indo-U.S. relations. In fact, it had to face a number of policy constraints regarding South Asia. Even under Kennedy, after its initial reservations about the military pacts, the U.S. administration tried to balance its involvement in India and Pakistan. Not infrequently the question was raised in the U.S. whether foreign aid should be tied to the resolution of the Kashmir dispute. As a result, not only were foreign aid debates in the U.S. Congress prolonged—even in 1962—but they also generated severe criticism of the Indian stand on Kashmir. On top of these continuing problems, sudden developments such as the use of force by India in Goa (1961), or the Indian decision to seek a Soviet-built MiG aircraft factory (1961)--actually finalized after refusal by the U.K. and the U.S.—affected the stability of Indo-U.S. interaction.

With the coming of the Kennedy administration, political ties between New Delhi and Washington further improved, due to the experience gained through the economic collaboration initiated under Eisenhower. In some areas of international diplomacy, e.g. UN operations in the Congo, the raging controversy about the UN Secretary-General's office, disarmament negotiations at Geneva, and the neutralization of Laos, Indian and American foreign policy goals tended to coincide. It was in the backdrop of this improved Indo-U.S. relationship that Nehru's third visit to the U.S. in November 1961 occurred. Despite initial expectations, the Nehru-Kennedy meeting hardly consolidated the gains in Indo-U.S. ties made earlier during the Republican presidency. While this was quite disappointing for the young American President,[119] talks between the two leaders did produce some common Indian and U.S. policy goals regarding South East Asia. This could be adduced not only to India's growing concern about the Chinese inroads into this region, but also to the American inclination to support liberal and non-aligned regimes, such as existed in India, presumably as a counter against Chinese communism.

This process of growing Indo-U.S. understanding received a severe jolt as a result of Washington's adverse reaction to Delhi's liberation of Goa from Portuguese colonial rule in December 1961. After Indian armed forces moved into Goa, Adlai Stevenson, the

U.S. ambassador to the United Nations, in a very angry and emotional speech against India, talked about the death of the UN What shocked the Indians most was that Stevenson did not even make a passing reference to Portuguese colonialism—as to why a handful of Europeans should rule several million Asian and African people.[120] In India his angry outbursts were explained in terms of the perceived anti-Indian bias of U.S. policymakers regarding issues of vital interest to India.[121]

Obviously, there were irritations between New Delhi and Washington in the wake of the Goa episode. But this episode did not prove to be a major obstacle in the way of further expanding interaction between the two countries. It would be wrong to suggest that Stevenson's reactions were representative of the general American position on Goa and other related colonial issues. Some important American participant observers believed that Goa should have been evacuated by Portugal about the same time the U.K. and France made a peaceful settlement with India "for Goa is a part of India." Other Americans also perceived the relevance of anti-colonialism in the arena of global politics.[122] Hence, it is hardly surprising that the Goa issue was not played up by the Kennedy administration. What is more, the matter was not allowed to impinge upon the more substantive bases of developing Indo-U.S. cooperation in the 1960s.

No sooner had the Goa issue subsided, than President Kennedy sent Dr. Henry Kissinger to the Subcontinent on a study mission. Presumably, Kennedy wanted to ease India's misgivings regarding the U.S. reaction to Goa. Speaking at New Delhi, Dr. Kissinger assured his audience that if the Kashmir question were raised in the United Nations, the U.S. would not seek to harm India because of Goa. More importantly, he offered America's sympathy for any action that India might deem necessary against China.

Despite initial American reservations, Pakistan was able to raise the Kashmir issue again at the UN Security Council (February 1962) with general Western support, particularly that of the U.K.[123] This was contrary to India's preference for bilateral talks without third party arbitration or good offices—for the eventual resolution of the problem. It is reasonable to assume that Pakistan's decision was timed to further exploit the existing tension between India and the Western powers (over the Goa issue) and thereby secure the latter's support in the UN for its position on Kashmir.

While there was a consensus among the Western countries for helping the disputants reach a settlement, there was no agreement for an imposed solution. While Washington sought to produce common reference frames by summarizing the common points of discussions in the Security Council, the Soviet Union charged that such a method was inadequate. Later, an Irish-sponsored resolution urging the parties to enter into negotiations was vetoed by the Soviet Union. India had strongly opposed the resolution.[124]

The UN debate on Kashmir did not lead to any dramatic changes in Indo-Pak relations or in those between South Asia as a whole and the major powers. Nevertheless, in the context of the accentuated Sino-Indian conflict (especially since the Tibetan revolt of 1959) and of then-growing tension between Moscow and Beijing, one could notice an evolving pattern of American policy toward South Asia. With the last few years of the Eisenhower administration, the United States seemed to have opted for a more balanced policy toward India and Pakistan. Admittedly, it called for considerable tightrope walking and also a certain degree of ingenuity on the part of American policymakers. This task implied reconciling the goals of two differing objectives: building bridges to a non-aligned India without compromising the more substantive U.S. military connection with an aligned Pakistan.

With the coming of the Kennedy administration this policy was carried out with greater vigor. During 1961-62, relations between India and the United States continued to develop on a more meaningful basis, notwithstanding the old conflicts: America's leaning toward Pakistan on the Kashmir issue, the U.S. supply of F-104 aircraft to Pakistan, America's annoyance with Indian action in Goa, and U.S. disapproval of India's decision to enter into an aircraft deal with Moscow. Establishment of closer rapport between the two governments (accelerated by the appointment of persons friendly to India in key positions of the new administration),[125] was followed by greater interaction between India and the U.S. Thus, moving from a position of hesitancy to one of formal commitment to the success of Indian developmental planning, the United States was inclined to undertake a greater role in supporting India's gigantic developmental efforts as envisaged under the Third Five Year Plan (1961-66). As the aid-giving activities of the different American agencies were integrated under the newly formed Agency of International Development (AID), the Kennedy administration not only committed a sizeable quantum of U.S. aid (on only nominal interest charges) to India, but also called upon other western aid-giving nations to do likewise.[126]

The subsequent improvement in Indo-U.S. relations around this time was somewhat affected by their mutually beneficial cooperation elsewhere. In the Congo, for instance, in early 1961,

Indian and American goals tended to coincide when UN peacekeeping operations were faced with a fiasco unless provided with further men and material support. In response to this common predicament, India's decision to support these operations with its own men and material was appreciated by the U.S. administration. In Southeast Asia, the U.S. was gradually subscribing to the policy of neutrality in Laos—as pursued by India.

In forging closer ties with India, U.S. Defense Secretary Robert S. McNamara had even sought Congressional authority to facilitate the supply of arms to "neutrals." It implied, that in the event of a contingency situation, non-aligned states such as India could hope to secure U.S. arms.[127] This possibility, along with India's growing prominence as an element in America's Asia policy, inevitably caused a good deal of anxiety and anger in Pakistan. The United States sought to allay Pakistan's misapprehension by offering more advanced aircraft. In addition, it promised not to provide military aid to India unless the security of the Subcontinent was in jeopardy and not without prior consultation with the Pakistan government. However, the U.S. administration refused to consider Pakistan's plea for forcing India to resolve the Kashmir dispute by making use of economic aid as an instrument of political pressure.[128]

In dealing with Pakistan and India the Kennedy administration, tried to pursue a policy which was as non-discriminatory as possible. Contrary to Pakistani apprehensions, U.S. interest in Pakistan did not decline. Despite its intention to develop closer cooperative ties with India, the new U.S. administration proceeded cautiously. It was only at the risk of losing the vital electronic surveillance facilities at Peshawar (for monitoring Soviet missile sites) that the Kennedy administration could have ignored Pakistani sensitivity regarding its role in the Subcontinent. Also, because the United States still had to deal with possible Soviet pressures along the "Northern tier" (thereby affecting the CENTO countries) and its threatening position in Europe (especially near Berlin) it exercised a certain caution to keep the overall alliance system in order.

These considerations were crucial in limiting changes in America's South Asia policy. While the Kennedy administration tended to underline the need for projecting India as a politically stable and economically viable element (considering the growing Chinese threat), it was unable to take a more neutral position on the Kashmir issue.[129] It was generally held in the U.S. that the settlement of the Kashmir was essential to Pakistan's national life and that certain agreements made regarding Kashmir should at least be honored by India until other alternatives were found.[130] Paradoxically, neither continued military aid nor enhanced economic aid from the U.S. inhibited Pakistan from "making efforts" to improve relations and develop friendly ties with China—as part of some long overdue changes in its foreign policy.[131]

For reasons stated above, Pakistan enjoyed a certain priority in Washington's overall South Asia policy. This was clearly indicative of the limits within which a closer Indo-U.S. relationship could develop. It was, however, assumed at that time by the U.S. that it could pursue a policy of continued support to Pakistan while making efforts to develop the Indo-U.S. relationship on a more enduring basis. Naturally, this two-pronged South Asia policy was tremendously difficult for American policymakers to coordinate.[132]

Yet, by virtue of its closer military ties with the U.S., Pakistan held an edge over India. The path of Indo-U.S. relations remained rather halting if not mutually irritating—in spite of the major U.S. foreign aid program in India and the high flying rhetoric about American stakes in the "strong constitutional democracy" in the Subcontinent.[133]

By autumn 1962, developments in South Asia seemed to be quite satisfactory from the U.S. standpoint. In the first place, the United States was slowly working its way toward a position of advantageous bilateral relationships with both India and Pakistan. Second, there were indications of developmental progress in the political and economic spheres of the Subcontinent. In particular, it appeared that the remarkable political stability achieved by India was likely to continue. An additional encouraging feature was that India showed signs of sustained economic growth. These promising trends were soon overshadowed by developments along the Himalayas. These posed a threat to peace in the Subcontinent, and in the process also put tremendous strains on India's policy of non-alignment.

Broadly speaking, the Sino-Indian conflict of October-November 1962 (like the Cuban missile crisis that occurred at the same time) symbolized a process of transformation in the global political system. In its more specific regional context, it generated some changes in the pattern of Indo-U.S. relationships, and in terms of level of interaction, this reached an all time high. Additionally, if it marked a new phase in America's South Asia policy, it also resulted in enhanced U.S. influence in the area. One notable feature of this phase is that unlike previous periods, American policy-making toward South Asia was no longer considered primarily in terms of a contest with the Soviet Union. In short, the Sino-Indian war and the subsequent U.S. response to the crisis indicated, in several ways, not only the growing autonomous significance of the Subcontinent, but also the varying patterns of Washington's ties with both India and Pakistan. The following chapter will deal with the policy process and the consequent American response pattern with reference to this crisis in South Asia.

Notes

1. Some observers have viewed South Asia and Southeast Asia as a single "subsystem"—Southern Asia. See Michael Brecher, *The New States of Asia: A Political Analysis* (New York: Oxford University Press, 1966), pp. 88-110. A "Subordinate State System" or the limits of a subsystem are determined more or less arbitrarily; nonetheless every subsystem has certain identifiable characteristics—denoted by the distribution of power within the region, the pattern of intra-regional interaction in the backdrop of the level of involvement of the major external powers. If we take note of these elements along with the geographical compactness of South Asia, our treatment of the latter as a separate subsystem seems more meaningful than the one conceptualized by Brecher that extends from Pakistan to Jakarta.

2. Wayne Wilcox, "American Policy toward South Asia," *Asian Affairs* 60 (June 1979), p. 129. Even in combination with other regional states, Pakistan is not in a position to match India. In light of this, Pakistan has been impelled to look for an external "equalizer." See Thomas P. Thornton, "South Asia and Great Powers," *World Affairs* 132 (March 1970), pp. 345-358.

3. A. Guy Hope, *America and Swaraj: U.S. Role in India* (Washington, D.C.: Public Affairs Press, 1968), p. 58.

4. During the war U.S. President Roosevelt made a number of attempts to persuade Britain to settle the question of India's independence, in order to secure India's support in allied war efforts against the Axis powers. For details see Hope, p. 58. Besides, the U.S. was also involved in the problem of relief operation in the Bengal Famine of 1943.

5. See Department of State, "U.S. interest in self-government for India, February 25, 1947," *Department of State Bulletin*, March 9, 1947, p. 450.

6. Secretary of State Marshall's secret communication to the U.S. Embassy in New Delhi, January 22, 1947; and U.S. Ambassador to India, Grady's evaluation of independent India's foreign policy direction, to the U.S. Secretary of State, July 9, 1947. See U.S. Department of State, *Foreign Relations of the United States*, Department of State Publication No. 8625 (Washington, D.C., 1972), pp. 139-140, 160-161 (hereafter *FRUS*).

7. Secretary of State Marshall's communication to the U.S. Embassy in India, January 22, 1947. See *FRUS*, p. 139.

8. Secret memorandum of conversation with the Indian Ambassador to the U.S., Asaf Ali, by the U.S. Secretary of State, February 26, 1947, *FRUS*, pp. 147-149.

9. Telegram from Secretary of State George Marshall to the Consulate at Madras, July 16, 1947, *FRUS*, pp. 162-163.

10. The following discussion is based on a secret memorandum between U.S. ambassadors in India (Grady), Pakistan (Alling), and Burma (Huddle), and the appropriate Department officers at the Division of South Asian Affairs, December 26, 1947. See *FRUS*, pp. 175-179.

11. See memorandum of conversations between U.S. envoys in South Asia *FRUS*, p. 178. According to the U.S. Ambassador in India, Grady, India's British Governor General Lord Mountbatten had "warned Nehru against dollar imperialism". See *FRUS*, p. 177. Britain thought that the U.S. role in South Asia conflicted with its own.

12. *FRUS*, p. 177.

13. See memorandum of conversation between the Indian Ambassador Asaf Ali and the Secretary of State in *FRUS*, pp.168-169. Evidently this conflicts with the contention of the Eisenhower administration that, since New Delhi did not want to cooperate with Washington in the containment of communist expansion and Pakistan was willing to do so , it was justified in rendering military assistance to the latter. On Kashmir, see telegram from the U.S. Ambassador to New Delhi, Grady, to the Secretary of State, November 3, 1947, *FRUS*, pp. 180-181.

14. *Ibid.*, p. 181.

15. See G. S. Bhargava, *U.S. Attitudes Toward India, 1947-1971: A Study in the Decisionmaking Process*, FAR2322-N (Cambridge, Mass.: Center for International Affairs, Harvard University, 1974), pp. 14-15.

16. The Franco-British invasion of the Suez Canal Zone in 1956 found the U.S. and India taking a common stand against this action. In some ways, this was a watershed in the Indo-U.S. relationship, which till then had been vitiated by the U.S. military alliance with Pakistan, as well as other differences.

17. See B. M. Kaul, pp. 97-98. Col. Kaul (during the war with China, Kaul, by then Lt. Gen., was held responsible for Indian military reverses) was military attache in the Indian Embassy in Washington. Paradoxically, in subsequent years Britain sold Canberra bombers to India.

18. It was on Britain's advice that India had decided to bring the dispute to the UN In contrast, the U.S. initially wanted "the Kashmir question to be settled by direct negotiations between India and Pakistan". See the State Department's confidential position paper on the Kashmir dispute transmitted to the U.S. Ambassador to India, December 2, 1947, *FRUS*, p. 182.

19. For an Indian perspective on the external powers' interests in this dispute, see Sisir Gupta, *Kashmir: A Study in India-Pakistan Relations* (Bombay: Asia Publishing House, 1967).

20. Indian Prime Minister Nehru's address to the Constituent Assembly, March 5, 1948. See S. L. Poplai, ed., *Select Documents on Asian Affairs: India 1947-50*, Vol. II (Bombay: Oxford University Press, 1950), p. 438

21. The Soviet Union, however, at this time maintained a very low profile in the UN deliberations on the Kashmir dispute. The Soviet delegate usually refrained from taking a categorical positiion.

22. Address at the National Publishers Association dinner, New York, January 17, 1947. The statement was later disowned by the State Department because Dulles spoke in his unofficial capacity. For an understanding of the impact of this remark, see the exchange of confidential communications between the U.S. Secretary of State and the U.S. Embassy in India, dated January 21, 1947 and January 22, 1947, respectively, *FRUS*, pp. 138-140.

23. See Bhargava, pp. 13-14.

24. According to one distinguished scholar on U.S. South Asia policy, as late as 1973 there was no "American policy consensus" regarding the "main questions" posed by the South Asian environment. Wayne Wilcox, *Emergence of Bangladesh* (Washington, D.C.: American Enterprise Institute for Public Policy Research, 1973), p. 1.

25. Wilcox, "China's Strategic Alternatives," p. 408.

26. Norman D. Palmer, *South Asia and United States Policy* (New York: Houghton Mifflin, 1965), pp. 2-11.

27. Thornton, p. 346; Wilcox, "China's Strategic Alternatives," pp. 408-409; also see Myron Weiner, "United States Policy in South and South East Asia," in Stephen D. Kertesz, ed. *American Diplomacy in a New Era* (Notre Dame: University of Notre Dame, 1961), p. 173.

28. Chester Bowles, "America and Russia in India," *Foreign Affairs* (July 1971), p. 639.

29. M. J. Desai's comments on Wilcox's paper in Tang Tsou, p. 437.

30. Harold Isaacs, *Scratches on Our Mind: American Images of China and India* (New York: John Day, 1958).

31. Sisir Gupta, "Indo-U.S. Relations: The Understanding Gap," *The Overseas Hindustan Times* (November 13, 1971); also see Baldev Raj Nayar, "Treat India Seriously," *Foreign Policy* (Spring 1975), pp. 133-154.

32. Based on an observation made by a high level U.S. diplomat.

33. Norman D. Palmer, "Ups and Downs in Indo-American Relations," *Annals* 294 (July 1954), pp. 113-123.

34. From Senate hearings on the nomination of Henry A. Kissinger as Secretary of State, September 1973, cited in Henry A. Kissinger, *American Foreign Policy* (New York: W. W. Norton, 1973), p. 234.

35. Phillips Talbot, *Understanding India* (New York: Foreign Association Headline series, No. 214, February 1973), pp. 62-69.

36. President Richard Nixon's *U.S. Foreign Policy Report to the Congress*, May 3, 1973. See *U.S. Foreign Policy for the 1970s: Shaping a Durable Peace* (Washington, D.C., 1973), p. 80. In the same report, however, he stated that the U.S. prefers to see democratic institutions flourish in India.

37. For these various points of view, see Selig S. Harrison, "Troubled India and Her Neighbors," *Foreign Affairs* (January 1965), pp.312-330; for McNamara's testimony of March 30, 1966, see U.S. Congress, House Committee on Foreign Affairs, *Foreign Assistance Act of 1966*, Hearings, 89th

Congress, 2nd Session, p.269; and President Richard Nixon's *Foreign Policy Report to the Congress*, May 3 , 1973. *U.S. Foreign Policy for the 1970s: Shaping a Durable Peace* (Washington, D.C., 1973), p.81.

38. Address to the Indian Council of World Affairs, New Delhi, October 28, 1974. See *Towards a Global Community: The Common Case of India and America*, (Washington, D.C.: Department of State, 1974), p. 2.

39. Kissinger, p. 235.

40. See report of a conference on India and the United States, May 4 and 5, 1959, in Selig S. Harrison, ed., *India and the United States* (New York: Macmillan, 1961), p. 63. Speaking in an interview in 1964, the Democratic Vice-Presidential nominee, Hubert Humphrey, had stated that the only "counterbalance of the Chinese power is a coalition of powers with India as its main force"(*The New York Times*, September 13, 1964).

41. U.S. Congress, Senate, 85th Congress, 2nd Session, March 25, 1958. *Congressional Record*, Vol. 104, p. 5248.

42. Address by Ambassador to India, George V. Allen, at the India League of America, New York, April 1, 1953 See *The New York Times*, April 2, 1953. One Congressman, Frank S. Thompson (New Jersey), making observations on India's "Crucial Role," stated: "If India goes down, all Asia may go down, and if Asia is lost the cause of freedom itself may be lost (U.S. Congress, House, 85th Congress, 2nd Session, January 27, 1958. *Congressional Record*, Vol. 104, p. 1100.

43. John Sherman Cooper, "India: Critical Test of Foreign Aid". U.S. Senate, 85th Congress, 2nd Session, March 18, 1958. *Congressional Record*, Vol. 104, p. 4613.

44. John D. Jernegan, "American Policy Toward India and Security of South Asia," *The Annals* 294 (July 1954), pp. 131-137. The author was formerly Deputy Assistant Secretary of State for Near Eastern, South Asian and African Affairs.

45. During the early phase of Pakistan's independence (before the conclusion of the military alliance), its relationship with the U.S. was only proper but "not close." Consequently, as a new nation, its "impact upon the American consciousness was virtually nil"(Palmer, p. 28).

46. See U.S. Library of Congress, Congressional Research Service, *Major U.S. Foreign and Defense Policy Issues* (a compilation of papers prepared for the Commission on the Operation of the Senate), Washington, D.C., 1977, pp. 219-221.

47. It is not possible to answer precisely whether South Asia is "as critical a focus of world politics" as other areas of great powers' contest. What is relevant, however, is that the major powers "demonstrate their foreign policy interests in the Subcontinent and regard it as an important area for maneuver." See Barnds, *India, Pakistan and the Great Powers*, p. 3.

48. Weiner, "United States Policy in South and South East Asia," p. 173. My research based on interviews with U.S. government officials also tends to confirm this observation.

49. Statement of Assistant Secretary of State for Near Eastern and South Asian Affairs, Joseph J. Sisco, March 12, 1973. See *United States Interests in and Policies Toward South Asia*, Hearings before House Subcommittee on the Near East and South Asia, 93rd Congress, 1st Session, March 12, 15 and 27, 1973, Washington, D.C., 1973, p. 4.

50. See *The United States and South Asia*, Report of the House Foreign Affairs Subcommittee on the Near East and South Asia, May 26, 1973, Washington, D.C., 1973, pp. 22-23. For the "background of American aid," also see John P. Lewis, *Quiet Crisis in India* (Bombay: Asia Publishing House, 1963), pp. 248-264.

51. This analysis is based on periodic statements by U.S. presidents, various State Department officials and Congressional leaders. For a compact presentation on this issue, see Sisco's statement, March 12, 1973, pp. 3-6.

52. One former member of the U.S. State Department Policy Planning Staff has seen certain merit in the Subcontinental power balance. He contends that "the most 'stable' period in South Asia was when the United States was most closely involved with Pakistan—the mid-1950s until 1963" (see Thornton, "South Asia and the Great Powers," p. 357, fn. 4). Interestingly, one biographer of Nixon insists that as Vice-President, Nixon had advocated arms aid to Pakistan not so much to ensure its security against possible communist threat but "as a counterforce to the confirmed neutralism of India." See Ralph Toledano, *Nixon* (New York: Henry Holt, 1956), p. 164.

53. Isaacs, pp. 276-279.

54. For a concise account of these developments, see Charles Heimsath and Surjit Mansingh, *A Diplomatic History of India* (New Delhi: Allied, 1971), pp. 66-74; also see Dana Adams Schmidt, "India Aid Status under Challenge," *The New York Times*, May 3, 1954.

55. N.R. Pillai, "Middle Ground Between America and Russia: An Indian View," *Foreign Affairs* 32 (January 1954), pp. 259-269.

56. According to a Pakistani analyst, "the attitude of the Labor Government was particularly apathetic towards Pakistan" See G. W. Choudhury, "Pakistan-India Relations," *Pakistan Horizon*, Vol. XI, 2 (June 1958), p. 8.

57. For a study of Pakistan's efforts in this direction, see Sisir Gupta, "Islam as a Factor in Pakistan Foreign Relations," *India Quarterly*, 18 (3), July-September 1962, pp. 230-253.

58. For text of these speeches see Liaquat Ali Khan, *Pakistan: Heart of Asia* (Harvard University Press, 1950), pp. 11-16.

59. Choudhury, *India, Pakistan, Bangladesh, and the Major Powers*, p. 79.

60. Choudhary, p.79.

61. Speaking at Gujranwala in March 1951, Liaquat Ali Khan had stated that Pakistan was neither tied to the Western bloc nor a camp follower of the Soviet bloc of nations. *Dawn*, March 10, 1951.

62. Pakistan was an "enthusiastic" participant in the San Francisco conference convened for the signing of the Japanese Peace Treaty, 1951

(Choudhury, *India, Pakistan, Bangladesh, and the Major Powers*, p. 80). India, in contrast, did not attend this conference and thereby reflected its policy differences with the U.S. India wanted not only recognition of Japanese sovereignty over the Ryukyu Islands (then under U.S. occupation) but stipulations for the return of Taiwan to the People's Republic of China.

63. Barnds, *India, Pakistan and the Great Powers*, p. 91.

64. U.S. Assistant Secretary of State, George C. McGhee, in the U.S. House of Representatives, Committee on Appropriations, *Mutual Security Appropriations for 1952*, Hearings before Subcommittee, 82nd Congress, 1st session, p. 648.

65. Writing in his autobiography, General Ayub Khan (later President of Pakistan) stated: "The political turmoil in the wake of the Prime Minister's death convinced me that we must not lose any time in building up the army which alone could hold the country together and defend it against any possible attack." See Mohammad Ayub Khan, *Friends Not Masters: A Political Autobiography* (New York: Oxford University Press, 1967), p. 42. As early as 1951, Ayub Khan had become quite convinced that to strengthen Pakistan's defense there was a need for "a strong and reliable friend." Fazal Muqueem Khan, *The Story of the Pakistan Army* (Karachi: Oxford University Press, 1963), p. 154.

66. Among U.S. officials, there was much respect for British thinking on strategic issues in unfamiliar lands. Barnds, p. 91. This has been also confirmed by former U.S. Ambassador to India, Professor John Kenneth Galbraith, in a personal communication to this author.

67. For instance, Chester Bowles and Selig S. Harrison. For Bowles' view, see his statement in the Joint Economic Committee of the U.S. Congress, January 18, 1971. *Economic Issues in Military Assistance, Hearings*, Subcommittee on Economy in Government, Joint Economic Committee, U.S. Congress, 92nd Congress, 1st session, 1971, Washington, D.C.,p.258. For Harrison's contention, see "Case History of a Mistake," *The New Republic*, August 10. 1959, pp.10-17. Sir Olaf Caroe's expertise on Asian questions primarily related to the Muslim countries to the west and northwest of Pakistan. His major works include *The Wells of Power*, *The Pathans*, and *Soviet Empire*.

68. Lionel Curtis, "Foreword" to Olaf Caroe's *The Wells of Power— The Oilfields of South-Western Asia* (London: Macmillan, 1951), v-vii. It would be oversimplistic to suggest that there was no variation in the British position on the question of the South-West Asian defense scheme as noted by Sir Olaf Caroe. In fact, many British government officials had some reservations regarding the efficacy of such a program. (Barnds, cited n. 9, p. 353.)

69. Caroe, *Wells of Power*, pp. 192-196. Caroe wanted the U.S. to share the responsibility of Britain in the task of adjustment in peace and defense in war, as discharged by it over a hundred years. There were others in Britain who tried to impress upon the U.S. the role that Pakistan could play in West Asia. Writing in the prestigious *Foreign Affairs* (January 1950), Sir William Barton noted among others the kind of role that Pakistan could play in helping

to set up a chain of Muslim nations as sort of a barrier against "international Communism" and its designs on South West Asian oilfields (pp. 299-308).

70. Caroe, *Wells of Power*, p. 193.

71. See, for instance, the views of Ian Stephens—a British journalist who lived in India and worked as editor of *The Statesman* ("The Image of Pakistan—II"), *Morning News* (Dacca), 25 February 1968. Cited in S. M. Burke, *Mainsprings of Indian and Pakistani Foreign Policies* (Minneapolis: University of Minnesota Press, 1974), p. 216.

72. See L. F. Rushbrook Williams, *The State of Pakistan* (Rev ed., London: Faber and Faber, 1966), pp. 118-119.

73. In particular, Henry A. Byroade (then Assistant Secretary of State for the Near East, South Asia and Africa), Theodore Tannenwold (Deputy to Mutual Security Administrator Averill Harriman), and Major General George Olmstead (Director of the Office of Military Assistance) were in favor of closer military links with Pakistan. Derived from Chaudhury, *India, Pakistan, Bangladesh, and the Major Powers*, p. 80. The author was a policy advisor to Yahya Khan.

74. Chester Bowles, *Promises to Keep: My Years in Public Life* (New York: Harper and Row, 1971), p. 478.

75. 1952 policy statement by U.S. on Goals in Southeast Asia, Document #2, *The Pentagon Papers* (New York: Bantam Books, 1971), p. 27.

76. In Washington, Pakistani Maj. Gen. Shahid Hamid negotiated with U.S. Army officials. In Pakistan, discussions took place around November 1952 between U.S. Admiral Arthur W. Radford, Chief of the Naval Staff, and Pakistan Governor-General Ghulam Mohammad and Commander in Chief General Ayub Khan. G. W. Choudhury, *India, Pakistan, Bangladesh, and the Major Powers*, pp. 80-81.

77. Barnds, p. 92.

78. Selig S. Harrison, "Case History of a Mistake," *The New Republic* (August 10, 1959); idem, "The United States, India and Pakistan," *The New Republic* (September 25, 1959); Arya, "America's Military Alliance with Pakistan: The Evolution and Course of an Uneasy Partnership," *International Studies* (July-September 1966), pp. 73-125; Jayanta K. Ray, *Public Policy and Global Reality: Some Aspects of American Alliance Policy* (New Delhi: Radiant, 1977), pp. 76-90.

79. Speech by Foster Dulles following his visit to West and South Asian countries, May 29, 1953. For text see *Documents on International Affairs 1953* (London: Royal Institute of International Affairs, 1956), p. 266. It appears Dulles had adapted his idea of "the Northern Tier" from the one coined by Caroe, "the Northern Screen."

80. Analysis based on Sarwar K. Hasan, "The Background of American Arms Aid to Pakistan," *Pakistan Horizon* (Vol. XX, No. 2, 1967), p. 123; Harrison, n. 102.

81. Stephen P. Cohen, *Security Decision-making in Pakistan* (a report prepared for the Office of External Research, Department of State, September 1980, Contract #1722-020167), pp. 70-78.

82. Some analysts have overstated the domestic considerations behind Pakistan's decision to enter into a military alliance with the United States. See Aswini K. Ray, *Domestic Compulsions and Foreign Policy: Pakistan in Indo-Soviet Relations* (New Delhi: Manas Publications, 1975), pp. 34-83.

83. Headquarters, 5235th Communication Group, U.S.A.F., North West Pakistan. Cited in Selig S. Harrison, "America, India and Pakistan: A Chance for a Fresh Start," *Harper's Magazine* (Vol. 233, No. 1394, July 1966), p. 54. It was from this base that Francis Gary Powers took off for his surveillance flight over the Soviet Union on May 9, 1960.

84. Baldev Raj Nayar, p. 140.

85. See dispatch by Karachi correspondent of *The New York Times*, November 21, 1953.

86. *The New York Times*, January 2, 1954.

87. *Ibid.*, December 20, 1953.

88. While justifying U.S. arms aid to Pakistan, Admiral Redford, Chairman of the Joint Chiefs of Staff, recognized Pakistan as a "very fine, loyal, anti-Communist ally." See U.S. Senate, 84th Congress, 2nd Session, Committee on Foreign Relations, Washington, D.C., 1956, p. 594.

89. See U.S. President Eisenhower's conference, November 18, 1953 (*The New York Times*, November 19, 1953).

90. As argued by Chester Bowles, U.S. Ambassador to India during the Truman administration (cited, Barnds, p. 92). For a subsequent reiteration of this point, see Chester Bowles' memoir, *Promises to Keep*, p. 277.

91. General Hoyt Vandenburg's testimony, U.S. House of Representatives, 83rd Congress, 1st Session, Committee of Appropriations, Hearings, *Department of the Air Force Appropriations for 1954* (Washington, D.C., 1953), p. 161.

92. Bowles, communication to Dulles, cited in *Promises to Keep*, p. 479.

93. Responding to the Indian Prime Minister's complaint, the Pakistani Prime Minister, Mohammad Ali, denied that any military arrangement was being conceived between Pakistan and the U.S. He had pointed out that only some consultations had taken place about the supply of U.S. arms to Pakistan. See his reply, dated December 17, 1953, in *White Paper on Kashmir: Meetings and Correspondence between the Prime Ministers of India and Pakistan, July 1953-October 1954* (New Delhi: Ministry of External Affairs, 1954). The Pakistani Foreign Minister, Zafrullah Khan, had asserted that Pakistan "never was and was not at present considering participating in a military alliance" (Interview to *Le Monde*, cited in *Pakistan Times*, January 5, 1954). In the United States, the Chairman of the Senate Foreign Relations Committee, Alexander Wiley, submitted that "no military alliance between the U.S. and Pakistan is under consideration" (*Amrita Bazar Patrika*, January 31, 1954).

94. For the text of the U.S.-Pakistan Mutual Assistance Agreement, May 19, 1954, see *United Nations Treaty Series*, Treaty No. 2736, Vol. 202, p. 302.

95. For the text of the Pakistan government press note, see *Dawn*, May 20, 1954.

96. See text of the operative clauses of the South-East Asian Collective Defense Treaty, signed at Manila, September 8, 1954, in United Nations Treaty Series, Treaty No. 2819, vol. 209, p. 28.

97. *Ibid.*, Treaty No. 3264, Vol. 233, p. 210. This defense arrangement failed to bring in other Arab states, apart from Iraq. What is more, in view of Israeli opposition, the U.S. did not join.

98. Selig S. Harrison, "South Asian and U.S. Policy," *The New Republic* (Washington, D. C.), December 11, 1961. The total value of the military hardware received by Pakistan from the U.S. was estimated around 1.5 billion dollars. See *Keesing's Contemporary Archives*, 1966, p. 21364.

99. Testimony of U.S. Defense Secretary Thomas Gates, U.S. Senate, Congress 85, Session 2, Committee on Foreign Relations Hearings, *Events Incident to the Summit Conference* (Washington, D.C. 1960), pp. 123-124, 126, 143.

100. The U.S. declaration regarding West Asia was made in the backdrop of the escalating crisis over Suez on November 29, 1956. This was the enunciation of the more commonly known Eisenhower Doctrine. For text see *Department of State Bulletin* (December 10, 1956), p. 918.

101. The Joint Resolution 117 to Promote Peace and Stability in the Middle East (Public Law 35-7).

102. For text of this agreement, see *United Nations Treaty Series*, Treaty No. 4726, Vol. 327, p. 286.

103. See comments of Pakistan Foreign Ministry in *Dawn*, March 7, 1959.

104. Statement by the Indian Prime Minister Nehru in the Parliament, March 13, 1959. For text see Jawaharlal Nehru, *India's Foreign Policy: Selected Speeches* September 1946-April 1961 (New Delhi: Publication Division, 1961), p. 475.

105. From an average below 2% of the G.N.P., India's defense spending rose to over 2% of the G.N.P. after 1954. Between 1954 and 1958, India was compelled to place orders for the purchase of Canberras and Gnats, and Mysteres from the U.K. and France respectively. Stockholm International Peace Research Institute, *The Arms Trade with the Third World* (Stockholm: Almquist & Wiksell, 1971), p. 475.

106. President Eisenhower's letter to Nehru concerning U.S. military aid to Pakistan, February 25, 1954. See U.S. President, *Public Papers of the Presidents of the United States* (Washington, D.C.: Office of the Federal Register, National Archives and Records Service, 1953). Dwight D. Eisenhower, 2956, p. 284. India was also assured that the U.S. would prevent Pakistan from using U.S. military equipment against India.

107. Prime Minister Nehru's letter to the Prime Minister of Pakistan, Mohammad Ali, March 5, 1954.

108. For an account of the process of Indo-Soviet rapprochement, see Richard B. Remnek, *Soviet Scholars and Soviet Foreign Policy* (Durham:

Carolina Academic Press, 1975), pp. 127-129; also see Arthur Stein, *India and the Soviet Union: The Nehru Era* (Chicago: The University of Chicago Press, 1969), pp. 62-84.

109. For a discussion, see Aswini K. Ray, *Domestic Compulsions and Foreign Policy: Pakistan in Indo-Soviet Relations 1947-58* (New Delhi: Manas, 1975), pp. 128-129.

110. According to the then Chinese Premier Chou En-lai, the Pakistani Prime Minister, Mohammed Ali, had assured him that Pakistan was not lined up against China and that if the United States launched a global war, Pakistan would not be involved in it. See Sarwar Hasan, ed., *Documents on the Foreign Policy of Pakistan: China, India and Pakistan* (Karachi: Pakistan Institute of International Affairs , 1966), pp. 361-62.

111. A. H. Raskin, "Meany Says Nehru and Tito Aid Reds," *The New York Times* (December 14, 1955).

112. Notwithstanding the U.S. intervention in Lebanon (1958), the U.S. stand on Kashmir in the UN Security Council (1957) the Indian "liberation of Goa" (1961), and the Bay of Pigs episode (1961).

113. U.S. economic aid to India started in 1951 with the shipment of food under the Point Four Program of the Truman administration. This administration had even intended to give $200 million as a loan for the fiscal year 1953-54, but the proposed loan was later cancelled by the Eisenhower administration which preferred military aid.

114. P. J. Eldridge, *The Politics of Foreign Aid in India* (Delhi: Vikas Publications, 1969), p. 31.

115. From 1951 to 1970 the U.S. contributed about $8 billion in loans and grants to India. It included $4.3 billion P.L. 480 agricultural commodities and $3 billion in low-interest loans. See *United States Foreign Policy, 1960-70, A Report of the Secretary of State*, Washington, D.C., 1971, p. 90. In aggregate terms India became the largest recipient of U.S. aid among the developing countries, though in per capita it was at the bottom because of its huge population.

116. To a great extent this consortium was established through the efforts of former ambassadors (to India) Bowles and Cooper, Prof. John K. Galbraith (later ambassador to New Delhi), Senators Kennedy (later President of the U.S.), Kefauver, Humphrey, Fulbright, and Mansfield. Eldrige, p. 32.

117. Prof. W. W. Rostow's statement before the Senate Foreign Relations Committee, February, 1958. W. W. Rostow, *The Diffusion of Power, 1957-1972: An Essay in Recent History* (New York: 19 72), p. 106.

118. W. Averill Harriman has called this development one of "parallel position" between Moscow and Washington. See his statement, U.S. Congress House Committee on Foreign Affairs, *U.S. Foreign Policy for the 1970s*, Hearings, 91st Congress, 2nd Session, May 25, 26, 27, and June 7, 1970, Washington, D.C., p. 21.

119. President Kennedy later described this meeting as "a disaster . . . the worst head-of-state (sic) visit I have had". Cited in Arthur M. Schlesinger,

Jr., *A Thousand Days: John F. Kennedy in the White House* (Boston: Houghton Mifflin, 1965), p. 526. Nehru, of course, was not India's head-of-state.

120. Speaking in the Security Council on 18 December 1961, Stevenson had stated that "what is at stake today is not colonialism . . . It is a lamentable departure not only from the Charter but from India's own professions of faith" (*United Nations SCOR*, 987th meeting, pp. 16-17). Arthur Schlesinger, Jr. indicates that the Department of State inhibited Stevenson from balancing his statement by making references to Portuguese colonialism (Schlesinger, n. 159, p. 527).

121. Jawaharlal Nehru's reply to foreign affairs debate, Rajya Sabha, June 23, 1962. See *Jawaharlal Nehru's Speeches*, Vol. 4, September 1957-April 1963 (New Delhi: Publications Division, August 1964), pp. 299-300.

122. Statement by Senator John Sherman Cooper inserted in Congressional Record, June 27, 1962 (Outgoing telegram, Department of State to U.S. Embassy, New Delhi, RE: Deptel 4391). Also see John Kenneth Galbraith, *Ambassador's Journal* (New York: New American Library, 1970), p. 252.

123. The leading American daily had commented: "Direct negotiations between the two countries offered the best hope for an eventual settlement" (*The New York Times*, January 24, 1962). President Kennedy wanted India and Pakistan to make use of the good offices of the World Bank President Eugene Black with a view to resolve the Kashmir question through direct negotiations. See *Asian Recorder* (New Delhi), 1962, p. 4452.

124. For an account of this debate on the Kashmir issue in the UN Security Council (February, April, May, and June 1962), see Gupta, *Kashmir: A Study in India-Pakistan Relations*, pp. 345-352.

125. Some of these persons, for instance, were John Kenneth Galbraith (Ambassador to India), Chester Bowles (Undersecretary of State) and Phillips Talbot (Assistant Secretary of State for Near East and South Asian Affairs). As a Senator, John F. Kennedy attached particular importance to India's political and economic stability.

126. The U.S. economic aid to India in 1961-62 was about $400 million (excluding surplus food) out of a total of $1 billion needed as foreign aid for India's Third Plan.

127. See the statement by U.S. Secretary of Defense, Robert S. McNamara, June 16, 1961, U.S. Congress, Senate Committee on Foreign Relations, *International Development and Security* (S. 1983: a Bill to promote the foreign policy, security and general welfare of the United States), Hearings, 87th Congress, 1st Session, 1961, p. 599.

128. In the course of his visit to the U.S. in July 1961, some of these issues were raised by President Ayub Khan in his talks with President Kennedy. For an account see Mohammad Ayub Khan, *Friends Not Masters: A Political Autobiography* (New York: Oxford University Press, 1967), pp. 136-138; also see William J. Barnds, *India, Pakistan and the Great Powers*, pp. 169-170. It is worth noting here that President Kennedy also did manage to overcome (in May

1962) a Congressional attempt to reduce foreign assistance to India, as an indication of American disapproval of the Indian action in Goa.

129. In a memorandum submitted to President Kennedy in May 1961, Vice-President Johnson called for continued U.S. support to Pakistan while attempting to develop more enduring friendly ties with India. See William S. White, *The Professional: Lyndon B. Johnson* (Boston: Houghton, Mifflin, 1964), pp. 240-244.

130. U.S. Assistant Secretary of State Phillips Talbot's interview with H. R. Vohra, Washington correspondent of the *Times of India*, on Indo-U.S. relations (Department of State, Memorandum of Conversation, July 5, 1962). But, interestingly Talbot also underscored the need for U.S. support for constructive efforts to achieve greater harmony between Pakistan and India since the former would find it difficult to exist if there were chaos in the other. In the same way, the latter would find it difficult to get on if there were chaos in the former.

131. Underlined by Pakistan Foreign Secretary Dehlavi in a news conference on May 30, 1962 (following a reported Cabinet level meeting reviewing Pakistan's foreign policy in light of new situations on May 26, 1962). Reported in a dispatch from the U.S. Embassy (Karachi) to the Department of State, June 4, 1962 (Dispatch No. 783).

132. Speaking at a press conference on July 12, 1962, U.S. Secretary of State Dean Rusk pointed out that "where two friends of the U.S. such as Pakistan and India have battles between themselves, that in itself, imposes some strains on relations with both." (Excerpts of this conference were sent for information to the U.S. embassies in New Delhi, Karachi and Kabul.) *Department of State Bulletin*, July 30, 1962, p. 176.

133. Dean Rusk, the Secretary of State, emphasized this aspect during an interview on July 8, 1962 (cited in a communication by Assistant Secretary of State Frederick G. Dutton to Congressman Lindly Beckworth, August 17, 1962).

3

India's China War:
The U.S. Response

There were two different (though interrelated) phases in the U.S. response to the momentous Sino-Indian war of October 1962. The initial phase was marked by emergency arms assistance and political support to India in response to an urgent appeal by the government of India. The second dealt with the possibility of working out an American arms aid program in light of the perceived threat posed by China.

There are a number of critical questions raised by the American response to the Sino-Indian conflict, and in particular, the decision to render military, economic, political, and moral support to India. What were the American decisionmakers' perceptions of the conflict between India and China? To what extent were they in conformity with their preconceived notions about U.S. interests in the area? What was the pattern of American response? How were the relevant decisions made and concomitant actions (in terms of scope, contents and priorities) determined? Who were the actors—individual and institutional—involved in the decision-making process? To what extent was the scope of Washington's decision determined or influenced by its major alliance partners? What broad conclusions can be drawn from this episode? Before we deal with these questions, a bit of background is in order.

Prelude

With hindsight we now know that—in spite of the conclusion of the Panchshila (five principles) agreement of 1954 and numerous cultural exchanges—the Sino-Indian relationship had been too thinly based. The 1954 agreement established procedures for trade between India and the Tibet region of China and stipulated peaceful co-existence as the basis of the relationship between the two countries, but it ignored the border question.[1]

By 1959, there were serious differences between India and China regarding their common border along the Himalayas. Their relations were further strained by the outbreak of the Tibetan rebellion in March 1959. India had contended that the Sino-Indian boundary had been historically sanctified by treaties and a long record of administrative jurisdiction. In their view, while the tripartite (India, Tibet and China) Simla agreement (1914) delimited the eastern sector boundary (known as the McMahon Line), census and revenue documents along with two treaties (those of 1684 and 1842) determined the boundary in the western sector (pertaining to India's Ladakh region). India was, however, not averse to negotiating minor adjustments. The Chinese, in contrast, viewed the entire Sino-Indian boundary issue as a complicated legacy that called for major rectification.[2] The two neighbors were on a collision course. The first armed clash between India and China took place in August 1959, at a border post called Longju in the eastern sector. This was soon followed by a similar incident in October near the Kongka pass in the western sector.

There are divergent opinions as to the basic factors that led to the war between China and India in October-November 1962. It is not our purpose to recapitulate this debate,[3] but it is reasonable to say that the war may have been triggered off by both India's and China's mutual misperception of each other's intentions.[4] In making this assertion certain qualifications are in order. First, there are reasons to believe that the dispute about the border was a symptom rather than the cause of the Sino-Indian confrontation. Second, mutual misperception was to a large extent generated as well as accentuated by differing foreign policy orientations.[5] Third, China and India had divergent conceptions of the changing world scene. To New Delhi, "new horizons" seemed to be opening up with the growing Soviet-U.S. detente and their economic and political commitments to India.[6] From the Chinese viewpoint this was India's "double alignment," and hence a threatening spectacle, especially in the light of a developing Sino-Soviet gap.

India perceived China's attempts to exploit Pakistan's antipathy toward India as a serious challenge to itself. Under President Kennedy, the U.S. had not only become reconciled to India's non-alignment, but was prepared to underwrite the political and economic stability of the latter, in spite of Pakistan's displeasure.[7] China was to find in a disenchanted Pakistan a useful way to put pressure on India. Beijing's willingness to enter into border negotiations with Pakistan in 1961—after some initial reluctance—was the first move in this direction. These complex relationships made up the setting in which the U.S. decided to render military aid and political support to India when it became involved in a war with China.

Washington and the Border Situation

In some Asian conflicts—notably the cases of Korea and Vietnam—the United States was and is directly involved. In contrast, the American approach to the potentially explosive border dispute between India and China—the two most populous states in the world—exhibited a certain element of paradox. The initial U.S. response was marked by an attitude of studied non-involvement, if not general indifference. Indeed, it was not until the major clashes of October-November 1962 that the American administration reacted with deep concern and a sense of urgency.

There were several considerations behind this initial reticence. The U.S. had to take into account the Nationalist Chinese regime position on the Sino-Indian border question.[8] Like Peking, Taiwan did not recognize the McMahon Line and disputed India's position. Thus, the Eisenhower administration had declared on at least two occasions that the U.S. was not quite certain about the existing status of the boundary. Once, in a news conference, President Eisenhower stated, "I don't think anyone has ever known exactly" the "exact spots" in which the McMahon Line was located. He thought the important issue was whether the nations were going to settle their disputes through negotiations.[9] His Secretary of State (Christian Herter) also made it clear that the United States had insufficient evidence on which to base an opinion regarding the "rightness or wrongness" in the dispute.[10]

Despite this standoffish posture, Eisenhower's five-day state visit to India in December 1959 marked a certain change in the American attitude. In some of his eloquent speeches during this visit, Eisenhower expressed support to India—at a time of increasing border tension along the Himalayas. In an apparent bid to assure India, Eisenhower had also reiterated U.S. opposition to any use of force for settling "international issues and quarrels."[11] However, in his meeting with Nehru, the American president made no direct comment when Nehru raised the issue of "the nature and potentialities of the current Chinese invasion into India."[12]

By mid-1962, Sino-Indian relations had become quite abrasive. Persistent small-scale armed incursions (in the wake of India's "forward strategy") on India's northwestern and northeastern frontiers reached invasion proportions on October 20, just at the time that the Cuban missile crisis blew up. Understandably, Indian and Chinese versions of the causes of the border war differ, but there were unmistakable signs of Chinese military preparedness, and their offensive was properly coordinated. In contrast, India's military operations were marked by piecemeal, uncoordinated logistics and a shocking inadequacy of hardware.[13]

India's predicament was underlined by utter confusion at the highest level of political leadership. What seems to have been particularly sloppy was that while the civilian authorities had given instructions to the Indian armed forces to "free our territory" from the Chinese,[14] they neither anticipated nor were psychologically prepared for a major Chinese offensive in reaction to their own forward strategy. Nehru's reaction to a Chinese attack was that "this type of aggression" was a "thing of the past."[15] If this suggests his profound shock at the Chinese decision to cross the escalation threshold, it also clearly underlines his inadequate understanding of the risks of a half-baked strategy. Though shocked and surprised, Nehru initially refused to endorse some of his cabinet colleagues' suggestion for "approaching any power" for help to fight the Chinese.[16]

How did America react? Initially, the U.S. approach was a continued aloofness. Though it "sympathized" with Indian concern about the "integrity of its northern frontier," the distance and the high altitude of the locale of the battle made it a "little hard to have exact information there."[17] It was only later—when India had requested military aid—that the approach changed. But again, despite America's willingness to render military assistance to India, American policymakers demonstrated a degree of discretion in handling India's requests.

The diaries and chronicles of the period by some of Kennedy's New Frontiersmen throw light on the evolving American approach to the conflict, and to India in particular.[18] With the Himalayan border conflict exploding into a series of shooting incidents, we get the first clear intimation of the U.S. approach in the journal of then American ambassador to India, John Kenneth Galbraith. True, the distance and remoteness of the conflict hindered the flow of hard information to Washington; however, these constraints sometimes provided "greater leeway" to the U.S. ambassador on the scene in using his personal "judgments and tactics" to shape U.S. policy.[19] Thus, Galbraith, in responding to the Sino-Indian struggle for forward posts, called it a dispute over "worthless territory,"[20] and on July 23, 1962, created guidelines for the U.S. approach: "Our (my) policy is to keep silent and seem to take no satisfaction out of the manifestation of the Cold War."[21] This was a clear indication that the U.S. was unwilling to exploit a new Cold War issue or to take a more categorical position in favor of New Delhi. For one thing, the border confrontation at that point did not seem to be significant enough for the United States to take an active interest. The idea was to watch, wait and keep a variety of options open.

It was on August 8, 1962, that the American ambassador to India unofficially signalled America's "full sympathy for India's predicament on its northern border." But then, quite in line with the ongoing policy of caution, Ambassador Galbraith also expressed "hope for a settlement and our desire to do nothing that might prejudice it."[22] Galbraith's low key "sympathy" suggested only minor modification in the U.S. approach toward the border question. It appears that the Kennedy administration's initial decision to pursue the policy of non-involvement was partially prompted by the urging of two of Galbraith's predecessors in New Delhi, Chester Bowles and John Sherman Cooper. Incidentally, both Bowles and Cooper were known for their sympathetic understanding of India. Their contention was that any direct U.S. interest in the dispute or support for the Indian position would have injected the Cold War into the Sino-Indian border issue and made it all the more unmanageable.[23]

There were other elements in the evolution of America's "wait and see" approach. Kennedy, it may be recalled, had perceived India as the key area in Asia; he wanted it to win the political and economic race against China. But despite his support for continued economic assistance, he was somewhat skeptical about Indian leadership. His skepticism was accentuated by a disappointing meeting with Nehru and disillusionment over the military operation in Goa. The Goa episode, in particular, had diminished Kennedy's expectations regarding India's ability to play any meaningful role in the "struggle for peace."[24]

Washington's attitude was also indicative of calculated unconcern about the issue. From available evidence it appears that this was the product of skepticism about a major Sino-Indian armed conflict occurring in the near future. Interestingly, around March 1962, while Bowles (then U.S. Undersecretary of State) was visiting New Delhi, he had a meeting with Lt. Gen. B. M. Kaul, then Chief of Staff of the Indian Army.[25] In the course of this meeting Kaul informed Bowles of the possibility of a major Chinese attack between the summer and fall of 1962, and stressed the need to work out a "deterrent" based on mutual cooperation with "some friends."[26] In response, Bowles expressed his "skepticism about such an attack," but asked him to put his query to Galbraith.[27]

Unfortunately, no appropriate follow-up steps were taken to bolster Indian defense capabilities. Writing to Kaul in 1963, Bowles stated that if India and the U.S. had "worked on the basis of cooperation to meet the situation in advance," as suggested by him (Kaul), the October-November 1962 events "might have taken a somewhat different turn."[28] Later, when Bowles came to India as the U.S. ambassador, he told Nehru about Kaul's accurate projection of the timing of the Chinese attack. Nehru's only comment was: "I wish he had told me too."[29] Incidentally, Kaul told Bowles in the course of the talks that he did not apprise Nehru about his suggested "possibilities."[30] Despite this denial, it is quite conceivable that the Indian Prime Minister was trying to inquire of the U.S. President through his favorite general (who was also a relative) about the possibility of U.S. military assistance to India in the context of the growing threat from China. On the other hand, it is equally reasonable to assume that Bowles had reported to Kennedy the contents of his discussions with Kaul. But Kennedy's silence on this, and the absence of any U.S. initiative in this direction, only suggest that his administration was not inclined to get involved in India's developing conflict.

From an alternative but more important standpoint, the Kennedy administration's initial caution was also designed to avoid any unnecessary difficulty with Pakistan. It is probable that any unilateral U.S. support of the Indian position at that stage would have been misinterpreted by Pakistan and by Congress as a move toward more substantive commitment. Paradoxically, though Kennedy initially had serious doubts about the rationale behind military pacts, especially with Pakistan, he seemed to have "modified" his views after becoming President.[31] According to Chester Bowles, Kennedy had "succumbed to the familiar pressures of his top advisers" in approving a supply of a squadron of F-104s after Ayub Khan had visited him in July 1961.[32]

More importantly, there was some rethinking about China policy within the Kennedy administration. It appears from Galbraith's communication to Kennedy that he was instructed to open up a new channel of communication with Peking; however, because of "various reasons," and the press speculation about the possible change in China policy, Galbraith decided to postpone any talks with China's ambassador in New Delhi.[33]

Though Kennedy was not in favor of communist China's immediate admission to the U.N., he was nonetheless prepared to take "a fresh look at China."[34] He clearly stated that the U.S. had no hostile policy toward China, and hoped that it "will be persuaded that a peaceful coexistence with its neighbors represents the best hope for us all."[35] Kennedy and Dean Rusk approved substantive steps, such as the opening of a reliable channel of communication and shipment of wheat to China in the midst of a food crisis.[36] This is not to understate the continued anti-China biases of many administration officials, Senators, and Congressmen, but it does help to delineate the evolving U.S. approach to India's China conflict.[37]

If one goes by the entries of events in Galbraith's journal, it is evident that he did not focus on the substantive issues of the confrontation until it blew up into a major war in October. In his entry of October 18, Galbraith for the first time mentions the American predicament in the border dispute by stating that the McMahon Line runs "in principle" along the Himalayan "peaks."[38] It should be noted that in the "convenient absence of instructions" from Washington, the U.S. ambassador in New Delhi seemed to have worked out an ad hoc American approach to the situation.[39] In one of his communications to President Kennedy, Galbraith advised: express quiet sympathy, make clear that we hope for settlement, and not feel any urgency about offering help. It will be far better if the Indians have to ask.[40] Later when the conflict intensified, the U.S. ambassador changed his stand.

Importantly, if the "absence of instructions" to the U.S. ambassador to India implied that the President could depend upon his judgment, it also meant that neither the White House nor the State Department was particularly perturbed by the developing Sino-Indian confrontation. In light of this, it is not surprising that only after the frantic Indian appeals for arms assistance did U.S. military aid start to trickle into India. For the policymakers in Washington it was not even then an easy choice. They had to decide on a level of new military commitment in an area of relatively marginal concern.

At the same time they had to relate this assistance for India to the perceived level of Chinese threat, and manage any Congressional opposition.

Though it involved a limited U.S. military commitment, this decision did not satisfy Pakistan. It triggered Pakistani protests against arms aid to India—a state considered consistently hostile to Pakistan. Faced with mounting Pakistani opposition, American policymakers had to stress the need for an early settlement of all outstanding Indo-Pak disputes in the hope of building up a more cost-effective joint subcontinental defense against China. Some U.S. Congressmen even suggested resolution of the Kashmir dispute as a precondition for arms aid to India.[41] What subsequently complicated the problem for India were the Kennedy administration's attempts "to reconcile military aid" to India and Pakistan with a stable balance in the region. This was, obviously, in deference to the standing Pakistani plea for a subcontinental military balance.[42]

India's Military Reverses and U.S. Military Aid

We have spelled out some of the operational constraints that determined the level of arms assistance to India. To the extent that these factors ruled out a sizeable American arms supply, any potential Congressional intervention or public debate was pre-empted.[43] In some ways, this explains why the question of arms aid to a non-aligned India could be handled within the Executive Branch. Here, we will examine the decision-making regarding the supply of American military hardware to New Delhi and make an attempt to locate the principal actors involved.

We noted earlier how the Sino-Indian clashes culminated in a major attack on India's northeastern and northwestern borders by October 20, 1962. This attack, of invasion proportions, took place at a time when the United States and the Soviet Union were facing each other over the emplacement of Soviet missiles in Cuba. According to his White House aide, Theodore Sorensen, President Kennedy wondered aloud, despite his preoccupation with the more "direct threat" to his nation, which crisis would be "more significant" in the long run. In New Delhi, Galbraith was concerned about the possibility of a joint Sino-Pakistani attack which would not only lead to India's "defeat" and "collapse" but also result in internal "anarchy." Hence his principal task was to help India and ensure peace between the Indians and the Pakistanis.

The Kennedy administration responded promptly to the Chinese attack of October 20, 1962. In a communique issued on October 21, the Department of State gave out the first official reaction. The United States was "shocked at the violent and aggressive action of the Chinese Communists against India." It further stated that any Indian request "would be considered sympathetically."[44] On October 23, Indian Foreign Secretary M. J. Desai told Galbraith that India will have "to turn" to the United States for "substantial assistance." Responding to his apprehension about any form of imposed aid arrangement, the American ambassador clarified the U.S. position. He, in fact, had "reassured" the Indian Foreign Secretary that the U.S. administration would neither "force them into an alliance" nor "impose security inspection procedures for the arms they received"--in disregard of their sovereignty. In return, Galbraith was able to secure some form of assurance from the Indian side regarding their willingness to support American efforts to get the Cuban missile sites inspected by the United Nations.[45]

Meanwhile, faced with the rapid collapse of the military front in the North-East Frontier Region, New Delhi was impelled to seek military equipment from the U.S., the U.K., and the Soviet Union. Initially, on October 26, India sent a general appeal for "sympathy as well as support" to all governments (with the exception of Portugal and South Africa). In making this appeal Nehru underscored the vital significance of the conflict between India and China. "This crisis is not only of India but of the world and will have far reaching consequences on the standards of international behavior and on the peace of the world."[46] In spite of his predicament, however, the Indian Prime Minister was reluctant to make a more direct request for military hardware from a major power. According to one White House insider's account, in presenting this message to President Kennedy,[47] the Indian ambassador in Washington, B. K. Nehru, explained that "the Prime Minister, after all these years in the neutralist pacifist camp, found it difficult to make a direct request for armaments from the United States. He was hoping, instead, that the President in his reply would offer 'support' instead of an alliance." The U.S. President in reply had assured that he had no wish to take advantage of India's misfortune for the sake of coercing her into an alliance.[48] However, in a note of caution, he also told the Indian ambassador that if Krishna Menon remained as India's Defense Minister, it "makes things difficult at home."[49]

Kennedy promptly sent an enthusiastic reply. While expressing his general concern about the South Asian crisis, he informed Prime Minister Nehru:

> I know I can speak for my whole country when I say that our sympathy in this situation is wholeheartedly with you. . . I want to give you support as well as sympathy. This is a practical matter, and if you wish, my ambassador in New Delhi can discuss with you and officials of your government what we can do to translate our support into terms that are practically most useful to you as soon as possible.[50]

Incidentally, when President Kennedy received Prime Minister Nehru's communication he was under the impression that this was sent exclusively to him. Later, his enthusiasm apparently "waned" as he came to know that the same message had been delivered to other world leaders.[51] Even then, Kennedy's reply did not imply an open-ended commitment of assistance to India. It would appear that procedural as well as substantive policy-making factors may have constrained the prompt announcement of the specific details of the contemplated American aid. The Kennedy administration was looking for a more specific Indian request for military aid. In addition, U.S. policymakers were apparently not considering assistance in terms of what the Indians were likely to ask for, but in accordance with the level of threat posed by China.

In some ways, British Prime Minister Harold Macmillan had been more prompt than Kennedy in giving assurances regarding practical help. After the Chinese invasion Macmillan had sent Nehru a message of sympathy, demonstrating the solidarity of the Commonwealth.[52] By October 22, British Commonwealth Secretary Sandys had not only deplored the Chinese attack on India but also praised India's patience and restraint and reiterated British recognition of the McMahon Line.[53] Nehru had been so moved by Macmillan's timely response that in his reply of October 24, he said "Your kind message and the assurance that you will do everything in your power to help us has further heartened us in our determination to resist the blatant Chinese aggression."[54] Indeed, Nehru had reasons to be moved by the British government's gesture. At that point, with the exception of the British, "everybody has been ambiguous in their support" of the Indians, writes Ambassador Galbraith in his diary.[55] Thus, by October 27, when Macmillan received Nehru's world wide appeal for help and sympathy, the U.K. was all set for "sending a lot of small arms, automatic rifles and ammunition" to India. A consignment of British military hardware—reportedly comprising small arms—arrived in New Delhi by two RAF aircraft on October 29, the first Western aid to reach India.[56]

There is, however, no need to overstate Britain's concern about the Chinese threat that faced India. In a speech on October 30, Macmillan told the House of Commons that as the winter months were drawing near it was unlikely that hostilities would continue on the existing scale, though he admitted a "serious situation will persist."[57] Further, the initial British response was not unexpected because of the imperative of the Commonwealth connection. Aside from Ghana, and to an extent Pakistan, most Commonwealth nations unequivocally deplored China's action and offered the much needed sympathy and support for India.[58]

By the last week of October a military relationship between non-aligned India and the U. S. began to emerge. On October 25, informal talks took place between Galbraith and India's Finance Minister, Morarji Desai, regarding the pros and cons of military aid programs for India. What is more, the Indian Defense Minister, Krishna Menon, and the Commander of the Indian forces in the NEFA area, Lieutenant General B. M. Kaul, were also in touch with the American ambassador. They underscored India's urgent need for arms supplies. Perhaps, a clearer indication of the growing Indo-U.S. military interaction was the Indian decision to exchange military information with the service attaches of the U.S. embassy. This was in marked contrast with the previous Indian practice of maintaining a distance in military relations.

The process of closer ties between New Delhi and Washington was hastened by the Kennedy administration's recognition of the Indian position on the McMahon Line. To eliminate any ambiguity in American support to India, Galbraith seems to have initiated the move for reversing the U.S. noncommittal stand on the McMahon Line.[59] On October 26, the Department of State directed the U.S. ambassador not to endorse the McMahon Line, since this question also involved a U.S. ally, the KMT government in Taiwan. However, in less than twenty-four hours, Galbraith was able to reverse this directive, presumably using his White House connection. On October 27, he made the first official declaration about recognition of the McMahon Line:

> The McMahon Line is an accepted international border and is sanctioned by modern usage. Accordingly, we regard it as the northern border of the NEFA area.[60]

The Kennedy administration approved this stand notwithstanding the expected protest from the KMT regime on Taiwan.[61] Evidently, the outcome was finally determined by expedient considerations for providing greater credibility to America's South Asia policy in an ongoing crisis.

Contingency planning for arms aid was already under way in Washington. On the advice of Galbraith, the Department of State waited to receive a formal request for assistance from the Indian government.[62] October 29 seems to have been a crucial day in Indo-U.S. relations. By the time President Kennedy's offer of help reached Nehru in a letter sent through Galbraith, New Delhi apparently had decided to request American arms. Anyway, in delivering the U.S. President's communication to Nehru, Galbraith told him that the American people would "respond to a request from him" as they would not to anyone else.[63] Whatever inhibition Nehru had (whether out of personal pride or otherwise) in making a formal request for arms aid, it was over by October 29. The continued military reverses against China seemed to shatter his resistance.[64]

The Indian Prime Minister told Galbraith on the same day that India "did indeed have to have aid and it would have to come from the United States." Though Nehru wanted to avoid irritating the Soviet Union, he admitted that the Soviets realized that U.S. assistance was "inevitable." The Prime Minister, however, hoped that this "would not mean a military alliance" between the United States and India. The American ambassador assured Nehru that the U.S. would not insist on such a thing.[65]

Nehru's request for U.S. arms aid came to Kennedy through Galbraith, changing India's earlier stand.[66] It appears from his journal that when Galbraith came to know in advance that an elaborate request for U.S. arms aid was coming from the Indian Defense Minister Krishna Menon, he was able to get it from Nehru.[67] Because of Menon's unfavorable image in the U.S., any request from him would have made it difficult for the Kennedy administration to expedite the supply of arms. It should be noted that despite a major armed escalation along the Sino-Indian border from October 20 till October 29, "no official exchange of views" on arms aid took place between New Delhi and Washington.[68] Nehru's unwillingness to seek arms was matched by Kennedy's reticence.

So much had to be dealt with on October 29 that Galbraith calls it "the longest of all days" for him. As the details of India's request came in, arrangements were made for airlifting the "most urgent" things needed, especially for fighting in hilly terrain. The mode of payment for this help was, however, not as yet worked out by the two parties. Aside from military matters, the U.S. ambassador was attempting to limit the likely impact of the arms supply agreement on Pakistani sensitivity. It appears he had impressed upon some senior officials of the Indian Ministry of External Affairs the "need for taking the Pakistanis into their confidence."[69]

If the U.S. administration had been rather reserved so far, it had now come out openly in favor of India. Galbraith claims that he, the U.S. ambassador in New Delhi, had given the lead to the decisionmakers in Washington. Yet, Arthur Schlesinger, then a White House aide, suggests that it was due to President Kennedy's "strong backing" that Galbraith was able to take the initiative in consolidating U.S. friendship with India.[70] This seems to imply that the U.S. ambassador was merely working out the details of U.S. arms aid on a basis that was in accordance with the President's general approach.

The evidence furnished by Sorensen also contradicts Galbraith's claims and suggests that Kennedy was in complete command of the situation.[71] He alone determined the direction of the U.S. policy toward the Sino-Indian conflict. It seems, encouraged by success in the Cuban missile crisis, "some" of Kennedy's aides had urged more "direct or extensive" U.S. action on the Himalayas against China's "expansion" in Asia. But the U.S. President, according to Sorensen: ". . . saw no gains for India, for the United States or for the free world in making this fight our fight in the Himalayas."[72] On another occasion, Kennedy quietly ignored one "excited recommendation"—in a midnight call for an emergency meeting—from Secretary of State Rusk[73]. This would have certainly put the U.S. on a collision course with China. This view does not understate Galbraith's role in the initial decisions, but underlines the simultaneous interaction that was also taking place in Washington itself.

Whatever the nature of the interaction, the "dilatory" Department of State remained the principal spokesman for the U.S. arms aid policy and it had to translate specific decisions into action. In doing this, it was concerned with several factors: What the extent of arms aid to India should be; how to expedite the arms supply; how to ensure that Pakistan would not create difficulties for India;

whether arms aid should be related to an early resolution of the Kashmir dispute, and the opening of a joint Indo-Pak front against China. An added concern of the Kennedy administration was, as noted above, not to get directly involved in the Himalayan conflict and thereby lose the wider perspective of its long term interests in Asia.

Having favorably responded to Nehru's request, the main concern of U.S. policymakers was how to estimate the intentions and reactions of not only the Indians and the Chinese, but also those of Moscow and Rawalpindi. Given Soviet ambivalence on the border conflict and their inability to force New Delhi and Peking to the negotiating table, Moscow was to have only a marginal role under the circumstances. It was speculated, however, in the event of massive U.S. arms aid (or if India became a full-fledged member of the U.S. alliance system) that the USSR could, though reluctantly, come out in full support of China. Regarding Peking, the U.S. calculated that Chinese "intentions were more political than military," and hence called for a level of response just sufficient to deter it from further probing.[74] In this context, the U.S. opted for a coordinated policy designed to work out an effective defense of the Subcontinent with minimal investment, and thereby not cause undue alarm in Moscow or Peking.[75] But the success of this policy was dependent on how well the complex relationship between the U.S., India and Pakistan was managed.

The U.S. wanted to make sure that Pakistan did not move against India, especially when India was engaged in armed conflict with China. Thus, on October 28, Kennedy sent a letter to Pakistani President Ayub Khan, informing him of the contemplated U.S. arms aid to India. He also requested Ayub to give his assurance to Nehru regarding Pakistan's intentions in Kashmir. To expedite the matter, the U.S. ambassador to Pakistan rushed from Karachi to Rawalpindi to meet Ayub, but only met Pakistan's Foreign Minister Mohammed Ali, who was unable to given him any official assurance. On November 5, in his reply to Kennedy, Ayub Khan expressed his inability to give assurance. He was particularly disappointed with the U.S. administration for having decided to provide arms aid to India without consulting Pakistan beforehand. What is more, India was informed prior to Pakistan.[76]

Faced with stiff Pakistani opposition to U.S. arms aid to New Delhi, ambassador McConaughty proposed a "strong" U.S. stand in support of Pakistan on the Kashmir question in exchange for Ayub's assurance to Nehru. On hearing this development Galbraith apprehended that this would be interpreted as a land grabbing move against India from all sides. While he agreed with this approach, he advised the Department of State and McConaughty not to press the Kashmir issue. This was later endorsed by the Department of State. Meanwhile, by making use of a "strong" U.S. position vis-a-vis New Delhi, Galbraith was able to persuade Nehru to personally request Ayub Khan for Pakistan's assurance.[77]

By October 31, ambassador McConaughty was able to secure from Mohammed Ali a promise of a "benign attitude" on U.S. arms to India with the understanding that the subcontinental "balance of power"will remain "unchanged."[78] But Pakistan continued to press the Kashmir question. Though official Pakistan policy was not to agree to Kennedy's proposition for Pakistani assurance to India, "through diplomatic channels" Ayub Khan had assured that Pakistan "would not aggravate India's problems."[79]

While the New Delhi-Washington-Pindi exchanges about a Pakistani assurance to India were taking place, on October 30 Galbraith signalled the Department of State regarding a "changed attitude" toward India. Obviously, this shift came in the aftermath of the Cuban missile crisis. From an earlier position of "delicate support," the United States now wanted to give an "impression of strength" that would deter Peking. At the same time, the United States sought to counter growing Indian (if not Soviet) apprehension regarding possible U.S. attempts to enroll India as a new alliance partner by exploiting the situation created by the Chinese attack. In a categorical statement issued on November 6, ambassador Galbraith made it clear that the American military aid to India was "not intended to involve India in a military alliance or otherwise influence her policy of non-alignment," but was designed primarily "to help defend India's independence."[80]

Meanwhile, an important change occurred in the U.S. perception of India when Indian Defense Minister Krishna Menon was demoted on October 31. The removal of a major irritant in Indo-U.S. relations not only underlined the possibility of better cooperation in procuring defense material but also helped relations with Pakistan.[81]

It was on November 3 that the United States started an emergency arms airlift to India; the first consignment of military supplies arrived at Dum Dum Airport (Calcutta) from U.S. depots in West Germany. For a week (November 3-10) 10 U.S. jet freighters—each with a payload of twenty tons of military hardware—airlifted on an around-the-clock basis 60 planeloads of automatic weapons and ammunition to India from various stocks in the U.S. and Europe.[82] The bulk of these materials were provided for operational utility in the mountain terrain. According to knowledgeable sources, the arms consignments consisted of light infantry weapons, mortars, 3.7 howitzers, ammunition, communication equipment, spares for Dakota and Fairchild Packet aircraft, snow clearing equipment, winter clothing, etc.[83]

The initial provision of U.S. military assistance was made under section 503 of the Foreign Assistance Act of 1961. It empowered the President to draw upon the existing stocks of U.S. arms to render arms assistance in a contingency situation without prior Congressional approval.[84] If the U.S. President did not have this authority, the supply of urgently needed hardware to India would have been delayed pending an answer to "Where is the money coming from?"[85] The emergency provision of the Foreign Assistance Act of 1961 enabled President Kennedy to promptly respond to Nehru's urgent request for moral and material support. Because the arms aid involved only a "modest amount," the Presidential decision permitted circumventing possible Congressional intervention.[86]

On November 14, 1962, U.S. defense assistance to India was formalized with an exchange of notes between the Indian ambassador to the United States, B. K. Nehru, and U.S. Assistant Secretary of State, Phillips Talbot. This exchange of notes, incidentally, supplanted agreements (of 1951 and 1958) for U.S. military sales to India.[87] In receiving U.S. arms aid, the Indian government not only agreed to allow U.S. diplomats stationed in India to inspect the equipment and obtain relevant information about its use, but also pledged not to use it except against the threat of Chinese attack. In addition, India was supposed to return those articles which might not be needed any more for their designated purpose.[88]

From the outset, the Kennedy administration was concerned about dispelling Pakistani apprehension over this new area of Indo-U.S. interaction. On November 17, the Department of State announced its assurances to Pakistan, indicating that if India "misused" American arms aid for aggressive purposes then the United States would take "appropriate action" to deter such aggression.[89] Around the same time, a Pakistani Cabinet source not only urged the Kennedy administration to put pressure on India to settle the Kashmir question, but also derided the U.S. for having suggested to Pakistan that it should freeze this issue.[90]

As the emergency arms airlift was completed by November 10, there followed renewed Indian requests for U.S. aircraft and machinery for production. The State Department on its part assured sympathetic consideration. In the following pages, we will deal with the process of implementing these American military assistance programs.

The Second Chinese Offensive and After

By mid-November, the Chinese were making a coordinated move to mount their second offensive against the remaining Indian positions in NEFA and Ladakh. Indian morale seems to have been bolstered by the U.S.-U.K. arms aid and indicated the possibility of a counter attack.[91] The U.S. ambassador in New Delhi apprehended that if the Chinese "big push" took place then it "could bring the British and ourselves into some kind of military action." Even at that stage, no one knew what the Chinese intended to do. Galbraith wanted the United States to "assume something more serious," on the grounds that it was less dangerous to retract from a dismal projection. In view of its long run implications, however, he hoped that the Chinese would not act in a manner that was likely to force the United States to face the "prospect of a new, large and extremely expensive ally."[92]

In contrast, some Kennedy White House aides seem to have been more sanguine about Chinese intentions; they felt that Nehru's requests for all sorts of American arms were rather "unrealistic." They believed that the Kennedy administration had rendered more than enough assistance to quiet down the border. Hence, anything over and above that level might cause a "real war" as well as "permanently alienate Pakistan." They underlined the need for relating further U.S. arms aid to a prior effect on Pakistani and Soviet perceptions of the developments. A London meeting of U.S. officials (including Assistant Secretary of State Phillips Talbot), produced some mild documents that concluded that the Chinese had "no disagreeable intentions." The assumption of this meeting contradicted Galbraith's guarded apprehension about possible Chinese action in NEFA. In particular, his argument was that after telling the Indians for years about the Chinese communist "aggressive tendencies," this was not the time to tell them that these "chaps are really lambs."[93]

Despite the U.S. Ambassador's "worst case" analysis of China's intentions, he was not in favor of an alliance with India as a counter against Chinese threats. His rationale against such a move was that an alignment with India could be "too expensive" for the

U.S. Paradoxically, President Kennedy seemed to have been displeased by news stories from New Delhi about Nehru's insistence that India's nonalignment had not changed and that even the U.S. wanted her to retain it. What might have caused further displeasure was that Nehru was presumably down playing U.S. arms aid so as not to hurt Soviet "sensitivity." Anyhow, the U.S. ambassador was able to preempt the issue by urging "patience"—in view of the wider implications of this problem—in his reply to Kennedy's query sent through Carl Kaysen of the White House staff.[94]

Despite promising developments, especially from the standpoint of Washington's South Asia policy, things seemed to have been heating up rather ominously along the Sino-Indian border areas on November 16. The Chinese launched a massive attack near the Walong sector of NEFA after the Indians had started some vigorous patrol action.[95] But even otherwise the Chinese had adequately prepared themselves for the "necessary and advantageous" second offensive.[96] After destroying the forward elements of the Indian army, the PLA launched its major offensive on November 18. By November 19, Indian resistance had collapsed completely in NEFA in the face of Chinese attacks along a broad front. With complete confusion at command level, the unorganized retreat of the Indian forces turned into a military debacle in less than forty-eight hours.

Things were hardly better in New Delhi where the government was stunned by this full-scale rout. Public morale seemed to have reached the lowest point. There was apprehension that the Chinese might cut off the link between Assam and the rest of the country, and carry out bombing raids on cities like New Delhi and Calcutta.[97] Faced with the renewed Chinese onslaught, by November 16 the India government started sending requests for all kinds of assistance to the U.S., the U.K. and the Soviet Union. Significantly, it was in this context that T. T. Krishnamachari, the newly appointed Indian coordinator of supply, requested of Galbraith a supply of U.S. fighter interceptors for Calcutta's protection against possible Chinese air attacks. In addition, he asked for a loan of a half billion dollars. What is more, by the next day the Indians were seeking U.S. airlift help for moving troops to the battlefront. Thus, India's NEFA debacle led it to approach Washington for more substantive material support and moral sustenance.

New Delhi was soon haunted by the specter of a Chinese blitzkrieg (across Assam's plains) coupled with possible air attacks on the northern cities. In fact, the second Chinese attack came as a rude awakening for the Indians. The Indian government feared that the Chinese were "going to overrun the plains."[98] In response to this alarming possibility Nehru had sent two frantic communications to President Kennedy on November 19 requesting massive assistance. In one of these communications he sought extensive Indo-U.S. military cooperation though not direct American support in defense of India's territorial integrity.[99] Essentially, Nehru's plan called for what Galbraith described as "full defensive intervention" by the U.S. Air Force; it envisaged "the immediate delivery of fourteen squadrons of U.S. fighter planes to protect the northern Indian cities, and three squadrons of bombers, which would enable the Indian Air Force to attack Chinese communication lines."[100] It may sound incredible but Nehru's Cabinet colleagues were not formally involved in the making of such a vital decision; nor did they have a hand in the drafting of this communication. It appears there were some "informal discussions" between the Indian Prime Minister and his senior ministerial colleagues.[101] Nehru's action, though, seems to have been influenced by the compulsions of the circumstances. Since the rapid developments constrained any form of decisionmaking process, the Indian Prime Minister seems to have used his discretion in sending the urgent message.

When Galbraith came to know of this proposal he was unenthusiastic about its implications.[102] His efforts during the following days were directed toward dissuading the Indians from initiating any "air action." Aside from India's lack of "effective" air strength to retaliate against the Chinese, there was technical difficulty in providing the immediate U.S. air protection Nehru sought. Hence, Galbraith thought that it would have been an unwise move for the Indians.[103] At the same time, however, the U.S. ambassador not only asked for twelve C-130 transport planes for India but also suggested (on his own) the dispatch of elements of the U.S. Seventh Fleet to the Bay of Bengal, presumably as a demonstration against the Chinese. It appears an aircraft carrier was already on its way when the Chinese announced unilateral ceasefire on November 21 and it had to turn back. Meanwhile, a message from President Kennedy to the U.S. ambassador promised replenishment of lost material and the supply of spares as requested by Nehru. In addition, it brought an interim offer of another airlift. More importantly, Kennedy proposed sending a high-level mission to New Delhi to study India's defense requirements, and wanted to send three more American teams to help the Indian government manage the war. Significantly, in sending this message the U.S.

President had sought Galbraith's reactions to his proposal which evidently meant Kennedy was trying to be as tactful as possible in conducting U.S. policy toward the South Asian crisis.

By the evening of November 21, Galbraith received Secretary of State Dean Rusk's telegram in response to Nehru's appeal. Most of the Rusk queries seemed to be on familiar lines: would New Delhi be accommodating toward Pakistan, and "more concerned" about "problems of communism" in South Asia? He also asked about the possibility of "mobilizing resources" through the Commonwealth.[104] After responding to these queries, Galbraith projected that the Chinese would not "press on all fronts," again because of logistics. He also expressed concern about the need for persuading the Indians to avoid unwarranted escalation. Thus when the ceasefire was announced from Peking, the government of India's measured response instead of total rejection was considerably influenced by the U.S.[105] The rationale behind America's plea for restraint was subsequently explained by Galbraith in the context of the raging controversy in the Indian Parliament over the reported presence of a U.S. aircraft carrier in the Bay of Bengal during the Sino-Indian conflict of 1962. Writing a letter to *The New York Times* in early 1965, Galbraith claimed that his "most useful contributions" were "toward avoidance of what might have been a costly and otherwise disastrous conflict." He points out that American policy "was to help the Indians and persuade them not to commit their prestige and that of the Chinese by carrying the attack into the air."[106]

On November 20, a New China News Agency (NCNA) broadcast announced the Chinese decision to halt armed conflict by midnight of the next day and then start withdrawing troops (from December 1) to a position 20 kilometers north of the McMahon Line. Under the prevailing situation, India's choices were rather limited; notwithstanding its reservations about the Chinese announcement, it did not reject their unilaterally declared ceasefire.[107] What then were the basic motivations behind the dramatic Chinese announcement of a unilateral ceasefire? In Nehru's perception "the unexpected anger" of the Indian people along with the rapidity of the U.S. response—aside from a certain Soviet "peacemaking influence"—seemed to have induced Peking to make this announcement. An alternative Indian viewpoint was that the Chinese offer was designed to avoid any pretext for massive American military aid to India. This also implied an attempt to malign New Delhi before the non-aligned group of nations. In contrast, others have interpreted the Chinese unilateral ceasefire *cum* withdrawal as a mechanism to bring about a checkmate through a "calculated military and political maneuver." It precluded retention of territorial gains and thereby preempted any possible Chinese entanglement in a prolonged conflict with Indian armed forces. Everything aside, the Chinese announcement produced uncertainty as to the real situation not only in New Delhi but also in the major western capitals.[108]

The Harriman Mission

The frantic Indian appeal for massive U.S. military aid following the NEFA debacle inevitably drew Presidential attention. Because it involved making a major decision, it was understandable that the President spread out decisionmaking on a wider interorganizational basis. Thus, when President Kennedy announced on November 20 that he was sending a high level U.S. team to New Delhi to assess India's needs, it was clear that his major policy decision would not be based merely on the U.S. Ambassador's judgment. While this was not unexpected under the circumstances, it also implied a relatively reduced role for the ambassador regarding important policy issues. It is conceivable that in apprehension of this possibility, Galbraith had earlier not only turned down "the proposals for new helpers" from the Department of State, but also forestalled the Pentagon's suggestions for "separate communications" with the U.S. military mission in New Delhi.[109] Obviously, he wanted to be in charge of the entire range of American activities in New Delhi, thereby having a major share of Presidential attention.[110]

As the firing ceased on the Himalayan battleground, Kennedy faced the task of responding to Nehru's request for long-term assistance to India to help build up its defense capability to effectively deter any further Chinese attacks. The policymakers were unsure of the type and volume of arms aid they should give to India, and of the likely reactions of Pakistan and Congress. A fact-finding political-military mission headed by Averill Harriman was dispatched to India on November 21. Its members were drawn from all the bureaucratic divisions of State and Defense. The mission comprised (besides Harriman) Roger Hilsman, Director, Bureau of Intelligence and Research in the Department of State; Paul Nitze, Assistant Secretary of Defense for International Security Affairs; General Paul Adams, Commander-in-Chief of the Strike Command; and Carl Kaysen of the White House Staff.

A similar politico-military mission from Britain, headed by Duncan Sandys (Minister for Commonwealth Affairs), was sent to the Subcontinent at this time to find out ways to bolster up India's defense with a possible Indo-Pakistan compromise over Kashmir. It would appear from British Prime Minister Macmillan's memoir that he was quite concerned about the likely impact of the Kashmir dispute on the Anglo-American supply of arms to India. He was, in fact, in agreement with the Prime Ministers of Australia and New Zealand that without a "compromise over Kashmir... it would be difficult for America and ourselves to increase our supply of arms and material beyond a modest level."[111] Evidently from the outset, Britain had set up the ground rules for its supply of arms to India; yet, this was based on a criterion not directly related to India's defense from China. Hindsight suggests that the Sandys mission was also an apparent British attempt to initiate Indo-Pak talks by exploiting India's urgent defense needs.

In a similar vein, President Kennedy had also laid down the reference frame for further arms supply to India. Thus in deciding to send a U.S. team to assess Indian requirements in response to the Chinese incursions, he categorically stated that the United States administration was "mindful" of its "alliance with Pakistan." He explained:

> Chinese incursions into the Subcontinent are a threat to Pakistan, as well as India, and both have a common interest in opposing it. We have urged this point on both governments, our help to India in no way diminishes or qualifies our commitment to Pakistan.[112]

Evidently, the U.S. President was not considering arms aid for India on a level that could upset the established guidelines of decisionmaking regarding South Asian affairs; he was trying to balance what was one of Washington's most difficult problems.[113]

In contrast to Galbraith's assessment noted earlier, Hilsman stated that "none of us" in Washington "was sure it would be wise" for India to accept China's unilaterally announced ceasefire. In a personal memorandum to Hilsman, the President sought his assessment of the "implications" of China's offer of a ceasefire: "If it were genuine would it be a good thing for the Indians to accept it or would it be better for them to refuse it in spite of military difficulties."[114]

Within this broad reference frame of U.S. South Asia policy, the Harriman mission was indicative of more substantive

American efforts to help India out of its predicament. According to Hilsman (a member of the team), this mission was conceived in part as an initial step to demonstrate American support for India and thereby to transmit to Peking "a signal of deterrence." He submitted, however, that future Chinese behavior was dependent on "whether or not effective deterrents could be created in the Subcontinent." In light of this requirement, the Kennedy administration had to find out in a general political context "what kind of help would be required from Britain and the United States to accomplish this . . . whether they (India and Pakistan) were willing to modify their hostility toward each other."

In this context, an Indo-Pakistan joint defense was perceived as the only effective defense of the Subcontinent against the threat posed by China. Theoretically this was on expected policy lines spelled out earlier by President Kennedy or even Prime Minister Macmillan. Hilsman contended that the U.S. in no way could "help rebuild India's strength if that strength were to continue to be dissipated in a quarrel with Pakistan, who was also a friend to whose defense the United States contributed."[115] From the outset, the Kennedy administration had certain reservations as to the extent to which the U.S. could provide military aid to India.

Arriving in New Delhi on November 22, the Harriman mission spent about ten days in the Subcontinent. Along with the Sandys mission it studied India's defense needs, but it also impressed upon New Delhi the need to resolve the Kashmir question with Pakistan. Though U.S. concern about Indo-Pakistan reconciliation as a prerequisite for subcontinental defense was understandable, the U.K.-U.S. joint Kashmir initiative appeared rather hasty. Nehru was reluctant to open up the Kashmir question in any Indo-Pakistan talks, but the combined Harriman-Sandys "pressure," considering India's reliance on the West for defense needs, impelled Nehru to agree to initiate talks with Pakistan for resolving differences on "Kashmir and related matters."[116] It would appear from various accounts that both Sandys and Harriman were overzealous in their attempts to resolve a long-standing and complicated issue in too short a time. Harriman had suggested that no President could recommend to Congress the appropriation of sizeable military assistance to two friends (one a military ally) of the U.S., who fail to cooperate against their common enemy and use up their resources against each other.[117] An effective joint defense of the Subcontinent, as delicately hinted by him, was no doubt a desirable goal from the American viewpoint, but it was not a viable proposition from the outset. In their insistence on an early resolution of the Indo-Pakistan differences, the Harriman mission apparently also ignored the developing Sino-Pakistan connection.

Significantly, on the very day (December 27, 1962) that talks began in Rawalpindi between Indian and Pakistani officials there was an announcement of a Sino-Pakistani border accord. There is also evidence which suggests that it was "the impetus given by the India-China conflict" that produced this agreement.[118] It is impressive that this aspect of a rather complicated subcontinental issue was neither anticipated nor taken into consideration by many U.S. policymakers. Instead, they tended to believe with Hilsman that Nehru's "Kashmiri Brahmin" obsession with Pakistan was the major cause of continued Indo-Pakistan differences over Kashmir. In contrast, there were others like Galbraith and Chester Bowles (then Undersecretary of State) who urged restraint and not force to make India concede (to Pakistan) when it was hard-pressed with defense needs against China. Galbraith had even suggested in his communication to Kennedy that the plebiscite had "no future" in regard to the settlement of the Kashmir question.[119] Even President Kennedy had on more than one occasion expressed his reluctance to intervene in the dispute between India and Pakistan. He believed there were limits on America's "power to bring about solutions."[120]

Given the above considerations, the Harriman mission's active role in the Kashmir initiative and its timing—in the context of India's other pressing priorities and Pakistan's developing connection with China—appear somewhat intriguing. Evidently the Kashmir initiative owed itself to the initial attempts made by British Minister for Commonwealth Relations, Duncan Sandys. Incidentally, on November 18 he had to postpone his South Asian mission to discuss the Kashmir issue because Ayub did not want to meet with him. At the same time he did not want to be seen as "confirming his pressures to the Indians." But by November 22 with the arrival of the Harriman Mission in New Delhi—in the wake of the Chinese announcement of a unilateral ceasefire in November—he wanted to make a joint U.K.-U.S. effort. He finally reached New Delhi on November 25 with a British politico-military team. Ironically, Sandys was reported to have felt the entire Sino-Indian conflict was indicative of their differences over a few acres of desert in Ladakh—which he wanted the Indians to surrender to the Chinese. Apparently, the British delegation attached greater priority to the resolution of the Kashmir issue than to India's appeal for help against the Chinese. As for the Harriman mission, it is conceivable that if the ceasefire had not been announced then, it would have been concerned only with India's defense needs. This is not to understate U.S. policymakers' concern about the Kashmir issue; in fact, despite Galbraith's counsel of caution regarding this matter, both the State Department and the White House staff had been trying to force the issue on New Delhi—presumably under the persuasion of their British allies. But paradoxically, both Duncan Sandys and Dean Rusk in the course of their New Delhi visits had assured Nehru that the question of their aid was not related to the settlement of Indo-Pak differences over Kashmir and other related matters.[121]

Even outside the context of Indo-Pak relations, some members of the Harriman mission perceived new elements in the situation which would have an important bearing on America's considerations of India's defense requirements. Hilsman's reaction to China's military triumph was that China "was now a force to be reckoned with," and that never again would anyone in the world be able to think about the Subcontinent without considering the interests of China and the fact of its power.[122] From this standpoint, it was perhaps inevitable that the Sino-Pakistan developments would not be seen by many of the China analysts within State as distorted, but indicative of the possibility of an alternative channel of communication.

One of the purposes of the Harriman mission was to underline U.S. political and military support to New Delhi vis-a-vis Peking. The dispatch of an aircraft carrier—which turned back after the ceasefire—was presumably part of this demonstration exercise. The obvious message was that the U.S. had a "deep interest" in what happened even to the "neutrals" like India.[123] It is, however, not definitively known whether China's unilateral ceasefire was effected by the demonstration of U.S. support to India. The answer is wrapped in a complex of military and political factors, in which American military assistance and support might have been one of the elements that influenced the Chinese.[124]

After coming to New Delhi, the Harriman mission had discussions with Indian leaders and senior civilian and military officials about India's defense requirements. At the same time the U.S. mission worked with the smaller British team brought by Duncan Sandys, and planned the framework for relatively modest military aid to India over the next three years under a U.K.-U.S. agreement—subsequently approved by Kennedy and Macmillan at Nassau. It seems that in these discussions Harriman repeatedly reminded Nehru and other Indian leaders that "the United States wanted to help, but India would have to be realistic about the cost and complexity of modern defenses."[125] Mostly, the political assessment of the Harriman mission only confirmed the views held in Washington, conforming with the U.S. approach to this conflictual situation. But, the military assessment showed an alarming shortage of spares and support equipment, and, excepting the airports of Calcutta and New Delhi, India did not possess radar. In addition, India had to ground its Harvard trainers and Vampire fighters.

Despite India's acute defense needs, American sensitivity about their Pakistan connection seems to have imposed limits on their ability to offer long-range sizeable military assistance to New Delhi. Thus the phase of instinctive Western response to Indian appeals was over with the conclusion of American and British emergency military shipments with the cessation of the Sino-Indian war. Hereafter, the U.S. administration started to drag its feet regarding the long overdue proposed modernization of India's defense forces. The Indian government sought financial assistance from the United States and the U.K. in support of their "relatively moderate" defense plan that involved an amount around $500 million spread over a period of five years. But unfortunately for India, U.S. officials in the State and Defense departments and on the White House staff, such as Rusk, McNamara and McGeorge Bundy (with the particular exception of Undersecretary of State Bowles), were "strongly opposed to a five-year program to help modernize the Indian armed forces." Their objection was "largely based on the assumption that it would disrupt U.S. relations with Pakistan and thereby jeopardize the American military base at Peshawar."[126] Even President Kennedy reportedly felt that India's request for U.S. financial assistance for their $500 million defense program was "unrealistic."[127]

What then were the basic elements of the assessment made by the Harriman mission?[128] First, it pointed out that the "problem" was not one of an immediate, large scale war, but "of creating an effective long-term deterrent power in the Subcontinent." Second, it stipulated aid on a contingency basis as long as the emergency was acute. Considering the high cost and complexity of an air defense system, India would for some time have to rely on foreign aid for air defense in the event of a crisis. The basic task, in the meantime, would be to bring the Indian ground forces into operational effectiveness.[129] Third, the mission maintained that it was in American interests that India not only remain non-aligned, but also maintain friendly relations with Moscow.[130] Fourth, the findings emphasized political settlement between India and Pakistan as a prerequisite for subcontinental security against the Chinese threat.

The report, however, neither spelled out the basis of a Kashmir settlement nor stipulated it as a precondition for U.S. arms to India. Fifth, it was stated that in the absence of Indo-Pak reconciliation, the more military aid the U.S. gave to India the greater the likelihood that Pakistan would move toward China. The general tenor of the Harriman report suggests that the extended or expanded supply of military hardware to India was constrained by the U.S. desire to maintain friendly ties with Pakistan. Finally, the report not only stressed the need for encouraging the "trend toward new and younger men in the Indian administration," but also indulged in considerable "romantic nonsense about the Commonwealth."[131]

It appears that the U.S. administration kept in close touch with the British in formulating its policy on arms aid to India and in dealing with the Kashmir issue. At one point, Kennedy was committed to the idea that the U.K. and the Commonwealth should take a lead in India's air defense arrangement. Also, echoing one of those Harriman mission proposals, he had reportedly suggested to Macmillan the need for appointing a British mediator on the Kashmir issue. Galbraith was opposed to this approach, believing it overstressed the importance of the Commonwealth. In particular, he was vehemently critical of an air defense scheme in which the Americans provide radar and airfields while the British put in the combat squadrons and take "credit for protection." What further bothered him was that the proposals sent to the British seemed to offer a "unilateral commitment" to India without any stipulation for consultation. He felt, however, that an implied "air defense" arrangement, suggested by Indian Foreign Secretary M. J. Desai, could well provide the long-run basis of a "political association of the first importance."[132]

At the National Security Council meeting on December 17, Galbraith, strongly opposed the proposal of the Joint Chiefs to divide the air defense deal with India: "We are taking the radar and other donkey work and the British are providing the air squadrons." After listening to Galbraith's argument President Kennedy seemed to have ruled out this air defense package for India, but during the following days of the executive committee meeting he was unable to make this decision stick. By then "everyone" had started sniping away at this decision. Later, a proposal for the association of U.S. air power with Indian defense—a scheme favored by Galbraith— was diluted almost to the extent of dispatching a military mission to New Delhi.[133]

Thus, less than a month after India's military debacle, concern in the U.S. administration regarding the Chinese threat seemed to have subsided, and there was a new emphasis on the urgency of a Kashmir settlement. In this changed context President Kennedy and British Prime Minister Macmillan met in Nassau, Bahamas (December 18-21, 1962) to review, among other things, the "defense problems of the Subcontinent."[134] To work out the specifics, Ambassador Galbraith was present along with others from the Departments of State and Defense and the White House staff. It seems that the British team only reluctantly entered into an extended discussion with its U.S. counterpart on problems relating to China and India; they did not think there was a major threat from China in the Subcontinent. As for the U.S., excepting Galbraith, Phillips Talbot, and President Kennedy, the defense aid program was not seen as an opportunity for a closer association between India and the Western community.

The British were more reserved on matters of the kind of assistance the Indians sought or the idea of a closer association between India and the West. Their reticence was apparently influenced by their "more limited resources," and also possibly from a better understanding."[135] Thus the U.S. President had to work out a low key agreement with Prime Minister Macmillan for the continuance of emergency military aid to India on a modest scale. It entailed grants of up to $120 million worth of military hardware shared equally by the U.S. and Britain (plus its Commonwealth partners).[136] Its essential feature was to help India in raising much needed mountain divisions and to provide some ancillary combat and engineering equipment. This modest amount of aid was an indication of the "diminishing concern" about the threat posed by China. It also signalled that neither the U.S. nor Britain was prepared for the kind of "closer association" with India favored by Galbraith.

Galbraith is right when he says that the British role was not decisive in the Nassau agreement on continued but modest aid to India.[137] However, it appears from other sources that the British had extensive support within the U.S. administration. While Americans who advocated this view were apparently influenced by the British assessment, their judgment must have been independently arrived at. One eminent scholar of China's foreign policy, Allen Whiting, who himself was a member of the Harriman mission to India, gives "special credit" to experts like Harriman and Hilsman for holding out against the "worst case" analysis of Chinese intentions against India. It is because of Harriman's "statesmanship and courage," says Whiting, that "middle-echelon experts" and the Bureau of Intelligence and Research (INR) of the

State Department in particular, were able to advocate views contrary to "Cold War orthodoxy." In this debate they were also ably defended by Ball.[138]

It is inconceivable, however, that this group's assessment by itself would have determined the final decision about the modest U.S. defense commitments to India. What did decide the issue was the pressure of the "Pakistan lobby" within the Departments of State and Defense. Because these two departments had attached considerable significance to the U.S. air base at Peshawar (West Pakistan), they wanted to limit U.S. aid to India to a level that would not lead Pakistan to revoke use of this facility.[139] Consequently, the U.S. administration "went out of their way to reassure Pakistan," commented one former member of the Pakistani government. It appears that Washington had categorically acknowledged that America's agreement to assist Pakistan in the event of aggression was "not limited to communist countries"; it also included India.[140] It is impressive that while the "Pakistan lobby" and the China experts (along with their mentors) proceeded from different premises, their prescriptions for the Himalayan conflict tended to coincide. Needless to say, both these groups wanted to keep the flow of arms to India within minimal limits. The coincidence of their suggested levels of commitment had presumably produced the wider basis of a policy consensus that had the support of both Secretary of State Dean Rusk and Secretary of Defense Robert McNamara.[141] This policy consensus finally persuaded President Kennedy to endorse only a modest U.S. commitment to India's defense needs, despite the fact that the President favored the view that the request for extensive arms aid provided an opportunity for closer association between India and the U.S. In endorsing a major policy decision, the President tended to see whether this was based on an overall policy consensus.

The Concluding Phase: More Talks

When the Nassau meeting ended, Macmillan conveyed his and Kennedy's concern about the safety of civilian population centers against air attacks in a message to Nehru on December 23. He proposed:

> . . . if it is agreeable to you, we would be willing to send a joint British-United States team to India to study with your

air staff the problem of strengthening your air defense system.

From this he made it clear that Anglo-American aid was not conditional on the resolution of outstanding Indo-Pak differences. Macmillan, however, reminded Nehru that popular enthusiasm for India was "bound to be a little dampened if many Indian resources are immobilized on the Pakistan border" which otherwise could be used for defense against China. At the same time, in another message to Ayub Khan, he not only urged for patience in the long-standing dispute but also tried to calm Pakistani "natural anxieties" about any increased U.S.-U.K. assistance to India.[142]

Meanwhile, by the end of the year, the U.S.-U.K. sponsored Indo-Pak talks had started in Rawalpindi on a rather dramatic note—the announcement of a Sino-Pak border accord. Despite this provocation, the Indian delegation did not back out of the talks, and the meeting was soon adjourned until January 1963.[143]

Despite the unsatisfactory outcome of the Nassau agreement, Nehru still wanted an air defense arrangement.[144] But during the next eleven months (i.e., until the end of the Kennedy administration) progress toward further U.S. arms aid to India was slow. Yet, a U.S. Military Supply Mission to India (USMSMI) headed by Brigadier General Kelly was set up in New Delhi by February 1, 1963 under the supervision of Galbraith. In the meantime, a series of talks started between the United States and Britain regarding India's defense needs and other related matters. A joint U.S.-U.K. Air Defense Mission visited New Delhi (January 29 to February 23, 1963) to examine with the Indian Air Force the technical requirements for organizing an effective air defense in the event of any "further Chinese aggression."[145]

For the United States, aside from the reluctance to furnish lethal military equipment to India because it could antagonize Pakistan, a major concern had been how far it could go in meeting Indian defense needs. Clarifying America's military assistance policy toward India, Galbraith had declared before an Indian audience:

When the Chinese came over the mountain last Fall, there was no appropriation for military aid to India. We have so far been meeting your emergency needs out of reserve stocks of the United States Army . . . Here we are responding to your requests. There is no question of our urging any particular arrangement. I have been firmly instructed to make clear to your Government that even the act of exploring the problems—which with Britain, Canada and Australia we are now doing—does not constitute a commitment.[146]

This statement suggested that Washington was not prepared to do anything unilaterally or in haste for India, nor was it willing to make a firm long-term commitment on account of domestic and external constraints.

From the Indian viewpoint, the Chinese threat in the Subcontinent urgently called for an effective air defense system, which, Nehru had argued, was supposed "to meet the emergency like the one created by the Chinese advance into NEFA" and to negotiate "the long-term threat posed by China." While explaining the basic rationale, he said:

Both these have to be kept in view; in either event the strengthening of the Indian Air Force has to be tackled immediately. In the event of sudden emergency arising, the Government will have to deal with it in the light of developments with support from friendly countries, which may become suddenly necessary and be available.

Though stressing air support, he ruled out the possible stationing of foreign air forces or the establishment of any foreign air bases in India as an "Air Umbrella."[147]

Evidently, there had been a gap between Indian expectations and what the U.S. and U.K. would give. From the outset, "it was difficult to handle the conflicting interests," submits Macmillan in his memoir. While Kennedy was disturbed about Pakistan's position, Macmillan was anxious not to get involved in "open-ended" British commitments beyond their means. In a communication to Macmillan on May 22, Kennedy took the position that the United States could possibly "go it alone," if Britain was reluctant to send a squadron to India; however, he wanted the U.S. to work in concert with the U.K. Later, Britain agreed to send one squadron on a visit to India "for training purposes" only. The British government ruled out any automatic "commitment to operate" in the event of a fresh conflict with the Chinese. Soon, Kennedy moved along this line; he seems to have been convinced that there was no need to make any firm commitment immediately. But then, he also believed that "American opinion would be serious" if the

Chinese were to launch a large scale attack on India and thereby put at risk the security of undefended urban centers.[148]

Apparently, the United States administration was unwilling to get involved in India's defense arrangement beyond a minimal level. This was indeed contrary to what the Indian government had been looking for since the NEFA debacle of November 1962. In early May of 1963, Rusk, Galbraith, Sandys, and the British High Commissioner to India, Paul Gore-Booth, had a number of meetings with members of the Indian government. They dealt with the general question of India's defense needs and the progress of joint Indo-Pak talks on Kashmir and other related issues. While explaining the American view, Rusk pointed out that the Chinese aggressive and expansionist policies situated a threat against the entire Subcontinent. Hence, the U.S. was interested in promoting friendly relations between India and Pakistan. India was not opposed to this, but apprehended that any inadvertent step could further worsen the climate between the two South Asian neighbors. No communique came out of these talks, though the Kashmir issue was the main topic of their discussions. Obviously, there were differences between India and both the U.S. and U.K. regarding the quantum of military assistance and the assessment of the threat posed by China. Anglo-American interest in the Kashmir problem had further complicated the defense talks.

Faced with a security threat created by the Sino-Indian War, India decided to double the size of its army in a few years, and also modernize and expand the air force. In addition, India wanted to improve its defense production base and communication logistics. The government sought to sustain this defense expansion and modernization program essentially through increased defense allocations. But in certain important areas—especially air defense and the field of defense technology and production—the government looked for assistance from the United States and Britain.[149] Indeed, there were Indian expectations that perhaps the United States and Britain would help India extensively, and these expectations had been raised by prompt Western responses to their appeal for help during the Sino-Indian war. In the process, they not only overlooked the differences in Western perceptions of the Chinese threat but also the basic saliency of their Pakistan connection, which tended to limit anything more than a modest level of sustained military aid to New Delhi. But then the choices available to India around that time were not unlimited.

From April to May 29, 1963, two important Indian missions visited Washington. The first was a team of experts led by S.

Boothalingam, Secretary, Ministry of Economic and Defense Coordination. Though it came to discuss India's defense requirements, this was essentially a mission for procuring defense equipment and stores needed for the Army's overhaul.[150] A more high-powered mission—consisting of Minister of Economy and Defense, T. T. Krishnamachari; Foreign Secretary, M. J. Desai; and advisor to the Ministry of External Affairs, Dr. K. S. Shelvankar—came to ask for assistance to increase the size of the Indian armed forces and to create an enhanced defense production base and better operational logistics during the next few years. More importantly, the mission also asked for modernizing Indian air defense. India was particularly in need of supersonic aircraft since certain areas could not be adequately covered by an early warning system. In its discussions with President Kennedy and his aides, the Krishnamachari mission reportedly sought $1.5 billion in aid from the U.S., the U.K. and others. Though the Indian requests were placed under consideration, American officials were hardly enthusiastic about what the Indian mission was seeking.[151] Nevertheless, the Americans agreed to help India with surplus U.S. machine tools and also agreed to provide a small arms plant, technical consultation and technical training facilities.[152]

In early June the President of India, Dr. S. Radhakrishnan, came to the U.S. on a state visit. In a joint statement issued on June 4, Presidents Kennedy and Radhakrishnan agreed that their two countries "share a mutual defensive concern to thwart the designs of Chinese aggression against the Subcontinent."[153] While this must have pleased some Indians, the expressed sentiment did not imply any increased military aid to India. Ambassador Galbraith, who was also in Washington at this time, argued for "more" in a meeting on U.S. military aid to India, but had no support. The proposed aid stipulated a "thoroughly inadequate amount."[154]

The Kennedy-Macmillan meeting in Birch Grove (Sussex, U.K.) merely formalized the Washington decision. The two statesmen reaffirmed their policy of "continuing" help to India by providing further military aid to strengthen its defense against the threat of renewed Chinese attack.[155] In specific terms, they agreed on a military aid program that stipulated a further $100 million dollars contributed equally by the U.S. and the Commonwealth. One of the important results of this meeting was the simultaneous announcement of a U.S.-India-U.K. agreement on joint radar training exercises.[156] The U.S. rationale was that joint exercises would "put the Chinese on warning" regarding a protective measure in the event of any renewed attack on their part. It "postponed" at least temporarily, addressing India's need for a high performance aircraft.[157] The Indians were certainly not looking for a soft air defense program; they wanted their own air defense capability. Ambassador Galbraith was finally able to persuade the Indians about its merits through his sustained efforts. This program again demonstrated the Kennedy administration's preference for minimal commitments to India. While agreeing to joint exercises and the supply of mobile radar equipment (to be replaced by permanent installations during the next 12 to 18 months), the United States did not make any commitment to come to India's aid if it were attacked by China. However, both the American and the British governments agreed to consult with the Indian government in the event of such a contingency, regarding further assistance in India's air defense. A joint air defense training exercise was carried out between November 9 and 19, 1963. A squadron of United States Air Force F-100 Super Sabres along with a squadron of Royal Air Force Javelins and two Australian Canberra bombers participated in these exercises with the Indian Air Force. From the western perspective, this U.S.-U.K. involvement was much less provocative or dangerous than what was implied in Nehru's appeal of November 19, 1962.[158]

In the fall of 1963, Chester Bowles succeeded Galbraith as the new American ambassador in New Delhi, and immediately had to wrestle with an Indian request for a $500 million (five year) defense modernization program. Bowles thought the plans were "relatively moderate"; yet, a "bitterly" fought contest occurred within the U.S. government.[159] In any event, thanks to the initiative taken by Bowles and the U.S. military mission in New Delhi, a second military assistance agreement (aside from the one stipulating emergency aid in November 1962) was tentatively worked out in cooperation with the Indian defense establishment. It envisaged a supply of modern aircraft, as well as further equipment for mountain divisions and the radar installations—amounting to $75 million a year for a period of five years. It is impressive that Bowles was able to persuade Nehru to take a more considerate position in Southeast Asia and to enter into negotiations with the Pakistanis for a ceiling on defense expenditure—in exchange for this proposed arms deal. President Kennedy was evidently quite pleased with this arrangement. He had left no doubts in Bowles' mind that he would support the proposed deal irrespective of Pakistani reactions, but in order to facilitate the deal encouraged Bowles to generate the broadest possible support for his views within the State Department and the Pentagon. Specifically, he was to get the support of Rusk and McNamara. Thus, preparations were under way to favorably respond to the Indian request; Kennedy had scheduled a National Security Council meeting on November 26, 1963.[160]

Admittedly, long years of high level Pakistani influence within the State and Defense Departments posed a formidable challenge to Bowles' initiative. However, what sealed the fate of the proposed arms deal were unforeseen events within a span of just over two months. Four days before the scheduled National Security Council meeting, President Kennedy was assassinated. This not only implied postponing the proposed agreement, but also called for a fresh evaluation of India's defense needs in light of the new President's perspective. It was not surprising that President Johnson decided to send General Maxwell Taylor, Chairman of the U.S. Joint Chiefs of Staff (apparently on Bowles' suggestion) to India for further assessment of India's defense needs. Arriving in New Delhi on December 16, 1963, Taylor had discussions with Indian Defense Minister Chavan, and with India's Chiefs of Army, Air Force and Navy staffs regarding the entire range of India's military requirements and defense program. General Taylor was evidently quite impressed by the Indians' "determination" to strike a balance between defense and preservation of the vital economic program. It appears from Bowles' memoir that General Taylor's report endorsed his recommendation.[161]

But the Taylor report did not expedite a decision in support of India's defense needs. Evidently, Washington did not understand the implications of delaying matters of India's vital security interests. This dilatory policy was somewhat indicative of America's assumption that "India was not powerful enough to be taken seriously for accommodation," and that "it was in any case helpless," as argued by some analysts. In fact, there seems to have been a prevalent notion within the administration that perhaps the options available to the Indians were rather limited. Consequently, most American policymakers failed to anticipate that—faced with continuous American delay—the Indian government might turn toward the Russians for military hardware. One American participant observer commented in his memoir that "the idea of the Soviet Union's giving military equipment on any basis was dismissed as unrealistic. India, it was said, had no place to go but to the United States." Because of the perceived importance of Pakistan, in view of the U.S. base at Peshawar, the American government found it difficult to take any significant steps in support of India's defense needs: in apprehension of adverse Pakistani reactions. Furthermore, continued pressure from the "Pakistan lobby" in the State Department, Pentagon, and Congress, impelled the new administration to postpone the decision regarding substantial U.S. commitment to India's long term defense program.[162]

Despite these impediments, Bowles seems to have persuaded the Johnson administration to work out a program in conformity with India's defense needs. Two weeks of negotiations in Washington in May 1964, between an Indian team led by Defense Minister Chavan and U.S. officials, including Ambassador Bowles, produced an acceptable U.S. military assistance program for India. But once again an unforeseen event intervened: the sudden death of Nehru on May 27. This interrupted the final White House meeting scheduled for May 28 and prompted the South Asia Bureau officials of the Pentagon and State Department to advise the President and the Secretaries of the two departments to postpone the matter until "the dust has a chance to settle down." But, by that time even the sober-minded State and White House officials had been convinced of the vital importance of the Peshawar base to U.S. security. In this context, the Indian government decided to seek Soviet military assistance—after eighteen months of frantic waiting for a favorable U.S. decision.[163]

It had become obvious to New Delhi that the U.S. government was unwilling to support India's defense program beyond a marginal point. While it generally agreed to provide a military grant at the current level (though subject to Congressional approval), and also sought to extend military sales credit to India, the U.S. left the vital question of sophisticated weapons systems, advanced aircraft, and other defense related issues to further discussion. In the backdrop of this halting U.S. response, the Indian Defense Minister received an invitation from the Soviet Defense Minister, Marshall Malinovsky, to visit the Soviet Union. He used this visit to discuss with the Soviet government the implementation of India's defense plan.[164]

In brief, the Indian government was disillusioned with the United States' modest offer. Any systematic development of India's defense potential as envisaged under a five-year defense plan (1964-69)—in view of the Chinese threat—called for sizeable capital and technical input. An additional Indian concern was to ensure the continued progress of its economic development. Under these circumstances they found Moscow quite understanding. Further, the growing Sino-Soviet rift underlined India's vital importance to the Soviet policymakers. One informed American observer stated:

"American officials were loath to see the Soviet Union gain a major foothold in the Indian military establishment, but were reluctant to supply India with the same quality aircraft Pakistan was receiving."[165]

The Indians found Moscow all set to favorably respond to their request. Writing in his memoir, Chester Bowles noted: "In mid-August 1964, the same Indian military negotiating team, headed by Defense Minister Chavan . . . departed for Moscow, and two weeks later they returned with all they had asked for, and more."[166] This ironically ended the tortuous course of the response to Indian requests for sizeable long-term American military assistance. The U.S. response that had begun with a bang of emergency arms airlift (to non-aligned India) ended with the whimper of non-decision. To some informed American observers this was a case of "lost opportunity."[167] However, modest U.S. military aid to India did continue until September 1965 when it was cancelled because of the Indo-Pak war.

What was the total quantum of U.S. military aid supplied to India as a result of the 1962 war? Between October 1962 and September 1965 the U.S. furnished a total of $76 million in aid plus $4 million under the credit sales program. This did not constitute more than 36 per cent of the American promises,[168] and covered only four to five per cent of India's defense needs.[169] It should be noted that $60 million stipulated under the Nassau agreement was repayable in rupees—10 per cent was due at the time the order was placed, and the rest in 18 equal semi-annual installments.[170] Comparatively speaking, U.S. military aid to India during this period was about one-twentieth of its military assistance to Pakistan during the preceding ten years.

The Role of Congress

As for Congress, its role in arms sales and aid had grown enormously. By the earlier years of the Kennedy administration it had developed certain reservations regarding increased foreign assistance.[171] Anticipating its mood, President Kennedy in his 1963-64 foreign aid message to Congress, put his request for arms aid to India in qualified terms. While Kennedy believed a Chinese attack would entail "additional" U.S. efforts to bolster subcontinental security, he wanted these to be "matched" by "appropriate" Indo-Pak efforts.

Even in a largely executive-dominated decisionmaking process, reactions of the legislature have to be anticipated. Hence, foreign policy objectives have to be placed before it in a manner that will secure the overall support of Congress. Presumably, this prompted President Kennedy to send a four-member Congressional fact-finding delegation to New Delhi prior to the Harriman mission. The purpose was to keep Congress informed about the administration's response to India's request. There was no direct opposition in Congress regarding military assistance to India, but rather to the overall size of the general economic and military programs.

Some of the objections raised by U.S. legislators were similar to those posed within the executive branch. The findings of one perceptive study show that the year 1963 was marked by a significant degree of Congressional "consensus" on the need to make U.S. arms aid to India conditional upon modifications of India's foreign policy behavior.[172] One commonly held view was that considering Chinese aggression against India and the prompt arms assistance rendered by the U.S. and U.K., India should give up non-alignment and join the West. The other condition stressed India's understanding that it would not use U.S. arms against Pakistan, and that it would resolve the Kashmir dispute with Pakistan. The Chairman of the House Committee on Foreign Affairs, Thomas Morgan, had said in exasperation: "I think somebody ought to do some arm twisting and get this [the Kashmir dispute] settled."[173] At least one House member, John Broomfield, felt that if the "present method" of bolstering Indian defenses against China continues then the U.S. might "lose" the friendship of Pakistan, "our staunchest ally in that part of the world."[174] A powerful southern Senator and Chairman of the Senate Armed Service Committee, Richard Russell, opposed all arms aid to India on the grounds that it might fall into the hands of the Chinese.[175] Unlike the House members, however, Senators in general made less biting remarks or dramatic suggestions about U.S. arms aid to India. Instead, some Senators had even questioned the wisdom of giving aid to Pakistan, especially when it was developing closer links with China.[176]

Notwithstanding its relative opposition to the aid policy in general, Congress on the whole endorsed the administration's arms assistance program in India. The House Committee on Foreign Affairs decided to keep the matter under constant review; however, it made it clear that unless there were signs of an "improvement in the situation," the Committee would recommend reductions in aid to "both parties" (i.e., India and Pakistan).[177]

Analysis and Conclusion

In spite of the conflictual nature of the issues raised by the 1962 War, its impact on U.S. foreign policy was not comparable to that of the near-simultaneous Cuban missile crisis or the Berlin blockade (1948). While President Kennedy did have an interest in India's developmental performance, that by itself was not sufficient to generate sustained Presidential attention in regard to a relatively limited conflict in a rather physically isolated rough terrain.[178] Most U.S. policymakers perceived the 1962 Sino-Indian conflict more as a symbolic contest without the potential of an all-out war. Though President Kennedy was disposed toward Galbraith's (and later Bowles') idea of closer Indo-U.S. ties, he was not prepared to go beyond the structural adjustments within America's South Asia policy that were evidently preferred by his principal advisers. Indeed, the U.S. President is not free to initiate "drastic" changes in an "on-going" policy unless the principal role-incumbents in general concur that the salient situation is so critical that it cannot be managed within the existing policy framework.[179]

It is not surprising therefore that Washington's decisions on arms aid to India in 1962-63 were largely routine transactions. In this process, the major elements were the White House, the Departments of State and Defense, and the U.S. ambassador in New Delhi. Neither the Congress nor public opinion had a major impact on the policy outcome. The role of Congress was one of endorsing a decision that had already been arrived at; it merely followed the lead.

Without overstressing the point, there is evidence to suggest that on many occasions the U.S. President tried to initiate a move on the basis of the brief given by his personal friend, Galbraith. But again, in making policy he did not rely entirely on the advice of his ambassador; he also considered the reactions of the principal role-incumbents in the various departments and in his own White House staff. In addition, he took into consideration the judgment of an alliance partner, the U.K., which was also involved in the arms aid program.

This episode shows that if there is broad consensus on the issue at stake, and the consequent commitment is relatively modest, decisionmaking tends to remain within the bounds of the executive branch. Clearly, neither the President nor the related departments were prepared to commit the U.S. in an area of marginal interest beyond permissible limits. Some of the related problems (like the continuing Indo-Pak differences or the domestic implications of unqualified arms aid) only further underlined the constraints. In short, the ground rules of the decisionmaking process were already established and the various actors worked within existing norms in a mutually complementary process. In this case, we have not been able to discern extensive signs of bureaucratic politics regarding U.S. arms aid to India; yet, it would be too simplistic to suggest that it was conspicuously absent. The opposition of the so-called "Pakistan lobby" (in both the State and Defense departments) and the reservations of the middle echelon China specialists (within the State Department), regarding sizeable arms aid to India, were indicative of a vertical as well as horizontal bureaucratic contest within the foreign policy process. Last but not least, there was continuous jockeying for Presidential attention on the part of the U.S. ambassador in New Delhi and Secretary of State Rusk. Galbraith in fact felt that Rusk "continues to regard me as a major inconvenience in an otherwise placid organization."[180]

True, the U.S. decision to furnish arms aid to India reflected a generally favorable public mood, but in endorsing the decision the U.S. President had to remain aware of Congressional reaction as well. The modest size of the aid and the qualified nature of the commitment suggest that the decisionmakers settled for the lowest possible commitment that would secure overall Congressional approval. The subsequent Congressional approval of the arms aid to India, as stated earlier, not only indicates the correctness of the administration's anticipation, but also demonstrates the extent to which their perceptions of the issue area coincided.

Notes

1. For text of the Panchshila Agreement (April 19, 1954) between India and China, see *Foreign Policy of India: Texts of Documents 1947-58* (New Delhi: Lok Sabha Secretariat, 1959), pp. 101-109. The five principles of peaceful coexistence were later reaffirmed by the Prime Ministers of India and China at New Delhi in June 1954 , pp. 111-114.

2. For details about the two countries' positions regarding the India-China border issue see *Report of the Officials of the Government of India and People's Republic of China on the Boundary Question* (New Delhi: Ministry of External Affairs, Government of India, 1961). Hereafter *Report on the Boundary Question*.

3. For an analytical overview of this debate, see Stephen P. Cohen, "India's China War and After: A Review Article," *Journal of Asian Studies*, Vol. XXX, No. 4, August 1971, pp. 850-852.

4. Allen S. Whiting, *The Chinese Calculus of Deterrence* (Ann Arbor: The University of Michigan Press, 1975), pp. 116-169.

5. On at least one occasion China had demanded Indian endorsement of its conception of the U.S. as the "principal enemy." India had however refused to "discard or vary" any one of its policies under "pressure." For an exchange on this issue, see *Notes, Memoranda and Letters Exchanged Between the Government of India and China 1954-1959, White Paper I* (New Delhi: Ministry of External Affairs, 1959), pp. 73-78.

6. This is how Nehru viewed it. See Jawaharlal Nehru, *India's Foreign Policy: Selected Speeches, September 1946-April 1961* (New Delhi: Publications Division, Government of India, 1961), p. 362.

7. Kennedy's biographer notes that he appreciated Indian non-alignment as being similar to "our policy of non-involvement in the great international controversies of the Nineteenth century." See Arthur Schlesinger, Jr., *A Thousand Days: John F. Kennedy in the White House* (Boston: Houghton Mifflin, 1965), p. 522.

8. Since 1947, the Chinese Nationalist regime raised, on a number of occasions, objections regarding the validity of the McMahon Line. See *Report on the Boundary Question*, P.C.R.-8.

9. December 2, 1959. See U.S. Department of State, Bureau of Public Affairs, *American Foreign Policy 1959: Current Documents* (Department of State Publications 7492, 1963), pp. 1191-1192. Hereafter *Current Documents*.

10. News conference, November 12, 1959. *Ibid.*, pp. 1190-1191. Subsequently (November 13) Herter called in the Indian Charge d'Affaires in Washington to clarify any possible misconception resulting from his comments on the Sino-Indian border issue. In this context, he told him that his news conference remarks were not meant to condone the use of force by the "Chinese Communists." See *Asian Recorder*, 1959, p. 3023.

11. For a report of some of his speeches see *Asian Recorder* (New Delhi, 1959), pp. 3072-3075. According to the noted American columnist Walter Lippmann, "the central objective of the President's trip was quite evidently to reach an understanding with India." *The Washington Post*, December 17, 1959.

12. Dwight D. Eisenhower, *Waging Peace: 1956-1961* (New York: Doubleday & Co., 1965), p. 501.

13. For a first hand account of this aspect, see (Brig.) J. P. Dalvi, *The Himalayan Blunder: The Curtain-raiser to the Sino-Indian War of 1962* (Bombay: Thacker and Co., 1969), pp. 76-399. In private, on October 20, Home Minister Lal Bahadur Shastri (later to succeed Nehru) stated: "If only we were better prepared." Cited in Kuldip Nayar, *Between the Lines* (New Delhi: Allied, 1969), p. 133. For a contrary view, see S. S. Khera, *India's Defence Problem* (New Delhi: Orient Longmans, 1968), pp. 195-234. Also, a recent Indian publication contends that the Indian forces were "much superior weapons-wise"

and enjoyed better logistics. See (Lt. Col.) J. R. Saigal, *The Unfought War of 1962* (New Delhi: Allied, 1979), Chapter X.

14. Nehru's statement to the press at Palam (New Delhi) October 12, 1962. See *The Times of India*, October 13, 1962.

15. Nehru's speech in the Lok Sabha while moving the resolution on Chinese aggression, November 8, 1962. See *Jawaharlal Nehru's Speeches, September 1957 - April 1963*, Vol. I (New Delhi: Ministry of Information and Broadcasting, Government of India, August 1964), p. 231.

16. Lal Bahadur Shastri's conversation with Kuldip Nayar. See Nayar, p. 133.

17. U.S. Secretary of State Dean Rusk's comments in a news conference, July 12, 1962. See *Department of State Bulletin*, 47 ,July 30, 1962, p. 117.

18. John Kenneth Galbraith, *Ambassador's Journal: A Personal Account of the Kennedy Years* (New York: The New American Library, 1969); Theodore Sorensen, *Kennedy* (New York: Harper and Row, 1965); Arthur M. Schlesinger, Jr., *A Thousand Days: John F. Kennedy in the White House* (Boston: Houston Mifflin, 1965); Roger Hilsman, *To Move a Nation* (New York: Harper and Row, 1971); Chester Bowles, *Promises to Keep: My Years in Public Life 1941-1969* (New York: Harper and Row, 1971).

19. Bowles, p. 436. The author twice served as U.S. ambassador to India (1951-53; 1963-68). For some time, he was Undersecretary of State in the Kennedy administration.

20. In this context, Galbraith believed that "part of the trouble stems from Indian troops taking up more advanced positions." See Galbraith, p. 349.

21. *Ibid*, p. 353.

22. Derived from a lecture delivered at a public forum in New Delhi. This speech was subsequently reported in an editorial in *Indian Express* (New Delhi), August 16, 1962. Reflecting on this speech in his personal account, Galbraith points out that "under staff pressure" he had "eliminated most of the content" from this speech "so that it got only the slight attention it deserves." (p. 356).

23. Revealed by Galbraith in his New Delhi lecture.

24. Schlesinger, pp. 522, 526-529.

25. According to Bowles he "did not know Kaul" and it was Kaul who had sought this meeting (Bowles, p. 474). In contrast, Kaul stated that it was Bowles who had expressed the desire through the Indian Prime Minister (Nehru) to meet him during his visit to New Delhi (Kaul, p. 340).

26. Kaul, p. 341.

27. Bowles, p. 474. Bowles is said to have written to Kaul later about his intention to apprise President Kennedy about India's contingency (Kaul, p. 341).

28. Letter cited in Kaul, p. 342.

29. Cited in Bowles, p. 474.

30. Bowles, p.474.

31. Choudhury, *India, Pakistan, Bangladesh, and the Major Powers* (New York: The Free Press, 1975), p. 481.

32. Bowles, p. 481.

33. Galbraith's communication to President Kennedy, July 11, 1961. For text, see Bowles, pp. 146-149. Later on, with President Kennedy's approval, Bowles tried to establish contacts with Peking through the Burmese Prime Minister U Nu; his efforts also failed because of a military coup in Burma (p. 402).

34. For an account of this process, see Bowles, pp. 391-402.

35. Sorensen, pp. 750-751.

36. *Ibid.*, p. 751. On May 23, 1963, Kennedy had hinted his interest in detente with Peking in a press conference response to the effect that U.S wheat was available to meet China's food crisis. China, however did not respond to his offer. See U.S., President , *Public Papers of the Presidents of the United States* (Washington, D.C.: Office of the Federal Register, National Archives and Record Service, 1961-1963); John F. Kennedy, 1963, pp.431. (Hereafter *Public Papers of the Presidents: John F. Kennedy*)

37. There was strong Congressional concern about Chinese pressure against India. Senator Sparkman, acting chairman of the Foreign Relations Committee, stated the context of assistance to India: "We know right now that India is pressing very hard against Communist China upon her north-eastern frontier," and then added that it would be imprudent to discourage India by reducing aid "at the very time that she is moving in the direction that we have been wanting her to move for a long time." Cited in *The New York Times*, June 10, 1962.

38. Galbraith, p. 373.

39. Galbraith's communication to Kennedy, October 16, 1962. For full text see Galbraith, pp. 373-375.

40. For a succinct statement on Galbraith's relationship with President Kennedy and the roles he played, see Schlesinger, pp. 523-524. "Cables from overseas," especially from a distant country like India, says a participant observer, often had a far greater impact on the White House and State Department than even the most carefully drafted "interdepartmental memoranda" (see Bowles, p. 436).

41. Based on Selig S. Harrison, *The Widening Gulf: Asian Nationalism and American Policy* (New York: The Free Press, 1978), p. 270. In some ways, there was an earlier implied U.S. endorsement of the Pakistani position, in the Kennedy-Ayub Joint Communique of July 1961. It permitted Pakistan to use U.S. military hardware for the maintenance of its "security" without making any reference to the usual anti-communist arrangement. For text of the communique, see *Documents on American Foreign Relations, 1961* (New York: 1962), pp. 287-288.

42. For an analysis of this aspect see Shivaji Ganguly, "U.S. Military Assistance to India 1962-63: A Study in Decisionmaking," *India Quarterly* 28 (July-September 1972), pp. 216-226.

43. *The New York Times*, October 22, 1962.

44. Galbraith, pp. 378-379.
45. The full text of this letter is available in former Defense Secretary to the Government of India, S. S. Khera's account of *India's Defence Problem* (Bombay: Orient Longmans, 1968), pp. 177-180.
46. This was the first of some fifteen letters which Prime Minister Nehru and President Kennedy exchanged during the next six months. See Sorensen, *Kennedy*, p. 748).
47. *Ibid.*, p. 663. Incidentally, Prime Minister Nehru had also raised this issue in his meeting with Ambassador Galbraith on October 29. See Galbraith, p. 390.
48. Cited in Kuldip Nayar, *India: The Critical Years* (Delhi: Vikas Publications, 1971), p. 171. The author was press officer to Indian Home Minister Shastri during this period.
49. Cited in Nayar, *Between the Lines,* p. 154. In the same letter Kennedy made it clear that he had no inclination to force India into a pact by exploiting her predicament.
50. Cited, Nayar, *India: The Critical Years*, p. 171. The confusion seems to have been created by an erroneous announcement by All India Radio that Nehru had made a special request for help to Kennedy. For details, see Khera, p. 176.
51. As mentioned in Harold Macmillan's memoir, *At the End of the Day 1961-1963* (New York: Harper and Row, 1973), p. 228.
52. Cited in *Keesing's Contemporary Archives*, 1963, p. 19194.
53. Extract on Nehru's reply cited in Macmillan, p. 228. Surprisingly, Macmillan makes a sarcastic remark about Nehru's reply in his memoir: "This was indeed a different tone from that adopted by the protagonists of non-resistance and non-alignment."
54. Galbraith, p. 381.
55. Based on Macmillan, p. 229. Also see *Keesing's*, 1963, p. 19194.
56. Great Britain, *Parliamentary Debates* (Hansard), Fifth Series, Vol. 666, House of Commons, Session 1962-63, Cols. 33-34.
57. For details about the reactions of various nations, aligned as well as non-aligned, regarding the Sino-Indian conflict, see *International Studies* (Special Issue), 5 (July-September), 1963.
58. Galbraith makes a passing reference to his journal regarding the rationale behind such a move, p. 186.
59. Cited in *India News* (Washington, D.C.: Indian Embassy, Special Supplement, October 30, 1962). For a background to this announcement, see Galbraith, pp. 382, 385-386.
60. Indeed, immediately after Galbraith's announcement a frantic protest came from the KMT regime. Galbraith, p. 386.
61. On October 27, Galbraith was able to get the Department of State's "assurance of contingency planning in the event we are asked for aid" by India. Immediately after this the U.S. Ambassador set the U.S. military attaches to work on a transfer schedule for elementary arms for the Indian Army. Galbraith, pp. 385-389.

62. *Ibid.*, p. 390.

63. Earlier Nehru had ruled out such possibilities on the grounds that it implied becoming "somebody else's dependent" and meant "joining some military bloc." See Prime Minister on *Sino-Indian Relations—I* (New Delhi: External Publicity Division, 1963), pp. 118-119. Also, Nehru's hesitance about U.S. military aid was also influenced by his apprehension of a likely adverse reaction in Moscow.

64. Galbraith, p. 390.

65. Details of Nehru's formal request to President Kennedy for U.S. military equipment remain officially classified in both New Delhi and Washington.

66. Galbraith, pp. 389-390.

67. Whiting, p. 167. The author was a member of a special studies group, Bureau of Intelligence and Research (INR) in the Department of State from September 1961 to August 1966. He was also a member of Harriman's mission to New Delhi in November 1962.

68. *Keesing's*, 1963, p. 19194; and also see Galbraith, pp. 389-392.

69. Galbraith, pp. 394-395.

70. Schlesinger, p. 531.

71. Based on Sorensen, p. 748.

72. Theodore Sorensen, *The Kennedy Legacy* (New York: Macmillan, 1969), p. 200. Kennedy believed that "patience" with "firmness" and not the risk of a "final showdown" was the correct approach with China until it reconciles to live at peace with the U.S. and the countries on its periphery. Incidentally, in mid-1962 by opposing the use of force, the U.S. under Kennedy was able to dissuade Chaing Kai-shek from invading mainland China (Sorensen, pp. 746-748).

73. Roger Hilsman, *To Move a Nation* (New York: Delta Books, 1967), pp. 324-326. The author was at that time Director, Bureau of Intelligence and Research (INR), U. S. Department of State.

74. Based on personal interviews.

75. For Ayub Khan's statement about his disappointment with the U.S. decision, see his autobiography, *Friends Not Masters: A Political Autobiography* (New York: Oxford University Press, 1967), p. 145. Also for a summary of Kennedy and text of Ayub's letters, see pp. 141-143. According to an American source, Ayub Khan seemed to have avoided the U.S. Ambassador to Pakistan by going on a hunting trip (Barnds, p. 185).

76. Galbraith's role in these events is based on *Ambassador's Journal*, pp. 386-388.

77. Kuldip Nayar, *Between the Lines*, p. 158. According to Galbraith, Mohammed Ali had also promised to carry out their negotiations with the Chinese in "low key". Galbraith, p. 396.

78. Choudhury, *India, Pakistan, Bangladesh, and the Major Powers*, p. 112.

79. Cited in *Keesing's*, 1963, p. 19194.

80. Kennedy was once reported to have said that the "two K's," Krishna Menon and Kashmir, constituted the "trouble" between India and the U.S. In a private conversations with Sudhir Ghosh, a Member of Parliament from India. Cited in Sudhir Ghosh, *Gandhi's Emissary* (Boston: Houghton Mifflin, 1967), p. 310.

81. *Keesing's*, 1963, p. 19194; also see *The New York Times*, November 6-11, 1962.

82. See testimony by General Robert J. Wood, Director of U.S. Military Assistance, Subcommittee on Appropriations, Foreign Assistance. U.S. Congress, *House and Related Agencies Appropriations for 1966, Hearings*, 89th Cong., 1st Sess., 1965, pp. 266-267; also see K. Subrahmanyam, "U.S. Policy Towards India," *China Report* (January-April 1972), especially the section on "Military Aid to India," pp. 43-44; *The Arms Trade with the Third World* (Stockholm: Stockholm International Peace Research Institute, 1971), p. 477.

83. Foreign Assistance Act, September 4, 1961. 87th Cong., 1st Sess., 1961. For text see *United States Statutes at Large* (Washington: Office of the Federal Register, National Archives and Record Services, 1961), especially Chapter 2, "Military Assistance in Part-II," pp. 435-438.

84. Statement by U.S. Secretary of Defense Robert S. McNamara, Senate Foreign Relations Committee, June 13, 1963. See U.S. Congress, Senate Foreign Relations Committee, *Foreign Assistance Act, 1963*, Hearings, 88th Cong., 1st Sess., 1963, p. 173.

85. Roger Hilsman, p. 324. This estimate contrasts with the exaggerated estimates of the quantum of U.S. arms aid to India given by high level Pakistani sources. They believed that since the Sino-Indian war arms had been flowing to India on a "substantial scale" (see Ayub Khan, p. 133), and thus "threatened" Pakistan's "territorial integrity." Z. A. Bhutto, *The Myth of Independence* (London: Oxford University Press, 1969), pp. 62, 68.

86. General Robert J. Wood's testimony, f.n. 96; former Ambassador to India, and U.S. Undersecretary of State Chester Bowles, p. 439. A *New York Times* report of November 11, 1962, put the value of U. S. arms (airlifted to India till November 10) around $5 million.

87. For text of notes as released on November 17, 1962, see *Department of State Bulletin* 47, December 3, 1962, pp. 838-839. On November 27, the U.K. signed similar agreements. The agreement of 1951 was effected by an exchange of notes, Washington, March 7 and 16, 1951 (Treaties and Other International Series Act, 2241); the agreement of 1958 also based on exchange of notes at New Delhi, April 16 and December 16, 1958 (Treaties and Other International Series Act, 4322).

88. The statement runs as follows: ". . . if our assistance to India should be misused and directed against another in aggression, the United States would undertake immediately, in accordance with constitutional authority, appropriate action both within and without the United Nations to thwart such aggression". See *Department of State Bulletin* 47, pp. 837-838. Earlier on January 26, 1962, President Kennedy had affirmed in an exchange of letters with

President Ayub Khan, regarding U.S. assurances on aggression against Pakistan. See Choudhury, p. 113. These letters have not yet been released for publication.

89. *The New York Times*, November 12, 1962.

90. On November 12, Indian Home Minister Lal Bahadur Shastri had declared in a public meeting that India was building its military might to drive the Chinese invaders from Indian soil" (*Times of India*, November 13, 1962). By November 10, an encouraging development for India was that the Soviet Union had not only returned to its neutral position on the border question, but promised to meet its agreement to supply MiG-21 fighter aircraft to India. Deliveries were expected to begin in December. (Nehru's statement on Khrushchev's letter to him, *The New York Times*, November 11, 1962.)

91. Galbraith, p. 404; also see his communication to President Kennedy, November 13, 1962 (p. 414).

92. Sorensen, p. 200; and about the London meeting and Galbraith's views, also see Galbraith, pp. 119-417.

93. Galbraith, pp. 118-416. It is inconceivable that Kennedy wanted India to join in an alliance with the U.S. He must have been more concerned about the likely impact of Nehru's behavior on Capitol Hill, where many of the legislators might have expected more spontaneous gestures in favor of the U.S. on the part of the Indian Prime Minister.

94. Galbraith, p. 477.

95. Galbraith comments in his *Journal*: "It was the day of ultimate panic in Delhi, the first time I have ever witnessed the disintegration of public morale" (p. 424). Throughout the month of November Nehru sent "agitated reports" both to Macmillan and Kennedy. See Macmillan, p. 230.

96. New Delhi seems to have kept major military units near Siliguri rather than move them up for the defense of Assam and NEFA. See Whiting, p. 147. According to Bowles, fear of Chinese retaliatory air raids had inhibited the Indian government from making use of its air force against extended communication lines. He believes use of the IAF could have prevented India's military debacle. See Bowles, p. 474.

97. Interview by A. K. Sen (former Law Minister in Nehru's Cabinet), March 1974, as cited in Michael Brecher, "The Super Powers and the India-China War: Nonalignment at the Brink," in M. S. Rajan and Shivaji Ganguly (eds.), *Great Power Relations, World Order and the Third World* (New Delhi: Vikas, 1981), p. 122.

98. To this day this communication has remained a "highly confidential" document. According to one commentator this was transmitted through Indian Ambassador B. K. Nehru in Washington. For reasons known only to Nehru, the copy of the letter was never sent to the Ministry of External Affairs; it was retained by the Prime Minister's Secretariat. See Nayar, *Between the Lines*, pp. 168-169. But the veracity of the communication has been confirmed by knowledgeable sources (Galbraith, p. 424; Bowles' revelations in Nayar, *India: The Critical Years*, pp. 178-179; President Kennedy's remarks in conversations with Sudhir Ghosh. Cited in Ghosh, pp. 312-313).

99. Bowles, p. 474. One informed British commentator has indicated that in his desperate appeal Nehru had asked for fifteen squadron of bombers to counter the advancing Chinese armed forces. See Michael Edwards, "Illusion and Reality in India's Foreign Policy," *International Affairs* (January 1965), p. 42.

100. Derived from Michael Brecher, "Non-Alignment Under Stress: The West and the India-China Border War," *Pacific Affairs*, Winter, Vol. 52, No. 4, 1979-80, pp. 617-618. According to one Indian observer, this was a Defense Ministry proposal "just initialled" by Nehru. In fact, following the NEFA debacle, the Defense Ministry had been asking for all kinds of military assistance, which the Indian Prime Minister had been forwarding under his signature to the United States and other major friendly countries. See Nayar, *India: The Crucial Years*, p. 178. V. K. Krishna Menon had insisted subsequently in an interview that Nehru "did not make this request." "So far as I know there is not an iota of truth in the story," he noted further (Michael Brecher, *India and World Politics: Krishna Menon's View of the World* (London: Oxford University Press, 1968), pp. 172-173.

101. Commenting on Nehru's urgent message, one of Kennedy's White House aides said, without specifying the contents: "Pleas for a vast arsenal of American armaments began to pour in" (Sorensen, *Kennedy*, p. 630). One other Kennedy aide remarked sarcastically: "Nehru, forgetting the virtues of non-alignment, sent a desperate appeal for American help" (Schlesinger, p. 461). The then British Prime Minister recalls in his memoir that the Americans considered Nehru's various requests for assistance indicative of a "'state of panic,' since they were far reaching in the extreme" (Macmillan p. 230).

102. Evidently, Galbraith's viewpoint on "air action" was different from that of Chester Bowles—who believed that an Indian air strike could have prevented India's military reverses in NEFA. See Bowles, *Promises to Keep*, p. 474.

103. Galbraith, pp. 426-427. It should be noted that Kennedy had not as yet replied to Nehru's urgent request for U.S. combat air support transmitted on November 19, 1962. The Indian request was twice repeated to Kennedy, including once by Nehru himself in early January 1963. (See Thomas Brady's reports in *The New York Times*, January 25 and February 21, 1963; also see editorial in *Times of India*, January 29, 1963.) It is conceivable that in view of the long range implications of such a request, President Kennedy was reluctant to enter into direct correspondence with Nehru.

104. One senior American military official was reportedly sitting at the Ministry of External Affairs a few days before the ceasefire (Nayar, *Between the Lines*, p. 178).

105. Cited in *The Statesman*, April 28, 1965.

106. For text of China's announcement, November 20, 1962, see *Peking Review*, November 30, 1962, pp. 5-7.

107. Nehru's views revealed by Galbraith, p. 427. The other Indian viewpoint as expressed by the then Indian Home Minister, Lal Bahadur Shastri. See Nayar, *Between the Lines*, p. 172. For a contrasting analysis of the Chinese move see Maxwell, p. 419. British Prime Minister Macmillan mentions in his

memoir how he and his colleagues felt so uncertain about the real situation—even after consultations with the U.S. President or Prime Ministers of Australia and New Zealand (Macmillan, p. 231).

108. The announcement was made by President Kennedy in a news conference statement. See *Department of State Bulletin* 47 (December 10, 1962), p. 874; and Galbraith, "The American Ambassador," *Foreign Service Journal* 46 (June 1969), p. 16.

109. It has been Galbraith's contention that the ambassador should be "representative" of the President and not as "partisan" of the Department of State and thereby get involved in the inter-departmental fights (Galbraith, "The American Ambassador," p, 15).

110. Macmillan, pp. 230-231.

111. Kennedy's announcement on November 30, 1962. For text see U.S. *Department of State Bulletin* 47 (July-December 1962), p. 874.

112. This is also confirmed by Secretary of State Dean Rusk's testimony of June 11, 1963: "The problem is how to put India in a position . . . . to deter any attack by the Chinese against India, without at the same time leaving Pakistan to fear that in some ways this build-up might be directed against Pakistan" See Senate Committee on Foreign Relations, *Hearings*, f.n. 45, p. 43.

113. Hilsman, p. 328.

114. Hilsman, *To Move a Nation*, pp. 329-330.

115. Nayar, *India: The Critical Years*, p. 190. Pakistan's President Ayub Khan mentions approvingly the "significant role" played by Harriman and Sandys. See Ayub Khan, *Autobiography*, p. 148. An Indo-Pakistan joint communique was simultaneously issued from New Delhi and Rawalpindi on November 30, 1962. For text see *Foreign Policy of India: Texts of Documents 1947-64* (Lok Sabha Secretariat: New Delhi, 1966), p. 368.

116. For a perceptive treatment, see G. S. Bhargava, *U.S. Attitudes Towards India 1947-71: A Study in Decisionmaking* (Cambridge, Mass.: Harvard University Press, 1974), pp. 45-56; also see Hilsman, pp. 330-332.

117. *White Paper on the Jammu and Kashmir Dispute* (Rawalpindi: Ministry of Foreign Affairs, Government of Pakistan, January 1977), p. 77. Earlier, Galbraith was surprised that while neutral India was facing Chinese Communist invasion, Pakistan, a member of the SEATO and CENTO, was "forming some kind of axis with Peking." He sent a telegram on this to Rusk, on October 25, 1962. See Galbraith, p. 381.

118. Galbraith, p. 415. But paradoxically, it was Galbraith who had put pressure on the Indian government regarding Kashmir. For Kennedy's disapproval, see Ghosh, p. 310.

119. Galbraith, pp. 422, 431.

120. At the outset Galbraith had even urged Duncan Sandys not to raise the Kashmir issue with Nehru. Besides, in a communication (December 6, 1962) to President Kennedy he had even underscored the need for the U.S. to be "responsive" to India's defense needs—its major source of anxiety (*Ibid.*, pp. 431, 455). According to the then Undersecretary of State, the U.S.

administration had "seized upon India's need for U.S. assistance as a lever to force the Indians to make concessions to the Pakistanis in regard to Kashmir" (Bowles, p. 439).

121. Hilsman, p. 324.

122. Dean Rusk's conversations with CBS, November 28, 1962. See *Department of State Bulletin* 47 (December 17, 1962), p. 915.

123. For an analysis of these aspects, see Khera, pp. 188-191. Ambassador Galbraith no longer believed this to be "entirely true." The Chinese retired after they had shown that they could "defend" their territorial claims See Galbraith, p. 436.

124. Cited in Hilsman, p. 331.

125. The above analysis is based on Bowles, pp. 439-440, 475. Incidentally, the U.S. opposition was the consensus of a meeting of high officials called by President Kennedy in April 1963.

126. Sorensen, *Kennedy*, p. 665.

127. The report of the Harriman mission had not been officially released. The following summary is based on Hilsman, pp. 331-338; and also Galbraith, pp. 449-450.

128. According to U.S. General Paul Adamson, the Indian Army would require a "great deal" of military hardware, and "air defenses would pose a particular problem" (Hilsman, p. 332).

129. Explaining the rationale behind this approach, Averill Harriman had stated in a television briefing (February 11, 1963): "If India would break with the Soviet Union, it would tend to bring the two countries (the Soviet Union and China) together" *Department of State Bulletin* 48 (February 25, 1963), p. 275.

130. Galbraith, p. 450.

131. *Ibid.*, pp. 438-449. Galbraith believed Secretary of State Rusk was primarily responsible for making suggestions that the Commonwealth could be utilized for useful work (p. 442). Around early December, India's Defense Minister Chavan stated in a news conference that India could possibly ask for American military advisers (*The Hindu*, December 7, 1962).

132. Galbraith, p.438.

133. Galbraith, p. 452. Those who opposed Galbraith's position included Secretary of State Rusk; Secretary of Defense Robert McNamara; special assistant to the President McGeorge Bundy; U.S. Ambassador to the UN, Adlai Stevenson; Director if AID, David Bell, etc.

134. Joint Communique issued by President Kennedy and Prime Minister Harold Macmillan, December 21, 1962. For text see *Department of State Bulletin*, Vol. 48 (1229), January 14, 1963, p. 43.

135. Personal communication to the author from Galbraith, May 27, 1977.

136. Details of the military aid were not released in the Kennedy-Macmillan joint communique on the Nassau Conference. This was disclosed by the U.K. House of Commons Estimate Committee, *Supplementary Estimates*, Spring, March 4, 1963. Earlier in a television interview with CBS on January

9, 1963, Harriman had revealed the amount and its purpose for raising mountain divisions. See *Department of State Bulletin*, 48 (February 1963), p. 276.

137. Personal communication from Galbraith, May 27, 1977.

138. As revealed by Allen S. Whiting, Preface.

139. Bowles, p. 482. Also see Bowles' statement to the Joint Economic Committee, Subcommittee on Economy in Government, *Economic Issues in Military Assistance*, Hearings 92nd Cong., 1st Sess., January 4, 5, 6, 18, and February 2, 1971 (Washington, D.C.: U.S. Government Printing Office, 1971), p. 270.

140. See Choudhury, p. 112. (In this context he mentioned how top ranking U.S. officials such as George Ball, Dean Rusk, Gen. Maxwell Taylor, and Averill Harriman, in various meetings with Pakistani leaders, had reiterated U.S. support and aid to Pakistan in the event of an Indian attack.) Specific reference to U.S. assurance is derived from a 1963 *aide-memoire*, passed along by the U.S. ambassador in Pakistan, and as revealed to Choudhury by the former U.S. Ambassador to Pakistan, Oehlert. Cited on p. 113.

141. Based on personal interviews. They were opposed to any extensive American military assistance to India. To Secretary of State Rusk, the problem was how to aid India "without leaving" Pakistan "to fear that in some way this build-up might be directed against Pakistan". U.S. Congress, Senate, Committee on Foreign Relations, *Foreign Assistance Act of 1963, Hearings*, 88th Cong., 1st Sess., June 11, 1963, p. 42.

142. Macmillan, p. 232.

143. Six rounds of ministerial talks were held between India and Pakistan during 1962 to 1965, but they failed to produce any substantive Indo-Pak understanding. Some American scholars believe that in conducting border negotiations with China following the Sino-Indian war, Pakistan tended to show (among others) not only its obsessive hostility toward India, but also its displeasure with the Western allies for having decided to help India. See Norman D. Palmer, *South Asia and United States Policy* (Boston: Houghton Mifflin, 1966), pp. 216-217.

144. Nehru had even expressed his willingness through Foreign Secretary M. J. Desai to Galbraith "to work with the United States" both "politically and military in the rest of Asia." But the State Department failed to respond promptly (conveyed on January 5, 1963). See Nayar, *India: The Critical Years*, p. 278.

145. A press release regarding the U.S.-Commonwealth Air Team's visit to India on the invitation of the government of India was issued on January 23, 1963. See White House announcement, January 23, 1963, in *Department of State Bulletin* 49 (January 27, 1963), p. 247. A U.S. defense expert team was also in India in early February 1963.

146. Speech delivered at the Indian School of International Studies, February 20, 1963. Cited in *Indian Affairs Record*, March 1963, pp. 100-101.

147. Prime Minister Nehru speaking on a "Call-attention Notice" regarding the visit of a joint United States-Commonwealth Air Mission to India, February 21, 1963. See *Foreign Affairs Record* (February 1963), pp. 71-72.

148. Based on Macmillan, pp. 234-235. Speaking to newsmen at Washington on February 21, 1963, Kennedy assumed that the U.S. would be responsive to India "when we have a clear idea of what the challenge is and what their desires are and what our capabilities are." See *Indian Affairs Record* (March 1963), p. 101.

149. For an outline of the defense program see Indian Defense Minister Y. B. Chavan's speech on the (1963-64) defense budget, April 8, 1963. See *Lok Sabha Debates*, April 8, 1963, Third Series, Vol. XVI, No. 37. There was a sharp increase in the 1963 defense budget. It rose from Rs. 473 crores in 1961-62 to Rs 867 crores. According to one informed defense analyst, the Indian Army program as such did not call for either heavy external assistance or heavy foreign exchange expenditure. See Raju G. C. Thomas, *The Defense of India* (Delhi: Macmillan, 1978), p. 106.

150. The team reportedly discussed with Pentagon officials a two phase plan for setting up a defense production base to support the increasing requirements of the armed forces. *The Hindu* (Madras), April 29, 1963.

151. Indian requests were spelled out by Krishnamachari at a news conference, May 22, 1963. Cited in *Indian Affairs Record* (New Delhi, June 1963), p. 193. India was reportedly interested in securing transport aircraft, fighter-bomber aircraft, and radar equipment. India expected to receive about $1,500 million from the United States and Britain as assistance in support of this defense program (p. 191).

152. Defense Minister Y. B. Chavan's statement to the Lok Sabha, September 16, 1963. See *Lok Sabha Debates*, 1963, Vol. XXI (21-30), Col. 6247.

153. For text, see *Foreign Affairs Record* (New Delhi: Minister of External Affairs, 1963), p. 438.

154. Galbraith, p. 499. Later he was able to secure from Washington a "military program" for India for the next fiscal year " (p. 501).

155. In a communique they had expressed their awareness about the importance of the settlement of Indo-Pak differences. See *Department of State Bulletin* 49 (1256), July 22, 1963.

156. The main features of this agreement were outlined in Nehru's statement in Lok Sabha on the Air Training Exercises Agreement, August 19, 1963. See *Lok Sabha Debates*, August 19, 1963, cols. 1213-1218.

157. Galbraith, *Foreign Service Journal*, p. 18.

158. For details of the training exercises see the official Indian note in *Foreign Affairs Record*, November 1963, pp. 264-265. One western scholar suggests that "China's unilateral ceasefire" and "the West's caution" helped India to retain its policy of ("a tarnished") non-alignment. See Michael Brecher, "The West and the Indo-China Border War," *Pacific Affairs*, Winter, Vol. 52, No. 4, 1979-80, p. 627.

159. For details see Bowles, *Promises to Keep*, pp. 475-481.

160. General Maxwell Taylor's news conference, December 19, 1963. Cited in *Indian Recorder and Digest* (New Delhi, January 1964), p. 9. Also see Bowles, pp. 481-482.

161. Nayar, p. 78; Bowles, pp. 440, 482.

162. For details see Bowles, pp. 483-484.

163. See Indo-U.S. Defense Aid Talks Communique, issued in New Delhi, June 6, 1964, *Foreign Policy of India: Texts of Documents 1947-64* (New Delhi: Lok Sabha Secretariat, 1966, pp. 484-485; for details see statement by Defense Minister Y. B. Chavan, September 21, 1964. See *Foreign Affairs Record*, Vol. X, No. 9, September 1964, pp. 200-202.

164. Barnds, p. 168.

165. Bowles, p. 484.

166. *Ibid.*, pp. 472-486. It is interesting to note that from the British viewpoint the United States was more concerned about the possible Chinese threat. Macmillan writes in his memoirs that "Washington was more nervous than London." He claims: "We with our longer experience, felt convinced that while it would be Chinese policy to take advantage of any troubles or difficulties in any adjacent area they would not themselves advance on an adventurous policy." See Macmillan, p. 239.

167. K. Subrahmanyam, "Planning and Defense," in Paul Streeton and Michael Lipton, *The Crisis in Indian Planning* (London: Oxford University Press, 1968), p. 353. Some sources suggest that the United States had provided India about $92 million worth of military hardware—essentially comprising air defense radar, communication equipment, and mountain warfare equipment. See Statement by Lt. Colonel Gross, U.S. House of Representatives, Committee on Foreign Affairs, *United States Interests in and Policies Toward South Asia*, Hearings before the Subcommittee on the Near East and South Asia, 93rd Cong., 1st Sess., March 12, 15, 20 and 27, 1973, p. 102.

168. Indian Foreign Minister M. C. Chagla's statement, Lok Sabha, December 11, 1966.

169. Brigadier General Stephen Fuqua's private testimony, House Subcommittee on Appropriations, May, 1963; also Department of State memorandum submitted to the same subcommittee. The expunged report of these hearings were released on October 7, 1963. Cited in *Asian Recorder*, 1963, p. 5496.

170. It is because of this that President Kennedy had instituted a committee in December 1962, headed by General Lucius Clay, to study the scope and distribution of U.S. military and economic aid programs. His idea was to mobilize opinion in support of increased assistance programs, but though the Clay committee endorsed the need for continued aid to India, it recommended the gradual reduction of assistance programs. See Ganguly, p. 222.

171. Congress had already opposed a public sector steel plant (involving more than $100 million) for India.

172. See Joanne F. Loomba, "U.S. Aid to India 1951-1967: A Study in Decisionmaking," *India Quarterly* 28 (October-December 1972), pp.305-331.

173. Hearings before the House Committee on Foreign Affairs, 1963, p. 416. Rep. Boltan and Rep. Zablocki also endorsed Morgan's viewpoint.

174. U.S. Congress, House, 88th Cong., 1st Sess., April 8, 1963. *Congressional Record*, Vol. 109, p. 5859.

175. *Asian Recorder*, 1963, p. 5046.
176. Senator Morse in particular. See Hearings Before the Senate Committee on Foreign Relations, 1963, pp. 691-692.
177. U.S. Congress, House Committee on Foreign Affairs, *Foreign Assistance Act 1963*, Report (Washington, D.C.: U.S. Government Printing Office), pp. 6-7.
178. On one occasion President Kennedy had remarked that "if I were in his (Nehru's) shoes, I'd give up those barren mountains (Ladakh) and keep the lush valley (Kashmir)." Private conversations with Sudhir Ghosh, an Indian M.P. See Ghosh, p. 311.
179. Roger Hilsman, *The Politics of Policy Making in Defense and Foreign Affairs* (New York: Harper and Row, 1971), p. 28.
180. Galbraith, p. 450. Schlesinger mentions that Galbraith was once "reproved" by the Department of State for attempting to assure Nehru that the U.S. was not looking for allies in South Asia (Schlesinger, p. 513). Despite his relatively greater accessibility to the President, Galbraith also admits to the difficulty of bringing any policy matters to Presidential notice (p. 41).

4

Conflict Management: The 1965 War

The 1965 war marked the end of a phase of restrained Cold War that had existed in South Asia since the Kashmir war of 1947-48.[1] The 1965 war also led directly to the 1971 war, and the break-up of Pakistan. But to the United States government, the 1965 war was the high point of disillusionment with South Asian affairs. There was a 180 degree swing from the euphoric expectations of the Kennedy years, which envisioned a politically stable and economically viable Subcontinent underwritten by American economic and military aid. Moreover, this negativism shaped American attitudes towards food aid to India in 1966-67 (as seen in the next chapter).

As a major world power, the United States could not remain unconcerned about the problem of peace and stability within the Subcontinent. But there were a number of constraints which tended to influence its actions. First, the Johnson administration was faced with a growing crisis in Vietnam and Congressional pressure against foreign assistance. Second, the U.S. was put in the position of having to fulfil its assurances to both Pakistan and India—ironically against each other.[2] Third, above all, U.S. exasperation with Indo-Pakistan hostility had increased to the point where it influenced the U.S. administration not to initiate any direct steps towards the resolution of Indo-Pakistani conflict; thus, despite misgivings, the more active Soviet peacekeeping effort coincided with U.S. intentions.[3]

It was the dialectics of what was desirable for the U.S. and the extent to which it was prepared to involve itself under the circumstances, that determined the U.S. response to the South Asian conflict. This response was a low profile conflict resolution effort on the part of the Johnson administration. In studying this effort we will focus on several questions: First, what was the American perception of the crisis? Second, at what level was the crisis approached? Third, what actions were taken by the U.S.? Fourth, what individuals and institutions were involved in decisions concerning these actions?

Prelude to War

The Sino-Indian war of 1962 had been seen by many Pakistanis as a missed opportunity to resolve the Kashmir issue through armed intervention. In fact, there was a strong view that there was no justification for Pakistan's neutrality in the China-India conflict. Pakistan, the argument ran, had "a valid reason, indeed the obligation, to intervene in order to ensure that its own interests in Jammu and Kashmir" were not put into jeopardy by the Sino-Indian conflict. More important, there did "not at that time exist the disparity in military strength between Pakistan and India" which was to later handicap Pakistan.[4] The psychology of missed opportunity coupled with an apprehension of the growing power gap between Pakistan and India seemed to have determined Pakistan's decision to escalate an armed conflict with India—for the ultimate goal of annexing Kashmir.

Notwithstanding President Ayub Khan's word to the U.S. that Pakistan would not attack India—when the latter was engaged in a conflict with China in the Fall of 1962—he had given only "a non-committal answer" to Nehru's appeal of support and sympathy of October 27, 1962. He not only called for the amicable settlement of the outstanding dispute between India and Pakistan but expressed the hope that the Sino-Indian conflict could be peacefully resolved.[5] In this context, the Western powers were able to persuade India to begin talks with Pakistan on Kashmir and other related issues at the ministerial level.[6] Evidently, both the U.S. and U.K. (as India's chief arms suppliers) enjoyed a certain degree of leverage over the Indian government. At the same time the Western initiative was based on their assumption that Indo-Pakistan amity was a prerequisite for the defense of the Subcontinent against external aggression. But Pakistan did not perceive this as a primary issue, notwithstanding the rhetoric of joint defense circulating this time. The Pakistani government saw an admirable opportunity to favorably settle the Kashmir question. Yet, there were no fresh ideas, and Pakistan's demands "remained far above the maximum that India had ever thought of conceding."[7]

It is significant that in the period following the 1962 war, Pakistan raised the level of its interactions with China. Aside from their conflictual relationships with India, there were other considerations that influenced Pakistan and China to enter into a close relationship. If Peking was shocked by the neutral Soviet stand on its border conflict with New Delhi, Pakistan was jolted by Western military assistance to India. Washington's decision to rush arms to India on a "massive" scale was, in Pakistan's view, not only "unjustified by the requirements of the situation," but was also expected to further strengthen India's military capability against Pakistan. They could not rely any longer on "U.S. assistance" if India were to attack Pakistan.[8] Pakistanis also argued that as India acquired military superiority over Pakistan, it would be less willing to negotiate on the Kashmir question.

America's arms aid for India had thus triggered widespread indignation in the Pakistani ruling elite. Zulfiqar Ali. Bhutto, who later became Pakistan's Foreign Minister, said that Pakistan would not join India in any action against China even if the Kashmir question were settled amicably. Pakistan's "friendship with China" was "unconditional" he declared.[9] The subsequent conclusion of a trade agreement (January 4, 1963) followed by a border agreement (March 2, 1963) with China, merely demonstrated the yawning gulf between India and Pakistan.

The growing Sino-Pakistani cooperation tended to harden India's attitude towards Pakistan.[10] Showing his annoyance in a speech made at Srinagar on June 18, 1963, Prime Minister Nehru said: ". . . In the history of the world you will find very few examples of such deceit and duplicity as Pakistan has shown in siding with China in the dispute between India and China." He warned however, "Pakistan is mistaken if it thinks that it can intimidate us because we are facing this threat from the Chinese."[11]

Admittedly, Pakistan did not feel threatened by China. On the contrary, Pakistan perceived India's adversity as its opportunity for putting pressure on the latter. Thus in Pakistan's view China was not only considered as a "friendly neighbor" but even as their "likely partner and ally" against India. Chinese Premier Chou En-lai's endorsement of Pakistan's position on Kashmir in early 1964 was indicative of the developing Sino-Pakistan detente.[12] But despite these developing relations with China, Pakistan felt that after having possibly settled its dispute with the Chinese, the Indians might resort to a policy of "intimidation" against Pakistan. There was also concern that in enhancing its defense capabilities vis-a-vis China, India might develop its armed forces to a level that would be detrimental to Pakistan's long run security interests. In the context of this possibility, Bhutto anticipated that time was running out for Pakistan; he projected that "with the passage of time, and with the further augmentation of India's aid, the situation will come to such a pass that any chance of a peaceful and honorable settlement of our outstanding disputes will gradually recede more and more."[13] This statement neatly summarized Pakistan's predicament.

Aside from Kashmir, there were other disputes between India and Pakistan.[14] An intermittent exchange of border firings took place on the East Pakistan-Assam border from December 9 to 20, 1963. In early 1964, widespread Hindu-Muslim communal violence occurred in East Pakistan and in some parts of West Bengal, Bihar and Orissa in India. This was triggered by organized public agitation that followed the theft of the Prophet's sacred relic (a hair) from a mosque near Srinagar in Kashmir. While communal peace was being restored, there was a mass exodus of Hindu, Buddhist and Christian minorities from East Pakistan to India. In fact by April, 1964, around 200,000 refugees had entered India in distress.[15] The eviction of illegal Pakistani aliens from the border districts of Assam cropped up as an additional complication in Indo-Pakistan relations.[16]

Meanwhile, "under the impetus" given by the Sino-Indian conflict and the subsequent conclusion of a Sino-Pak border agreement, Pakistani leaders appear to have concluded that this "new element" would enable them to resolve the Kashmir issue on their terms.[17] Basically, they assumed that two-pronged pressure would ultimately bring India to its knees regarding Kashmir. The initial Pakistani move was on the global diplomatic front. In January 1964, Pakistan called for an immediate meeting of the UN Security Council to deal with the Kashmir question. While their justification was the failure of the direct Indo-Pakistan talks, essentially, it was to inhibit India's attempts to reduce international significance by further integrating the state. They also wanted to highlight the political turbulence within Jammu and Kashmir at that time, caused by the theft of the sacred relic.

Notwithstanding these efforts, Pakistan derived little political mileage. The Security Council meeting that went on from February 3 to May 18, 1964 (with several adjournments in between), produced a mere summation of contending views. But in raising the Kashmir issue before the United Nations, Pakistan had warned that unless the world body was able to prevent the Indian government from taking "unlawful steps" regarding Kashmir, the people of Azad ("Free") Kashmir and Pakistan might turn to other courses in desperation.[18] Subsequent events were to prove that this was not an empty threat, a brief interlude of reconciliation.

While the Kashmir issue was still being debated in the UN Security Council, there was a dramatic development in the state of Jammu and Kashmir. On April 8, 1964 the detained Kashmiri leader Sheikh Abdullah was released by the Government of Jammu and Kashmir. Subsequently, he came to New Delhi and met Nehru and other Indian leaders regarding the Kashmir question. On May 24, he went to Rawalpindi to discuss the matter with Ayub Khan.[19] While in Pakistan, he had announced on May 25 that Nehru and Ayub Khan were going to meet in June to deal with Indo-Pak problems. But the possibility of any lasting solution to their differences was dashed with the sudden death of Nehru on May 27, 1964.[20] Though sentiments regarding mutual understanding were expressed by both Ayub Khan and the new Indian Prime Minister Lal Bahadur Shastri, these were not enough to dispel the general atmosphere of discord and rivalry that existed between the two states.[21]

One measure of continued tension between the two countries was the frequency of armed clashes that had taken place in 1964 along the ceasefire line in Kashmir. By early 1965, such incidents had increased considerably. In March of that year, there were not only reports of firing incidents on the Cooch-Behar-East Pakistan border, but also intrusions by Pakistani Rangers in the Kutch District of Gujarat (India). In April, 1965, the most alarming border conflicts took place in Rann of Kutch, on the frontier between the Indian state of Gujarat and the West Pakistan province of Sind. The immediate cause of the conflict were the mutual claims over the undelineated Kutch-Sind boundary.[22] The fighting continued at intervals till the end of the month when a de facto ceasefire came into operation. It was through the mediation of British Prime Minister Harold Wilson, that a formal ceasefire agreement was signed on June 30.[23] The agreement envisaged that the Indo-Pakistan dispute be submitted to an international tribunal if direct talks failed. When India called off the ministerial talks on August 18, the dispute was immediately referred to a tribunal. In the meantime the two countries had by early July decided to withdraw their troops from other sectors of the border—where they were massed at the height of the Kutch escalation.

The Kutch escalation anticipated the full scale war between India and Pakistan in September 1965. It also gave both India and Pakistan a taste of the major external powers' likely response to future subcontinental conflict. In the Kutch escalation the British

Prime Minister took the initiative in diffusing the crisis. His mediatory efforts had the full support of the U.S. administration. While the U.S. kept in touch, it preferred to maintain a neutral posture.[24] The Soviet Union (to India's surprise, if not concern) also took a neutral stand on the crisis, even after China had taken Pakistan's side.[25] The editorials of *Pravda* and *Izvestia* had in fact helped in preparing the climate for Britain's mediatory efforts.[26] China sympathized with Pakistan and accused India of an armed provocation in the Rann of Kutch.[27]

There was one element of surprise for Pakistan in the outcome of the Kutch conflict: Shastri's willingness to refer the Rann of Kutch dispute to an international tribunal (India persistently refused to agree on any kind of international arbitration on Kashmir). If in this case, India had gone more than half-way to defuse the situation, Pakistan must have thought of the possibility of using this procedure for the Kashmir question.

One other result of the Kutch episode was that it had made Pakistan "dangerously overconfident" and India "dangerously frustrated."[28] Kutch shattered Shastri's illusion that it was easier to settle with Pakistan than with China. Explaining his reactions later to Kuldip Nayar, Shastri stated that "Pakistan mistook my desire not to fight as a sign of weakness."[29] In any event it had two consequences: first, it emboldened Pakistan to escalate the Kashmir dispute and thereby internationalize it for a final settlement; second, it put tremendous domestic pressure on the Indian government for a hard line in case of an aggressive Pakistani move. Earlier, during the Kutch conflict, Shastri's cabinet colleagues favored an all-out offensive on this sector. But on grounds of unfavorable military logistics and an uncertain diplomatic situation, both Shastri and the Army Chief-of-Staff, General J. N. Chaudhury, were opposed to this idea.[30] What must have particularly bothered New Delhi was Pakistan's apparent edge on the diplomatic front. While Pakistan had the full backing of a major external power like China, India lacked direct support from any one of the major powers.

Apart from India's diplomatic predicament, Pakistan was further encouraged (and perhaps misled) by India's internal political and economic difficulties. These included: the demands for autonomy by the DMK in Madras and for a separate state for the Sikhs in Punjab, and hostile activities by Naga guerrillas in northeast India. This was seen as evidence of India's "superficial" or "tenuous" unity. The death of Nehru had released centrifugal forces in India on an unprecedented scale. There were many in Pakistan who believed that India was on the brink of collapse.[31] This suggested that a determined push could settle the Kashmir dispute to Pakistan's advantage.

But time was not on Pakistan's side. Though India was bigger and had greater military and economic potential than Pakistan, its defense industries had not yet gone into full production. But, with the passage of time, as India's military and economic strength increased, it would try to dictate its own terms in the disputes with Pakistan.[32] From this perspective, time was running out. Some Pakistani analysts had concluded as early as 1963: "If we did not face up to it and prepare ourselves immediately," India could reach a position whereby it could "achieve her political objectives" without going to war. In a worst-case analysis, they even expected Pakistan to lose its status as an independent factor in international politics.[33] Faced with this predicament, Pakistani policymakers started their search for an appropriate answer.

There were additional reasons behind Pakistan's immediate discomfiture (if not direct concern.) First, India had decided by December, 1964, to extend Presidential rule to the state of Jammu and Kashmir—in the event of a breakdown in the constitutional machinery of the state. Second on January 9, 1965, the Jammu and Kashmir National Conference Party had decided to dissolve itself and become integrated with the Congress Party.[34] These actions were perceived in Pakistan as part of a move to fully integrate Kashmir with India, foreclosing any change in its status. These mergers, in the context of existing tension, evoked hostile reactions in Pakistan, including threats of Jehad (Holy War) against India.[35]

The Operational Scheme

The specter of growing power differences between India and Pakistan seemed to have influenced the Pakistani decision to seize Kashmir as early as possible—through a scheme of controlled escalation. Incidentally, this was to be done at a time when India was still busy on its China front and thus not able to react with its full weight and power.[36] Available evidence suggests that the political unrest in Kashmir in early 1964—following the theft of the holy relic—had greatly tempted President Ayub and his advisers. Their calculations were based on the assumption of a weakened India under "little" Shastri after the death of Nehru. By late 1964, the Pakistan Foreign Office and the Inter-Services Intelligence Directorate had jointly worked out an operational plan—called

"Operation Gibraltar"—to grab Kashmir. Though this was initially vetoed by President Ayub, there is no doubt that "the Kashmir operation was under active consideration by the end of 1964," as concedes the then Pakistani Information Secretary.[37]

President Ayub Khan was not initially eager to risk a major escalation over the Kashmir question, but subsequent events demonstrated that he was evidently convinced or "misled" by the arguments of his Foreign Minister Bhutto and Foreign Secretary Aziz Ahmed.[38] By then, certain contextual factors had also convinced Ayub of the need for a bolder course of action. Ayub's government was under popular pressure for firmer action against India, and the issue figured in the Pakistani presidential election of early 1965. But more importantly, Pakistan's tactical success in the Rann of Kutch had created—through flattery and the showering of praises by the news media—"an atmosphere of triumph and invincibility." Emboldened by the results of the Kutch conflict, Ayub made the vital decision to "play for larger stakes" by sending armed guerrillas into Indian-held Kashmir.[39] The Kutch episode was a dress rehearsal for the implementation of the Foreign Office plan in August-September, 1965. Pakistan's policymakers were hopeful that they could trigger a national liberation movement within the state, resolving the Kashmir question to their advantage with a minimum of Pakistani military involvement.

It seems some of the basic considerations behind the Kashmir operational plan were spelled out earlier by Bhutto in a communication to President Ayub. His main points can be summarized here:

—India is not in a position "at present" to risk a "general war of unlimited duration" with Pakistan;

—Pakistan has the "relative superiority of the military forces" over India, in terms of quality and equipment;

—The fact that India's "capacity increases with the passage of every single day" makes the situation more and more difficult for Pakistan.

Hence, Bhutto concluded that Pakistan's best option was "to react more boldly and courageously" against India.[40]

After the Kutch conflict, President Ayub Khan had become quite receptive to the idea of a bolder approach towards New Delhi. This in turn had prompted the Foreign Office to take a harder line on Pakistan's relations with India. In this context, the General

Headquarters of the Army (GHQ) was persuaded to produce a specific action plan. Thus "Operation Gibraltar" was conceived—a guerrilla war plan—entrusted for implementation to Major-General Akhtar Malik who was in command of the 12th Division, covering the Kashmir area. His task entailed training a large number of armed infiltrators and saboteurs, who were supposed to slip across at carefully selected points on the 470-mile long cease-fire line into Jammu and the Kashmir area for the ultimate capture of power. The plan of action was based on three simplistic assumptions: there would be spontaneous popular support for the armed guerrillas inside the Kashmir Valley; India would not launch a counter-attack across the ceasefire line; and India was also unlikely to cross the international boundary with Pakistan. Subsequent events were to prove them all incorrect.[41]

It is amazing that this plan was approved by Ayub, given the likelihood of a major escalation with India. Admittedly, "criminal Foreign Office advice" as well as Bhutto's assurances—regarding diplomatic deterrence against any possible decisive Indian reactions—had influenced Ayub's decision to authorize the plan. Also, it is possible that the Army high command might have been pressured into a risky venture by an appeal to their valor.[42] However, Ayub was responsible for this wrongly conceived move. If this is how Pakistan stumbled into the September 1965 war, then it was without any systematic decision-making.

Pakistani's strategy based on an over-optimistic assessment: that India was unlikely to react strongly to the Pakistani move. The rationale was that any major Indian counter-move, if not deterred by diplomatic means, would be constrained by the Chinese. Above all, Pakistan was itself materially well-equipped to defend against any vigorous Indian response. It is not definitely known whether it was because of Bhutto's persuasiveness that Ayub Khan gave the signal for infiltration across the ceasefire line, but there is reason to believe that domestic pressures as well as his own overconfidence—due to his uninterrupted political successes—had a bearing on his decision to take the "attendant risks".[43] For Pakistan it looked like the finest hour was at hand.

Pakistani leadership had miscalculated the extent to which India would hit back militarily against a strategy of infiltration. India had on many occasions categorically pointed out that it would not remain unconcerned if there was any attempt to resolve the Kashmir question by force. In fact, as early as 1952, the then Indian Prime Minister Nehru had warned: "If Pakistan by mistake invades Kashmir, we will not only meet them in Kashmir, but it will be a full-scale war between India and Pakistan."[44]

The Nehru doctrine had spelled out India's stand so clearly as to leave no room for misinterpretation. But the only question before Pakistan in 1965 was whether India at that point could really afford a full-scale war against a militarily better equipped Pakistan. It seems Pakistan had decided to act on the basis of the apparent gap between India's current capability—vis-a-vis Pakistan—and Indian intentions based on old assumptions, when India had a clear edge.[45]

From Infiltration to Full-Scale War

On August 5, 1965, several thousand Pakistani armed infiltrators started moving into Indian parts of Jammu and Kashmir in an attempt to foment a local rebellion against the Indian government. Further groups of infiltrators entered on August 18, despite Indian protests. Many of the infiltrators were picked up by Indian security forces but some of them made their way into Srinagar and its neighborhood. They blew up some installations and bridges, but these sporadic acts of destruction and the distribution of arms to the local people did not stir up an anti-Indian revolt. Faced with repeated Indian charges of Pakistan's connivance in the infiltration, the Pakistan government, not unexpectedly, denied all responsibility; instead it described the entire episode as a massive uprising by Kashmir freedom fighters, but as the days passed there was no evidence to support the Pakistani contentions.[46]

The Pakistani "expectations that the Kashmiris would rise with sufficient ferocity" to seriously undermine military positions or that "it would remain confined to Kashmir proved fallacious", says a former Pakistani diplomat.[47] Some informed American analysts have contended that it was the "traditional Kashmiri timidity" coupled with punishing measures against the infiltrators that caused the undoing of Ayub Khan's plan to liberate Kashmir.[48] While one can go along with the second argument, the first appears somewhat impressionistic. Pakistani attempts to set off a state-wide liberation struggle failed because none of the infiltrators were Kashmiris, and thereby violated the first rule of guerrilla warfare.[49]

What happened afterwards was a classic example of military escalation. Pakistani infiltration was first detected by the Indian security forces on August 5 following an armed encounter with the infiltrators at Poonch—where several of them were killed. While this matter was brought to the attention of the United Nations

Military Group in Kashmir (UNMGIP) and the UN Secretary-General, there was a blatant denial by Pakistan regarding its complicity.[50] A clandestine radio station calling itself the *Sada-e-Kashmir* (Voice of Kashmir) came on the air to propagate the myth of a successful local uprising. By the middle of August some 5,000 armed infiltrators were operating within Indian Kashmir. At one point, Srinagar was threatened by the main body of Pakistani infiltrators moving from the north, northwest and southwest. They tried to cut the vital Srinagar-Leh road near Kargil, the Indian lifeline to Ladakh.

Responding to the Pakistani "invasion" of Kashmir, the Indian security forces decided to move across the ceasefire line with a view to sealing off further infiltration. From mid-August onwards, Indian armed forces occupied a number of key Pakistani posts (including the vital Haji Pir salient) across the ceasefire line. With the Indians bent upon carrying the fight to the other side in hot pursuit of the infiltrators[51] and the majority of the Kashmiris not providing any assistance to them, Pakistan's "Operation Gibraltar" faltered. Furthermore, Pakistan was now faced with the task of bringing back the entrapped infiltrators from the net of mopping-up operations carried out by the Indian security forces.

The infiltration operation having failed, Pakistan had to choose between either backing down or further escalation. Pakistan chose the latter. It once again took the initiative and on September 1 launched "Operation Grand Slam"—a major armored attack across the junction point of the ceasefire line and the international boundary line near the Southern part of Indian Kashmir. The operation was designed to cut off Kashmir from the rest of India.[52] It did not take long for India to activate its own "Operation Riddle" that signalled an all-out attack on West Pakistan. On September 6, India launched an offensive across the Punjab border on a wide front. The immediate purpose was to compel Pakistan to release the pressure on the Indian communication line with Kashmir.[53] On the same day, in a broadcast to the nation, President Ayub Khan declared "we are at war" with India and "will not rest until India's guns are silenced forever."[54] In response, an Indian government official spokesman stated that India was "not at war with Pakistan," but that its operations were "intended to destroy Pakistan military bases from where they attacked India."[55] The war continued all along the Western Pakistan-India border until September 23; except for some stray Pakistani bombing raids near Calcutta, neither Pakistan nor India extended the conflict to the eastern region.

Meanwhile, China had not only pledged full support to Pakistan but on September 8th, alerted its guards along the Indo-Tibetan border.[56] The possibility of a graver conflict was then raised by the Chinese ultimatum to India on September 16. Peking demanded that India dismantle all "military works" on the Sikkim-Tibetan border within three days or India would have to bear full responsibility for all the "grave consequences arising therefrom."[57] This also alerted the two superpowers. The specter of Chinese involvement produced an expected U.S. warning to China, and also created a sense of urgency in both Washington and Moscow concerning the need for an immediate ceasefire. It was credibly reported that the U.S. Ambassador to Poland, Cabot Lodge, had formally warned the Chinese envoy Wang Kuo-Chang to stay out of the Indo-Pakistan war.[58]

The U.S. Approach

Washington's approach to the 1965 Indo-Pakistan conflict was largely predetermined by a certain trend of events within the Subcontinent. It also demonstrates the limits of American influence on these events. The Sino-Indian border war of 1962 and the subsequent U.S. arms aid to India—especially since the conclusion of a modest long-term arms aid program in 1964—had marked a new phase in Washington's South Asia policy. The Americans then observed with concern Pakistan's increasing attachment to Peking and the renewal of a hostile policy towards India.[59] There seemed to have been a sharp divergence between American and Pakistani perceptions of the priorities for the Subcontinent. Pakistan felt that the U.S. should have made economic and military aid to India subject to resolution of the Kashmir question.[60] By contrast, the U.S. expected some patience from Pakistan. Instead of moving closer to China, the U.S. wanted Pakistan to sort out its differences with India and contribute towards a joint South Asian effort against any possible communist threat.

On more than one occasion the U.S. administration expressed its displeasure about Pakistani attempts to draw closer to Peking—presumably with a view to settling scores with India. On March 1, 1964, Undersecretary of State George Ball warned Pakistan that "we very much hope President Ayub will not carry relations with Red China to a point" where it "impairs" the U.S.-Pakistan alliance relationship.[61] Around the same time, the Secretary of Defense (Robert McNamara) conceded that U.S.

military aid to India had "deeply troubled" Pakistan, but felt that it was "important that India be able to defend itself against communist Chinese aggression."[62] While the U.S. made clear its concern to Pakistan, it also underlined that it was seeking to "balance" the various facets of its South Asian relationship.[63] Needless to say, this was not what the Pakistan government wanted from the U.S. Consequently, Pakistan's alliance with the U.S. hereafter "lingered on in name only", observes a former Pakistani diplomat.[64]

If Pakistan's attitude was causing concern to U.S. policymakers, U.S. policy towards India was also faced with certain problems. There were already growing doubts among some officials as to the rationale[65] behind continued U.S. arms supply to India. First, to them, the Chinese threat to India seemed to have been declining. Second, although India appreciated the U.S. move to counter Chinese activities in Southeast Asia, it was not willing to become directly involved in these efforts.[66] Third, despite U.S. military aid, India continued to rely on substantial arms supplies from Moscow. While Soviet and U.S. interests coincided—so far as China was concerned—one of the basic considerations behind U.S. aid to India was to reduce its dependence on the Soviet Union.[67]

All these naturally produced Congressional skepticism in the U.S. as to the extent it could derive benefit out of its continued economic and military assistance to South Asia.[68] More importantly, if military aid to India and Pakistan was working at cross purposes, officials in support of their respective stand points were unable to produce any coordinated policy. It would appear from available sources that there was an impasse within the South Asian division.[69] In order to sort out the complexities of America's South Asia policy, what was needed was extraordinary diplomacy. The problem was to produce a meaningful understanding between India and Pakistan and then to prevent them from getting closer to the Soviet Union and China, respectively. For a time the U.S. administration had expressed the hope that if only India and Pakistan could find peace with each other, the Subcontinent could be made "impregnable"—from the standpoint of "defense and safety"—from the outside.[70] Events were unfolding contrary to these expectations.

In spite of American political and economic pressures, Pakistan made it clear that it was not ready to scrap its new relationship with Peking. Apart from George Ball and Dean Rusk's candid warnings—presumably in private—to Pakistan regarding the consequence of its growing cordiality with Peking, the U.S. had brought on other pressure.[71] America had earlier suspended a $4.3

million loan for the Dacca Airport (in Fall, 1963) and then later postponed (July, 1965) the Aid-to-Pakistan consortium meeting. The latter action was ostensibly taken to convey U.S. disapproval of Ayub's visit to Peking (March 1965) where he had criticized "the schemes for creating two Chinas."[72] Then on April 16, 1965, President Johnson abruptly postponed Ayub Khan's official visit to the U.S., scheduled for April 23. Although the White House explained that if the visit took place before the enactment of the aid bills President Johnson could not speak with authority,[73] few officials believed that the matter was that simple. "The President simply lost his temper," said one man connected with the episode.[74] Johnson was increasingly annoyed with Pakistan's pro-China moves and its inability to support, even as an alliance partner, the American efforts against the communist threat in Southeast Asia.

Ironically, in order to make the U.S. President's decision look less insulting to Pakistan, Indian Prime Minister Shastri's scheduled visit of early June was also cancelled. This act was indicative of the American administration's tendency to bracket India and Pakistan—irrespective of their size, importance, or problems.[75] The cancellation of the state visits produced anguish and irritation in both India and Pakistan. India reacted with scathing criticism of Johnson's Vietnam policy, as if to express its disappointment with the U.S.[76]

Evidently, both the White House and Congress had become exasperated by the continuing Indo-Pakistan quarrel. They also felt that U.S. aid to these countries called for acceptable behavior as well as economic performance. The Congress periodically threatened that if India and Pakistan "don't get down to business and settle their quarrels we should lessen the ratio or stop aid altogether."[77] Yet, it was not easy for the administration to contemplate such action in a normal situation. Besides, the U.S. was not prepared to take any stern action against Pakistan because of the possibility of losing its surveillance facilities. On the other hand, the U.S. was equally reluctant to forego India's "goodwill by openly taking Pakistan's side."[78]

These diverse pulls and pressures impelled the Johnson administration to take a posture which satisfied neither Pakistan nor India, but antagonized both. And it is because of these contradictory interests that the U.S. decided not to take any direct initiative in the Indo-Pakistani war of 1965. As we shall see, the Johnson administration decided to throw Washington's weight behind the UN's efforts to bring about a ceasefire—in cooperation with Moscow. Just as important, the war provided a reason for the U.S.

to suspend its military and economic aid to both India and Pakistan.[79] In short, America's approach to the war was determined by a complex of considerations, only one of which was the imperative of peace in the Subcontinent. It also indicated the extent to which the U.S. would alter regional interests, concerns, and policies—especially the aid programs—because of its escalating involvement in Vietnam. Thus, growing U.S. involvement in Vietnam, and increasing congressional opposition to military and economic aid, and residual U.S. regional interests determined the level as well as the nature of U.S. response to the 1965 Indo-Pakistan war.

Responses and Priorities

In the case of Kutch, the U.S. wanted to dissolve the crisis by backing the peacemaking efforts of the U.K. During the bigger September conflict, Washington's entire political weight as well as diplomatic efforts were designed to reinforce—in cooperation with the U.K. and the Soviet Union—the UN Security Council peacekeeping initiative in the Subcontinent. This was one of the rare occasions after the Second World War that the major powers handled a crisis through concerted policies. Ironically, in spite of its economic and arms aid programs in India and Pakistan, the U.S. had been unable to dissuade the two neighbors from going to war. In fact, in the course of developing a closer relationship with each it had lost its leverage over both. Washington's reliance on the UN was the consequence of its predicament.

Around the time of the first stage of the Indo-Pakistan escalation in Kashmir, President Johnson had clearly stipulated the role contemplated by the U.S. in regard to the "tense and difficult situation" there. Speaking in a news conference on August 29, 1965, the U.S. President had stated that America's "long standing" goal and its consistent stance had always been that the Kashmir issue "must and should be", solved by peaceful means. "The UN is involved" and he added, "we hope that the constructive efforts of the Secretary General may be successful here".[80] From this point onward (with one exception) the U.S. President was neither heard nor seen publicly taking any personal interest in the crisis.[81] He passed the responsibility to Dean Rusk (Secretary of State), Arthur Goldberg (U.S. Ambassador to the UN), and George Ball (Undersecretary of State).

The sporadic armed clashes that had started between India and Pakistan in Kashmir since the beginning of August, 1965, escalated into a full scale war by early September, and caused understandable concern in Washington, Moscow, London and at the UN. The UN was involved in the crisis maintained the ceasefire line in the disputed Kashmir territory. Among the major external powers, only China sought to exploit the conflict between two of its neighbors, for it had committed itself to the Pakistani position at the beginning of the crisis.[82] Between September 1-7, a series of appeals were made by the U.S., Britain, the Soviet Union and the UN Secretary General U Thant, to India and Pakistan to halt their fighting.

However, despite the rapid escalation of the situation, the United Nations took no timely or appropriate peacekeeping initiative. While the members of the UN Security Council were not unaware of the gravity of the developing situation, a Council meeting to deal with the matter could not be convened because of their disagreement. The then American ambassador to the U.N., Arthur Goldberg explains in a personal communication to a Pakistani scholar:

> India, Pakistan and the Soviet Union, in particular, strongly opposed the convening of any meeting on the grounds that events would be normalized without intervention by the UN My recollection is that Pakistan was opposed to UN action because it thought, wrongly, that it could contain the matter by military means, India because it had confidence in its own armed forces, and the Soviet Union because it tilted towards India. In the light of these developments, it was not possible to mobilize opinion in the council for an early ceasefire.[83]

It is curious that Goldberg does not refer to the UN Security Council's initial inaction on political grounds. On August 31, the UN Secretary General had presented a "confidential paper" to the Council members, informing them about the grave situation caused by extensive ceasefire violations since August 5.[84] But, the Security Council remained inactive.

Incidentally, this confidential paper was based on a report of an investigation (August 30, 1965) that the UN Secretary General had received earlier from the Chief Military Observer of the United Nations Observers Group in India and Pakistan (UNMOGIP). This report had indicated how, since August 5, armed men from the Pakistan side crossed the ceasefire line for the purpose of armed action on the Indian side.[85] But contrary to India's expectations this report was not promptly published, nor for that matter, were Pakistan's aggressive activities condemned. The UN's high officials were convinced that if the report were publicized, Pakistan would be driven into a corner and a negotiated peace would become impossible.[86]

In any event, on September 1 identical messages were sent by U Thant to Prime Minister Shastri and President Ayub Khan, asking both countries to respect the ceasefire line and to withdraw forces that had crossed the line. The UN Secretary General failed to obtain any assurances from the Pakistan government, but he got an oral assurance from the Indian Representative in the UN that India would act with restraint and would respect the ceasefire line if Pakistan did likewise.[87] While it was indicative of India's willingness to abide by the UN appeal, without Pakistan's assurance, the possibility of an early ceasefire and the restoration of the status quo ante was very remote.

The 1965 war underlined an important gap in America's South Asia policy. Even those within the U.S. administration who were quite skeptical about a meaningful understanding between India and Pakistan had favored economic and military aid to both countries, believing that these two neighboring countries would not start a major war. The 1965 conflict destroyed even this assumption. The growing feeling in the U.S. was that India and Pakistan were frittering away their energy over mutual hostility.[88] It inevitably set into motion a process of rethinking regarding the basis of America's South Asia policy. In short, the conflict produced "deeper disillusionment" within the administration and it raised "grave doubts about military as well as economic aid" to India and Pakistan.[89] The visible irritant was that U.S. arms provided to both for use against an outside threat were being used against each other, in support of their narrowly conceived objectives.

In its response to the 1965 Indo-Pak war, the U.S. government did establish a set of priorities. Americans saw the first and foremost task as bringing, about an immediate ceasefire between India and Pakistan. But the prospects of directly dealing with and persuading Rawalpindi and New Delhi to stop shooting were slim. Hence the U.S. decided to work through the UN Security Council—acting in concert with other major powers.

Initially, the U.S. was hesitant to get the Security Council involved in the resolution of the conflict. But once escalation began, and when Pakistan and India both failed to comply with the Secretary General's appeal for a ceasefire, the U.S. decided to take

the matter to the Security Council.[90] Speaking on this decision
before the Senate Appropriations Committee on September 8,
Secretary of State Rusk stated that:

> We are going to give the Security Council maximum support
> here, do our best to insist that they comply with the Security
> Council action and thereby vacate the problem of aggression
> . . . We look upon it . . . as a breach of the peace in which
> both sides have their share of responsibility.[91]

Apart from indicating the U.S. decision to rely on the UN Security
Council, Rusk's statement implied that the U.S. would bracket its
ally and friend in the same category.

The second important U.S. priority was to limit the area of
conflict. In specific terms this meant the prevention of the outbreak
of hostilities along the East Pakistan-India borders and the
suspension of the supply of U.S. arms to both India and Pakistan.
It also meant preventing Chinese involvement. The diplomatic style
of this policy was to confine a low public profile with pressure
through private communications. This was designed to dissuade not
only Peking from intervening on Pakistan's behalf, but also to impel
India and Pakistan to agree to a ceasefire.[92]

Stages of Action

Meanwhile the Johnson administration had correctly sensed
the mood of Congress regarding military and economic aid, and
their concern with the Indo-Pak war. There was bipartisan
consensus that the U.S. aid to India and Pakistan should be
suspended and that they should be given proper warning about their
irresponsible behavior. One Republican Representative suggested
that the President should give a "ceasefire-or-else" urgent message
to the two governments in the interest of world peace.[93] A
Democratic senator not only suggested suspension of economic aid,
but called upon the government to ascertain whether a "cessation" of
food shipments would "help promote an end to war". The senator
also advised that the U.S. should support every effort of the the UN
or that of "any other quarters".[94]

On September 8, Dean Rusk announced the suspension of
military aid to India and Pakistan. In keeping with its support of the
UN effort, the administration also decided to make no new
economic loans or grants to India and Pakistan excepting those

which were already in the pipeline because of past agreements. In announcing this decision, Rusk made it clear that the executive branch "will consult fully with the appropriate members of the Congress"[95] regarding the conditions under which military aid shipments may be resumed or new economic aid may be provided. He also requested that Congress not foreclose alternative policies available to the U.S. administration by legislative action on the pending aid bill for 1966.[96]

Needless to say, Congress enthusiastically endorsed the entire line of action contemplated by the executive branch. In a bipartisan concurrent resolution it resolved that:

1. The United States should support and encourage United Nations efforts and take other appropriate measures, as the President determines, to bring an end to the armed conflict between India and Pakistan at the earliest possible moment.

2. The Congress supports and approves the interim action of the President in withholding military assistance during the continuation of military hostilities between India and Pakistan and invites the President to consider making a determination . . . with respect to the temporary suspension of economic and military assistance during the continuation of military hostilities between them Congress was willing to give the administration the necessary freedom to protect U.S. interests as well as international peace.

In suspending military and economic aid to both India and Pakistan, the Johnson administration tried to take an evenhanded position on the conflict. Consequently, it shied away from the question of who started the conflict or whether Pakistan was justified in using U.S. arms against a non-communist adversary. According to Chester Bowles (who had by then become U.S. Ambassador to New Delhi) the possibility of losing the Peshawar base still swayed America's South Asia policy. In view of this, it appears that the Johnson administration tried to avoid the consequences of its earlier assurances that it would dissuade Pakistan from using U.S. arms in aggression against India. On India's complaint, the U.S. ambassador in Pakistan had lodged a private protest in the "mildest terms."[97] Underplaying the arms issue was an understandable part of the American predicament. On September 8, in a message to the U.S. Ambassador in Rawalpindi, Pakistan reminded him about the confidential assurances (presumably given by the Kennedy administration) that the U.S. would help Pakistan even if it faced "aggression from India." The U.S. position was that "it did not wish to apportion relative blame in the present case" and did not accept that "aggression was the responsibility of one party alone." In response to Pakistan's formal invocation of earlier U.S. assurances, the Johnson administration pointed out that U.S. action was designed to meet this "common danger" by supporting the UN peacekeeping efforts. It strongly urged Pakistan to abide by the UN appeal.[98]

With these diplomatic exchanges and the U.S. embargo on military aid to India and Pakistan, the Johnson administration put pressure on both states to avoid further military escalation. On August 10, Pakistan was told not to extend the war to the East Pakistan-India border on "humanitarian grounds." Around the same time New Delhi was also told not to extend the war to East Pakistan. It appears from available sources that Pakistan did not want to accept the American proposition. But, though Pakistan did not initiate conflict in this sector, it did carry out a bombing raid on an Indian air base near Calcutta. India on its part refused to be drawn into conflict in the east.[99] It is possible that Indian inaction in the east grew out of a desire to avoid provoking an overt Chinese reaction on Pakistan's behalf.

The Security Council Acts

The coincidence of America's "even-handed" position with the Soviet's neutral stance vis-a-vis India and Pakistan enabled the UN to effect a ceasefire on the Subcontinent. Since the Kutch episode in the Spring of 1965, there were signs that Moscow was moving towards a more flexible position in the Indo-Pakistan relationship—presumably designed to preempt the growing Sino-Pak detente. This was not overlooked by the Johnson administration, hence, the latter must have anticipated a relatively supportive Soviet role in the Security Council peacemaking efforts. This must have encouraged active American interest in UN Secretary General U Thant's attempts to restore peace in the Subcontinent. On September 1, the permanent U.S. representative in the U.N., Arthur Goldberg, promptly endorsed U Thant's initial peace appeal (S/6651, dated September 1, 1965) to President Ayub Khan and Prime Minister Shastri.[100]

It may be recalled that U Thant's appeal, having gone unheeded in both New Delhi and Rawalpindi, resulted in Arthur Goldberg calling an emergency session of the UN Security Council (he was president for the month of September). The Security Council was convened on September 4 to consider the question of military escalation in the Subcontinent. Goldberg attached particular importance to the effective supervision of the ceasefire by the United Nation's military observers, as underlined in U Thant's report.[101] He had clearly pointed out that:

> the cooperation with the military observers in the discharge of their functions, which is one of the Secretary General's proposals, must mean full freedom of movement and access for the observers in their discharge of functions. These functions are to observe and report any violations of the ceasefire and ceasefire line and to supervise the ceasefire orders.[102]

Evidently, this step was not uniformly appreciated by other members of the Security Council. The resolution adopted by the Council on the same day merely sought the cooperation of India and Pakistan regarding the UN observers.

In a non-permanent member sponsored resolution unanimously passed on September 4, the Security Council called upon India and Pakistan to cease armed hostilities immediately and to withdraw all armed personnel to their respective sides. The resolution also called upon the two governments to cooperate fully with the United Nations observer group in the task of supervising the observance of the ceasefire in Kashmir.[103] In a certain sense, this was a resolution without teeth, as it did not deal with the issues at stake in the conflict. Without making any reference to Pakistan's role in initiating the war, and Pakistani and Indian escalation, the resolution merely expressed the Council's wish for an immediate end to the fighting.

At the same time, parallel efforts were initiated by the Soviet Union to manage the conflict between India and Pakistan. On that very day (September 4), Soviet Premier Kosygin's messages for a ceasefire reached Shastri and Ayub Khan. After calling for a ceasefire, Kosygin stated that:

> ...the first step after immediate cessation of hostilities could be the reciprocal withdrawal of troops to positions behind the ceasefire line established by agreement between Pakistan and India in July 1949. Acting in the spirit of the United Nations Charter and the Bandung principles, the parties should enter into negotiations for the peaceful settlement of the differences that have risen between them. As for the Soviet Union, both sides could count on its willing cooperation, or to use the accepted expression on its 'good

offices' in this matter. We are ready for this if both sides consider it useful.[104]

Though there was no immediate response from New Delhi or Islamabad, the two superpowers were coordinating their efforts to persuade two warring neighbors to accept the UN resolution and come to the conference table.

The most remarkable feature of these developments was that the Soviet Union was willing to concur with the procedure preferred by the majority of the Security Council members.[105] Concerned with the Chinese role in the Subcontinent, the Soviet Union was eager to prevent China from exploiting the conflict and thereby come too close to Pakistan. Soviet concern also led it to call for an immediate ceasefire rather than to provide support to India's position as in earlier years.

The Secretary General was requested by the Council to report about the implementation of the ceasefire resolution. In the absence of any positive response to the UN resolution and in the light of the escalation outside the territory, the Security Council again met on September 6. On that day, the UN Secretary General reported about the three-pronged Indian counter-attack against Pakistan—designed to relieve the pressure of major Pakistani offensives on India's vital Chhamb-Jaurian Link with the Kashmir valley. Incidentally, Pakistan had also called for the Security Council to immediately convene to consider the situation.[106] Following a protracted debate the Security Council unanimously adopted a more elaborate second resolution; in it the Council repeated its ceasefire call and requested U Thant "to exert every possible effort" to implement it.[107]

Armed with this mandate the UN Secretary General visited the Subcontinent and conferred with government leaders of India and Pakistan, and also the head of the UN military observers group, General Robert H. Nimmo (Australia). Though his trip coincided with American and later British suspension of military and economic aid, U Thant failed to secure compliance with the ceasefire directives. Apparently, both India and Pakistan wanted to attach conditions to a ceasefire which were unacceptable to the other.[108]

After the abortive U Thant mission, Ayub Khan introduced an element of diplomatic confusion by inviting Washington. to take a more direct peace initiative. Ayub's proposal was evidently an attempt to secure U.S. support for a settlement advantageous to Pakistan, but it failed to produce any substantial response from Washington.[109] On the top of this came the Chinese ultimatum to

India on September 16. It called upon the Indian government to withdraw from certain border areas in dispute and to dismantle certain "military works" within 72 hours, a development that lent a sense of urgency to the various peace moves.

The motives behind the Chinese ultimatum as well as the extent of China's coordination with Pakistan are beyond the scope of this book. However certain relevant observations may be made in passing. Contrary to the assertions of some scholars, it is unlikely (in the light of Ayub's proposal for the U.S. initiative a day before the Chinese ultimatum) that there was a substantive Sino-Pakistan understanding regarding specific action. Available evidence suggests that there were differences between President Ayub Khan and Foreign Minister Bhutto as to the extent to which Pakistan could go along with China.[110]

It appears from the account of Air Marshal Asghar Khan (who went on an equipment procurement mission to Peking during the war) that Pakistan initially wanted China to concentrate its forces on India's borders "without any overt military action." In response, Premier Chou En-lai had expressed China's interest in Pakistan's security, the Chinese leaders wanted to have direct talks with Ayub on this matter. Apparently, before making any commitment, they wanted to find out whether Pakistan really intended to continue its struggle for political objectives. But events were to demonstrate that Pakistan was not in a position to enter into any concerted military scheme with China and annoy its Western allies.[111] Thus, as the pressure of the superpowers started to build in the wake of the Chinese ultimatum against India, Pakistan panicked. In the midst of the conflict, Ayub paid a secret visit to Peking with a view to dissuade them from any possible intervention and also to make them understand about Pakistan's decision to accept the ceasefire as proposed by the U.N.[112] It is however still not definitively known whether Peking would have carried out its threat even after Pakistan had made its commitments on terms acceptable to China. In a certain sense, the ultimatum was designed to test Pakistan's ability to defy the superpowers in support of Chinese posture.[113]

The ultimatum did not achieve much except to put the Pakistan government in a difficult position. Pakistan was accused of an act of collusion with the Chinese—who were allegedly looking for a pretext to initiate "aggressive" activities against India.[114] The Indians responded by consulting with the British, American and Soviet governments, handling the ultimatum with caution. India expressed its willingness to submit the complaint to a neutral or joint investigation. Also, while China was privately warned by the U.S.

through its Warsaw connection, Pakistan was also rebuked privately. On September 19, Undersecretary of State George Ball told the Minister of the Pakistan Embassy in Washington to clear up that "Chinese alignment was not at Pakistan's bidding." The same day, when the British High Commissioner in Pakistan sought Ayub Khan's clarifications, the Pakistan President denied any allegations about Sino-Pakistan collusion. The High Commissioner reminded Ayub Khan that in a "remarkable way" he was prepared to sacrifice not only Pakistan's "political position" but also its "national existence" for the sake of Kashmir. Later Ayub Khan confirmed to the UK envoy that he had told China to keep out of the current conflict.[115]

In the meantime, on September 17, Kosygin in a second message to Ayub and Shastri, called upon them to halt the hostilities. While supporting UN peacemaking efforts, he also reiterated his offer of good offices for direct talks between India and Pakistan. It was obvious that like the U.S. or Britain, the Soviet Union also stressed the urgency of an immediate ceasefire.[116] Earlier, Secretary of State Rusk had condemned the Chinese attempts to "fish in troubled water" and lauded Soviet policies.[117] At the same time, the U.S. Secretary of State had categorically stated:

> The United States welcomes Soviet support for the efforts of the UN to bring about a peaceful settlement of the Indo-Pakistan conflict over Kashmir . . . The U.S. would go to extreme limits to have a problem dealt with by the Security Council. India and Pakistan should take note of the fact that the Security Council was united and they should be ready to work for a peaceful settlement.[118]

Evidently, the basic aim of the two superpowers had been to inhibit Peking from any possible intervention. Hence they stressed the need for an immediate ceasefire between India and Pakistan.

In the face of these rapid developments the Security Council reconvened on September 17. Speaking in the reconvened session, the U.S. Representative in the U.N., Goldberg, deplored the use of U.S. arms in the conflict and stressed the need for a sense of "urgency and responsibility" for the Council to diffuse the conflict. In order to work out the line of action, the Council (on Goldberg's suggestion) went into private consultation. On September 18, Goldberg underlined the need for an immediate Indo-Pakistan ceasefire before the Chinese communists "aggravate the already grave situation".[119] He also called for a firm Security Council stand—in implied reference to the Chinese ultimatum, the U.S. did not want to get itself involved in a "second war" in Asia.[120] Hence, Goldberg was trying to make use of the Security Council as "the appropriate and most effective agency to meet the crisis."[121]

In its endeavor to achieve peace between India and Pakistan, the Council was also helped by the guideline provided by the UN Secretary General U Thant in his report following his mission to the Subcontinent. While he was not particularly successful in making the warring states accept the Council's call for a ceasefire, his report of September 16, 1965 did outline the relevant course of action that the Security Council could successfully pursue to restore peace. He had impressed upon the Council the need to take firm steps to defuse the explosive situation. U Thant suggested that the Security Council could order the concerned states to immediately desist from further armed hostilities in accordance with Article 40 of the UN Charter. This called for a concomitant Security Council declaration that the two concerned states' non-compliance with this order would constitute a breach of peace as stipulated under Article 39 (that entailed imposition of UN sanctions). His second suggestion envisaged a Security Council request to the heads of government in India and Pakistan for an early summit to sort out their outstanding differences.[122]

Thus when the Council met on September 17, there was a hectic debate whether to consider the suggestions made by U Thant. Evidently, there was a clear consensus that as an initial step, the situation called for an immediate ceasefire on the basis of Article 40 of the UN Charter. As the first two resolutions of the Security Council had failed earlier to impose a ceasefire, a stronger resolution was adopted on September 20. The resolution stated inter alia:

> The Security Council . . . demands that a ceasefire should take effect on Wednesday, September 22, 1965, at 0700 hours GMT, and calls upon governments to issue orders for a ceasefire at that moment and a subsequent withdrawal of all armed personnel . . .[123]

This resolution was certainly stronger in tone and spirit than those adopted by the Council on September 4 and 6.[124] It also urged the two governments to resolve their outstanding problems through bilateral negotiations. This resolution gave an implied warning to China to refrain from any action that might precipitate further armed escalation in the region.

By making a demand for a ceasefire on behalf of the international community, the Security Council was able to control the Indo-Pakistan war. Though the Council's resolution did not contain provisions for enforcement, it was not just another statement. The word "demand" is not often used with reference to sovereign nations; from the Council's standpoint it was "justified" in the interest of peace.[125] Needless to add, the adoption of this strong resolution was possible because the major powers were behind it. These powers demonstrated "rare unity on how to deal with the present situation."[126] Thus with the concerted insistence on the cessation of the conflict, the U.S., U.K., and the Soviet Union were able to control and manage a major conflict situation. In a certain sense, it was the "herculean diplomatic efforts" of Ambassador Goldberg that enabled the Security Council to work out a strong but flexible resolution that secured the belligerents' compliance.[127] The third ceasefire resolution reflected an "evenhanded" emphasis that characterized the overall American approach to the 1965 conflict.[128]

In the U.S., the role of the Security Council generated euphoric reactions. President Johnson appreciated the Security Council's role in diffusing the conflict and thanked "our own gifted Ambassador Goldberg" and the members of his team, and the UN Secretary General.[129] The administration's action was approved by the Congress, whose members hailed it as a UN triumph, and expressed their indebtedness to Johnson and Goldberg for the part they had played in averting a much broader conflict. They commended the wisdom of "multilateral intervention" and appreciated the Soviet role in the entire crisis.[130] On his part, President Johnson had remarked that being spokesman for the "most powerful nation" in the world had helped Goldberg to bring about an end to this crisis.[131]

The Security Council, having enforced the ceasefire, provided an opportunity for the Soviet Union to emerge as the conciliator of the Subcontinent. For different reasons, neither the Americans nor the British could take the initiative to work out a settlement of the Indo-Pakistan dispute. For Britain, the difficulty was that she had lost her credibility as a mediator with New Delhi by virtue of Prime Minister Wilson's one-sided criticism of India's counter-attack across the international boundary. As for the United States, the Johnson administration had decided to avoid direct diplomatic intervention, presumably out of weariness and frustration with the affairs of the Subcontinent. It was, indeed, a difficult choice for the administration to move into a situation where two states both friendly to the U.S. and also recipients of their economic and military aid, were militarily engaged. Hence, the American policy that developed was mostly an exercise in damage limitations—through minimum political investment. Therefore, it was left for Soviet Premier Kosygin to sponsor a summit meeting for Ayub and Shastri at Tashkent in January, 1966. The phase ended with the signing of an Indo-Pakistan declaration on January 10, 1966. First, it renounced force in the settlement of Indo-Pakistan disputes. Second, it provided for the troops' withdrawal to positions held before August 5, 1965. Third, both countries agreed to normalize their diplomatic relations. Needless to say, the reduction of tension was welcomed by the U.S. even though it meant a diplomatic gain for the Soviet Union.[132]

Conclusion

Washington's pattern of response to the 1965 conflict was largely determined by certain specific contextual limitations of the Johnson administration's South Asia policy. Some of them were partly inherited, considering American policy was shaped by the earlier ambivalent, if not negative, attitude towards the region and deep U.S. involvement, in particular. But, more importantly, the U.S. administration was also overtaken by several external and domestic developments that had bearing on America's South Asia policy.

First, the administration was faced with growing congressional criticism of economic and military assistance programs in the region. Second, President Johnson was exasperated by the continuing Indo-Pakistan conflict and of their poor economic performance. Third, the U.S. was becoming increasingly involved in the Vietnam War. Fourth, Chinese militancy caused additional concern. Finally, because of U.S. arms aid to India, Pakistan was trying to develop a closer relationship with China. There were, however, certain encouraging signs that the Soviet Union was moving to a more balanced position vis-a-vis India and Pakistan in view of its conflict with China. In fact, to the extent that the Soviet Union demonstrated its strong non-partisan interest in the resolution of a crisis involving a country aligned to the U.S., its role was not unacceptable to the Johnson administration. Also, with China making warlike noises, the U.S. favored a more concerted response of the major powers in regard to this emerging threat to South Asian stability. Given this priority, the U.S.

administration wanted to avoid any form of dissension by not pushing for the resolution of the Kashmir issue under the auspices of the UN Secretary General—an idea not favored by Moscow.

But, whatever the range of constraints, neither the Johnson administration, nor any U.S. administration could remain totally aloof from the developments within the region. Even though South Asia has usually been of marginal importance in comparison with Southeast Asia in the 1960s, or the Middle East in the 1970s and 1980s, a major power such as the U.S. finds it difficult to abstain from playing a role in consonance with its power and perceived interests. Paradoxically, this constitutes an additional constraint on the independence of U.S. foreign policy.

In this case, the U.S. response was indirect and supportive of the efforts of others. However, the administration did consult and take into confidence members of Congress. On its part, Congress was willing to give the President the necessary freedom of action, in deciding to suspend military and economic aid to India and Pakistan, the administration consulted Congress.

In the later stages of the crisis U.S. policy was implemented at two levels: private bilateral diplomatic pressure was generated by the Department of State, while public pressure for an immediate ceasefire was applied through the UN Security Council by the U.S. Ambassador to the UN This coordinated strategy was also used to prevent any Chinese intervention. One interesting aspect of this strategy was that the President did not become publicly involved in the U.S. efforts at conflict resolution. While one could argue that this only reflected the unimportance of the issue, it is more likely that this was designed to project the impartial role of the UN Security Council—then ably guided by Arthur Goldberg.

It is clear that in this case the Security Council was effective because of the emergence of parallel interests between the U.S. and the Soviet Union. Without the major powers' near-identical views regarding the imperative of an immediate ceasefire in South Asia it is inconceivable that the UN would have played an effective role. The unanimity of the superpowers' position on the conflict of 1965 also had a profound impact on the thinking within the U.S. administration. The "parallel efforts of the United States and the Soviet Union in the Pakistan-India conflict," along with the "efforts of the U.N.," said, Defense Secretary McNamara, "point to the peacekeeping pattern of the future."[133] These expectations were, however, belied by subsequent developments in South Asia— notably the Indo-Pakistan war of 1971.

Notes

1. See the article by a student of Indo-Pakistani affairs, Sisir Gupta, "Tashkent and After" in *India Quarterly*, 22 (January-March 1966), p. 3.

2. As an alliance partner, Pakistan claimed that the U.S. should have supported her in the war against India. India on the other hand reminded the U.S. to fulfill its assurances as to dissuading Pakistan from using U.S. supplied weapons against India.

3. Commenting on the Soviet success in bringing India and Pakistan to the conference table, *The Times* (London) commented on January 3, 1966: "How strange and intolerable it would have seemed to Curzon that the affairs of the Subcontinent he ruled should be taken to Tashkent to be discussed under the patronage of a Russian."

4. See *White Paper on the Jammu and Kashmir Dispute*, Ministry of Foreign Affairs, Government of Pakistan, Islamabad, January 1977, pp. 67-68. There are Pakistani military analysts who believe that as the Indian and the Pakistani armed forces were more or less equally matched at the time of partition, it is "highly doubtful that if we had made an all-out effort in Kashmir to save it from Indian occupation, India would have attacked Pakistan across the international border." And, even if it had led to an all-out war in 1947, India would not have fared better than it did in 1965. (Brig. A. A. K. Choudhry, *September 1965: Before and After*, (Lahore: Ferozsons, 1977), p. 15.

5. See, Galbraith, *Journal*, p. 63. For Ayub's response to Nehru's appeal, see *White Paper on the Jammu and Kashmir Dispute*, pp. 63-64.

6. Six rounds of talks were held between an Indian delegation led by Sardar Swaran Singh and a Pakistani delegation led by Z. A. Bhutto, from December 27, 1962 to May 16, 1963. (for an account see *Keesing's*, 1963-64, pp. 1953-54).

7. Sisir Gupta, *Kashmir: A Study in India-Pakistan Relations* (Bombay: Asia Publishing House, 1966), p. 353.

8. See Ayub Khan, *Autobiography*, p. 158.

9. *Pakistan National Assembly Debates*, Vol. 2, 1962, p. 93. Speaking in the National Assembly of Pakistan, July 17, 1963, Foreign Minister Bhutto had declared: ". . . if India in her frustration turned her guns against the international situation is such today that Pakistan would not be alone in that conflict . . . An attack by India on Pakistan involves the territorial integrity and security of the largest state in Asia." (*Pakistan National Assembly Debates*, July 17, 1963, p. 1666).

10. For an analytical study of the Sino-Pakistan collaboration, see Shivaji Ganguly, *Pakistan-China Relations: A Study in Interaction* (Urbana: Asian Studies Center, University of Illinois, 1971).

11. Jawaharlal Nehru, Pakistan Seeks to Profit from Chinese Aggression (New Delhi, 1963).

12. *Dawn*, January 14, 1964. See Ayub-Chou En-Lai Joint Communique, February 23, 1964. (Issued following the Chinese Premier Chou En-lai's visit to Pakistan in February), in *Dawn*, February 24, 1964.

13. See Mohammad Ayub Khan, "The Pakistan-American Alliance: Stresses and Strains," *Foreign Affairs*, January 1964, pp. 199-206; also see Z. A. Bhutto's speech in Pakistan Parliament, July 17, 1963. (cited in Sisir Gupta, *Kashmir*, p. 434.

14. For an analysis of the bases of Indo-Pak discord, see Sisir Gupta, "Indo-Pakistan Relations," *International Studies* (New Delhi), Vol. V, Nos. 1-2, July-October 1963, pp. 174-179.

15. Regarding the firing incidents on Assam-East Pakistan border, see *Indian Recorder and Digest* (New Delhi), January 1964, p. 23, as for the exodus, at one point, between 3,000 and 4,000 refugees were coming into India everyday from East Pakistan. See, the Indian Home Minister Gulzari Lal Nanda's statement at the Indo-Pakistan Home Ministers' Conference (convened to deal with the problem of communal violence), April 7, 1964, at New Delhi. *Foreign Affairs Record*, Vol. X, No. 4, (April 1964), pp. 108-112.

16. The 1961 census figures for Assam and Tripura revealed a drastic change in the population structure. A subsequent survey indicated that there had been a large-scale influx of Muslims from East Pakistan. The figure for Assam was about 300,000 and for Tripura 50,000. Therefore, expulsion proceedings were instituted against them in accordance to the Foreigners Act (*The Paradox of India-Pakistan Relations*, (New Delhi: Publication Division, Ministry of Information and Broadcasting, Government of India, September 1965), p. 37.

17. Some of these possibilities have been noted in the *White Paper on Jammu and Kashmir* (Government of Pakistan) pp. 77-78.

18. Letter from the Foreign Minister of Pakistan to the President of the UN Security Council, January 16, 1964 (S/5517).

19. Nehru Welcomed Sheikh Abdullah's efforts to bring about Indo-Pakistan rapprochement. He believed that unless "something was done to improve the relations" between India and Pakistan," there may be occasion for conflicts arising between them." See his statement at a meeting of the All-India Congress Committee, Bombay, May 17, 1964, in *Congress Bulletin*, issued by the Indian National Congress, New Delhi, March-June 1964, pp. 246-7.

20. According to one informed Pakistani observer, even if Nehru had lived longer it would not have made any difference to the Indo-Pakistan "feud." He argues that what Abdullah had offered to Ayub was some sort of a confederation between India, Pakistan and Kashmir. "To Pakistanis this meant 'the destruction of Pakistan." S. M. Burke, *Mainsprings of Indian and Pakistani Foreign Policies*, (Minneapolis: University of Minnesota Press, 1974), p. 185.

21. President Ayub Khan's monthly broadcast, June 1, 1964; and Lal Bahadur Shastri's first broadcast to the nation as the Prime Minister, June 11, 1964.

22. Indian Foreign Minister, Sardar Swaran Singh's statement in Parliament on Pakistani intrusions in Kutch district in Kutch (India), March 3, 1965. (*Foreign Affairs Record*, Vol. XI, No. 3, March 1965, pp. 49-50); his

statements on the Cooch-Behar firing incidents, in Lok Sabha March 19, 1965 (*Foreign Affairs Record*, Vol. XI, No. 3, March 1965, pp. 49-51). For a documentary outline of the Kutch episode, see S. K. Rana, (ed.), *Rann of Kutch: India, Pakistan and China* (New Delhi: The Book Times Co., 1965). Also for an analytical overview of the 1965 conflict, see D. D. Khanna, Kutch Dispute and Pakistani Infiltration in Jammu and Kashmir 1965, *Defence Studies Papers* No. 1 (Allahabad: Department of Defence Studies, University of Allahabad, 1981).

23. Indian Foreign Minister, Sardar Swaran Singh's statement in Parliament on Pakistani intrusions in Kutch district in Kutch (India), March 3, 1965. (*Foreign Affairs Record*, Vol. XI, No. 3, March 1965, pp. 49-50); his statements on the Cooch-Behar firing incidents, in Lok Sabha March 19, 1965 (*Foreign Affairs Record*, Vol. XI, No. 3, March 1965, pp. 49-51). For a documentary outline of the Kutch episode, see S. K. Rana, (ed.), *Rann of Kutch: India, Pakistan and China* (New Delhi: The Book Times Co., 1965). Also for an analytical overview of the 1965 conflict, see D. D. Khanna, Kutch Dispute and Pakistani Infiltration in Jammu and Kashmir 1965, *Defence Studies Papers* No. 1 (Allahabad: Department of Defence Studies, University of Allahabad, 1981).

24. Secretary of State, Dean Rusk's News conference, May 26, 1965. See *Department of State Bulletin* 52 (June 14, 1965), p. 945.

25. The Soviet news agency, *Tass* found the Indo-Pakistan conflict "deplorable." It did not criticize Pakistan in any way (*Pravda*, May 9, 1965) cited Hemen Ray, *Indo-Soviet Relations 1955-1971* (Bombay: Jaico, 1973), pp. 136-37.

26. "Tashkent and After," *India Quarterly*, January-March 1966, p. 9. It was after Ayub Khan's visit to the Soviet Union in early April that Pakistan was able to "establish direct contact" with Moscow. While discussing Indo-Pak problems with Ayub Khan, Soviet Premier Kosygin seemed to have advocated "direct negotiations" between the two countries. See Mohammad Ayub Khan, *Friends Not Masters: A Political Autobiography* (New York: Oxford University Press, 1967), pp. 168-174.

27. New China News Agency official communique, May 4, 1965. Cited *Peking Review* (May 14, 1965), p. 4.

28. William J. Barnds, *India, Pakistan and the Great Powers*, (New York: Praeger Publishers, 1972), p. 200.

29. Kuldip Nayar, *India the Critical Years*, (Delhi: Vikas Publications, 1971), p. 210.

30. Cited, Kuldip Nayar, *Distant Neighbors: A Tale of the Subcontinent* (Delhi: Vikas Publishing House, 1972), pp. 113-14. The mood of the country was reflected in one informed Indian commentator's statement: "Time was running out for a punishing counter-attack in Kutch." See Ramesh Thapar "Why we did not hit back," *Economic and Political Weekly* (Bombay), May 15, 1965, p. 805. General Chaudhury reveals that Pakistan's own plan was for getting India to panic and move down heavy reinforcements from the main Punjab theater to Kutch." Once they had the Indians there, the guerrilla's would

have gone into Kashmir, supported by the capture of the key point of Akhnur by the Pakistani regular army. See General J. N. Chaudhury, *India's Problems of National Security in the Seventies*. (New Delhi: United Service Institution, 1973), p. 12.

31. Aziz Beg, *Pakistan Faces India* (Lahore: Babur and Amer Publications, 1966), p. 207. Also Z. A. Bhutto, "Nehru An Appraisal," in the *Quest for Peace: Selection from Speeches and Writings, 1963-65* (Karachi: Pakistan Institute of International Affairs, 1966), p. 61.

32. See statement by the then Pakistan Foreign Minister, Z. A. Bhutto in Pakistan National Assembly, July 17, 1963, in Z. A. Bhutto, *Foreign Policy of Pakistan; Speeches in National Assembly 1962-64* (Karachi: Pakistan Institute of International Affairs, 1964), p. 74. A former Pakistani Air Marshal has revealed that in 1963 an Inter-Services Intelligence briefing had indicated the possibility that by 1966/1967 India would have a broad enough industrial base and adequate indigenous resources to be able to launch a "military adventure against Pakistan." See Air Marshal (Ret'd.) M. Asghar Khan, *The First Round: Indo-Pakistan War 1965* (Ghaziabad: Vikas, 1979), p. 7.

33. Asghar Khan, pp. 7-8.

34. Since its accession to India in 1947, the State of Jammu and Kashmir had a separate constitution. This enabled it to have a certain degree of internal autonomy.

35. "Let us prepare for war, a Jehad," declared the daily *Dawn* (Karachi), March 22, 1965. Another major daily *Pakistan Times* (Lahore, April 28, 1965) underlined: "Jehad is the only way to solve the Kashmir problem."

36. At the time of the Sino-Indian war, Pakistan refrained from taking any advantage of India's predicament. But, Pakistani analysts have been apparently divided as to whether Pakistan should not have made an all out effort to seize Jammu and Kashmir. Some of them believe, Pakistan could have accomplished this task without the undue risk of an Indian attack across the international boundary. (Brig.) A. A. K. Chaudhury, *September 1965: Before and After* (Lahore: Ferozsons, 1977), p. 15. Others contend that this was a wise decision; for such an action, Pakistan would have been "blamed for a stab in the back," (Maj. Gen.) Shakat Riza, Izzat-O-Iqbal, *History of Pakistan Artillery, 1947-1971* (Nowshera: School of Artillery, 1980), p. 133.

37. G. W. Chaudhury, *The Last Days of United Pakistan* (Bloomington: Indiana University Press, 1974), p. 20. For comments by the then Pakistani Information Secretary, Altaf Gauhar, see his Foreword in Asghar Khan, p. X.

38. G. W. Chaudhury, p. 20.

39. Asghar Khan, pp. 74-75. One Pakistani general called the Kutch conflict purely a "curtain raiser;" success in the operation had generated a feeling at the "lower level" that "we could do exceptionally well if a major conflict did break out." Lieutenant General M. Attiqur Rahman, *Our Defense Cause: An Analysis of Pakistan's Past and Future Military Role* (London: White Lion Publishers, 1976), p. 36. See, Barnds, p. 201.

40. Derived from Foreign Minister Bhutto's communication to President Ayub Khan, May 12, 1965. See, *White Paper on the Jammu and Kashmir Dispute*, pp. 82-83. General J. N. Chaudhury claims that "It was on May 5, 1965 that the larger pattern of Pakistan's intentions to seize Kashmir before we got too strong became apparent," though the actual details of how they would do it were not yet clear. (General J. N. Chaudhury, *India's Problems of National Security in the Seventies* (New Delhi: U.S.I., 1972), p. 13.

41. The above account is based on M. Asghar Khan, pp. 75-76.

42. See, Altaf Gauhar's Forword Asghar Khan; also see M. Attiqur Rahman, *Our Defense Cause*, p. 36. It is interesting that in recent years there has been a spate of writings in Pakistan in support of a conspiracy theory of the 1965 war. They accuse Bhutto and Aziz Ahmed for having deliberately dragged Pakistan into an ill-conceived armed conflict. For an overview see Brig. Abdul Rahman Siddiqi, "1965 War: Was it a Conspiracy?" in *Defence Journal*, Vol. IV, No. 89-10, 1978, pp. 1-10.

43. Bhutto in an interview with an Indian journalist had stated that he persuaded Ayub Khan to send the infiltrators into the Kashmir valley. Cited, Kuldip Nayar, *Distant Neighbors*, p. 187. President Ayub had also addressed the officers of this operation in the second week of July, 1965, explaining to them their tasks.

44. Prime Minister Nehru's New Year's message to the Nation, 1952.

45. The Nehru doctrine, though later reconfirmed, was actually formulated before Pakistan received the massive U.S. military aid.

46. The Indian allegations were largely substantiated by the subsequent UN investigation of the flare-up in Kashmir. See, Report of the UN Secretary General (U Thant), September 3, 1965, (*UN Doc. S/6651*).

47. Burke, p. 186.

48. Barnds, p. 203.

49. (Gen.) J. N. Chaudhuri, *Arms, Aims and Aspects* (Bombay: Manaktalas, 1966), p. 228. The author was the Indian Army Chief of Staff during 1965 war.

50. Pakistan Foreign Minister Z. A. Bhutto had declared on August 10 that "the responsibility for whatever is happening in Kashmir could not by any stretch of the imagination be attributed to Pakistan." Cited *Kashmir Answers Pakistan* (New Delhi: Publications Division, Government of India, September 1965), p. 4.

51. See Prime Minister Shastri's statement in an interview with *The New York Times*, August 22, 1965. The Indian position regarding the crossing of the ceasefire line was later reiterated by Defense Minister Chavan in a statement in the Parliament on August 25, 1965.

52. There are different Pakistani versions regarding the genesis of "Operation Grand Slam." Some believe that this was part of a two-stage plan drafted by Major General Akhtar Malik. According to another version it did not form part of Malik's original draft plan of operation. Incidentally, in launching its attack, Pakistan had in fact crossed the international border, though it wanted

to give the impression that the operation was confined to the Jammu and Kashmir ceasefire line.

53. This action was in conformity with the government's stand that in the event of persistent Pakistani "aggressive activities," the Indian Army "will decide its own strategy and the employment of its manpower and equipment in the manner it deems best." See Prime Minister Shastri's statement in Lok Sabha April 28, 1965, in When Freedom is Menaced: *Speeches of Lal Bahadur Shastri, August 13-September 26* (New Delhi: Publications Divisions, October 2, 1965), p. 142. The then Indian Army Chief of Staff has revealed that since May 5, 1965, when the likelihood of a Pakistani attack became quite apparent, he had secured the necessary "clearance" about retaliatory action after discussing the matter with both the Prime Minister and the Defense Minister. See Chaudhuri, *India's Problem*, pp. 43-44.

54. *The New York Times*, September 7, 1965.

55. *Pakistan: From 1947 to the Creation of Bangladesh, Keesing's Research Report 9* (New York: Charles Scribner's Sons, 1973), p. 90.

56. *Manchester Guardian*, September 9, 1965.

57. Chinese Foreign Ministry's note to the government of India, September 16, 1965. See, *Current Documents*, 1965, pp. 752:754.

58. See *The New York Times*, September 21, 1965.

59. Aside from Chinese support to Pakistan's Chhamb operation, it was their ultimatum that "really shook India" claims one informed Pakistani observer. See, S. M. Burke *Mainsprings of Indian and Pakistani Foreign Policies* (Minneapolis: University of Minnesota Press, 1974), p. 189. Also see White Paper on Kashmir, p. 97; M. A. H. Ispahani, "Pakistan and Regional Arrangements," *Pakistan Horizon*, 22 (Third Quarter 1969), p. 201. One Pakistani insider reveals that Ayub Khan did not want to have talks with Chinese leaders—despite their requests—regarding China's possible commitment, for fear of annoying Pakistan's Western allies. See Asghar Khan, p. 49.

60. For a representative Pakistani exposition of the problem see, Z. A. Bhutto, *The Myth of Independence* (London: Oxford University Press, 1969), pp. 62-65.

61. *Ibid.*, p. 69.

62. Statement before the Senate Committee on Foreign Relations, June 23, 1964. See, *Foreign Assistance, 1964, hearings before the Senate Committee on Foreign Relations*, 88th Congress 2nd Session, June 23, 1964 (Washington, D.C.: U.S. Government Printing Office, 1964) p. 519.

63. Assistant Secretary of State, Phillips Talbot's testimony on Foreign Assistance Act of 1964, House Committee on Foreign Affairs. See, *Foreign Assistance Act of 1964, Hearings before House Foreign Affairs Committee*, 88th Congress, 2nd Session, April 8, 1964 (Washington, D.C.: U.S. Government Printing Office, 1964), pp. 238-239.

64. See, Burke, p. 177.

65. Barnds, p. 195.

66. According to Chester Bowles, initially India was not averse to the idea of supporting U.S. efforts in the event of a Chinese invasion of Southeast Asian nations. It was later, when the U.S. introduced combat troops that India decided to "move away" from the U.S. (Bowles, p. 476).

67. Statement by AID Administrator, David E. Bell, in Senate Foreign Relations Committee, March 10, 1965. See, U.S. Congress, *Senate Committee on Foreign Relations, Foreign Assistance, 1965*, Hearings, 89th Congress, 1st Session, 1965, p. 96.

68. Senator Wayne Morse's statement of March 19, 1965, was symbolic of this skepticism: "I do not want to be pouring military aid into India or into Pakistan to put them in a position where they can call the tune as to whether or not we go to a military war as a result of their actions . . . I think we have to reappraise this year as we never have, to a greater degree than we ever have before this whole military aid program of the United States." See U.S. Congress, *Senate Committee on Foreign Relations, Foreign Assistance, 1965,* Hearings, 89th Congress, 1st Session 1965, pp. 399-400.

69. Barnds, 195. Also based on personal interviews.

70. Dean Rusk's interview with N.B.C. in September 1965, was symbolic of the U.S. priorities in South Asia, see, *Department of State Bulletin* 53 (March 27, 1965), p. 511.

71. Conveyed to the Pakistani ambassador to U.S. Cited, G. W. Chaudhury, p. 117. "Considerable pressure," was put on Pakistan by the Johnson administration to change its China policy, claimed Pakistani Prime Minister Bhutto in 1977. See Zulfikar Ali Bhutto, *Bilateralism: New Directions* (Islamabad: Ministry of Information and Broadcasting, 1970, p. 20.

72. See Sino-Pakistan joint Communique, March 7, 1965, in *Pakistan Horizon* XVII (2nd Quarter 1965), p. 181.

73. President Johnson's news conference, April 27, 1965. U.S. President, *Public Papers of the Presidents of the United States* (Washington, D.C.: Office of the Federal Register, National Archives and Record Service, 1963-68), Lyndon B. Johnson, 1966, p. 455. (Hereafter, *Public Papers of the Presidents: Lyndon B. Johnson*).

74. Derived from Philip L. Geyelin, *Lyndon B. Johnson and the World* (New York: Frederick A. Praeger, 1966), p. 266.

75. Bowles, pp. 498-499.

76. *The New York Times*, April 21, 1965.

77. Remarks by Chairman of the House Committee on Foreign Affairs, Thomas E. Morgan, April 7, 1964. U.S. Congress, *House Committee on Foreign Affairs, Foreign Assistance Act of 1964*, Hearings, 88th Congress, 2nd Session, 1964, pp. 238-39.

78. See Richard P. Stebbins, *The United States in World Affairs 1965*, (New York: Harper and Row, published for the Council on Foreign Relations, 1966) pp. 215-16.

79. See Geyelin, pp. 268-269.

80. *Public Papers on the Presidents, 1965, Lyndon B. Johnson*, 1966, p. 452.

81. Incidentally, in his memoir, Johnson has made only a one sentence reference to the Indo-Pakistan Conflict of 1965. (See, *Vantage Point*, p. 225).

82. Chinese Vice-Premier Chen Yi had turned up in Pakistan on September 4. He praised Pakistan's "just action" and came out in full-throated support of its demand on Kashmir. See *The New York Times*, September 5, 1965. Later, Peking threatened India with dire consequences if it continued its "aggression." See Chinese government statement of September 7, 1965, *Peking Review*, No. 37, September 10, 1965.

83. Goldberg's letter dated July 5, 1977. Cited Shafquat Hussain Chaudhry, "The UN Strategy for a Ceasefire in the 1965 War," in *Strategic Studies* (Islamabad), Vol. III, No. 4, Summer, 1980, p. 70. A Soviet tilt towards India is not supported by actual Soviet behavior during this crisis.

84. Cited in Report of the Secretary General to the Security Council on the situation in Kashmir, 3 September 1965 (*UN Doc. S/6651*).

85. See, letter dated August 30, 1965 from the Chief Military Observer of UNMOGIP to the Secretary General, with annexed annotated list of incidents of violation, in *Kashmir in Security Council: Texts of Documents September 2-7, 1965*. (New Delhi: External Publicity, September 1965), Part II.

86. Bowles, p. 502.

87. UN Secretary General U Thant's first report on the Indo-Pakistan Conflict submitted to the Security Council, September 3, 1965 (*UN Doc. S/6651*).

88. Barnds, p. 205.

89. Johnson, *Vantage Point: Perspectives of the Presidency 1963-1969* (New York: Holt, Rinehart and Winston, 1971), p. 225.

90. The UN Security Council met on September 4 in an emergency session at the call of the U.S. Representative to the UN, Arthur Goldberg.

91. See, U.S. Congress, *Senate Committee on Appropriations, Foreign Assistance and Related Appropriations for 1966*, H. R. 10871, Hearings, 89th Congress, 1st Session, 1965, p. 20.

92. For a discussion on the various facets of the "war diplomacy" of the 1965 Indo-Pakistan conflict see Russell Brines, *The Indo-Pakistan Conflict* (London: Pall Mall, 1968), pp. 353-381.

93. Remarks in the House by Representative Gerald R. Ford, 89th Congress, 1st Session September 7, 1965. *Congressional Record,* Vol. III, p. 23021.

94. Remarks by Senator Frank Church in the Senate, 89th Congress 1st Session, September 8, 1965. *Congressional Record*, Vol. III, pp. 23059-60.

95. Statement by Dean Rusk, Senate Committee on Appropriations, September 8, 1965. On the same day Britain had also imposed a "ban on the special arms aid to India, but licenses for commercial orders were not revoked." Britain did not have any arms agreement with Pakistan. See *Times* (London), September 17, 1965.

96. U.S. Congress, Senate Resolution 58, 89th Congress, 1st Session, September 9, 1965. *Congressional Record*, Vol. III, p. 23374.

97. Bowles, p. 504. Pakistan had also lodged a complaint against India's use of U.S. arms.

98. Based on some of the diplomatic exchanges published in parts in White Paper on Kashmir, pp. 86-87. A former Ayub aide G. W. Choudhury has also discussed the question of U.S. assurances. (Choudhury, pp. 112-13; 120-21). Until the entire diplomatic exchanges are declassified, it will be difficult to form a balanced judgement about the scope and extent of American assurances to Pakistan.

99. White Paper on Kashmir, Kuldip Nayar, *India: The Critical Years*, p. 225. In a statement in the Parliament on September 8, the Indian Defense Minister Chavan assured that India did not visualize taking action to escalate the war along the Indo-East Pakistan border. *Lok Sabha Debates* 45 (September 8, 1965), Col. 4612.

100. Statement by U.S. Representative Goldberg, September 1, 1965. *Department of State Bulletin* 53 (September 27, 1965), p. 526. In his statement of September 4, he made it clear that he was authorized by President Johnson to endorse U Thant's appeal. *Department of State Bulletin* 53 (September 27, 1965), p. 527.

101. UN Secretary-General U Thant's report of September 3, 1965 (*UN Doc.3/6651*).

102. S/PV 1237, September 4, 1965.

103. Security Council Resolution S/Res./209(1965).

104. Cited in (*UN doc. S/6685*).

105. Stebbins, p. 219.

106. Secretary General U Thant's report of September 6, 1965 in S/6661; for Pakistan's request see S/6699. September 6, 1965.

107. *UN Document 5/Res./210 (1965.*

108. Secretary General U Thant's reports to the Security Council, *UN Doc. S/6683 and S/6686.* There was, however, one difference; while India was willing to accept a ceasefire—though not with reference to the infiltrators—Pakistan flatly refused without a guarantee on the resolution of the Kashmir dispute. Incidentally, the United States was willing to give the Secretary General greater authority in this matter, but this was not supported by the Soviet Union and certain other Council members. (Derived from Goldberg's communication, cited, fn. 83, p. 75).

109. *White Paper on Kashmir*, p. 88.

110. *Ibid.*, pp. 88-92. It is also evident from informed Pakistani sources that Ayub was not eager to enter into any formal understanding with China regarding concerted action against India. In fact, for sometime he avoided any direct meeting with the Chinese leaders despite their repeated requests. (Asghar Khan, p. 49.).

111. See Asghar Khan, pp. 40-41, 47-49.

112. See G. W. Choudhury, *India, Pakistan, Bangladesh and the Major Powers*, pp. 189-91.

113. One informed observer contends that China's ultimatum was not a mere "paper threat." *Ibid.*, p. 190.

114. See Indian Prime Minister Lal Bahadur Shastri's statement in the Lok Sabha, September 20, 1965. *Lok Sabha Debates* 46 (Nos. 21-29), September 20, 1965, Cols. 6570-6571. Speaking to an Indian journalist subsequently, the then Chief of the Army Staff of India, General Chaudhury, had stated that he was sure that the Chinese would not attack India. Cited Kuldip Nayar, *India: The Critical Years*, p. 238.

115. From record of a meeting between President Ayub Khan and the British High Commissioner in Pakistan. Cited, *White Paper on Kashmir*, pp. 93-96.

116. Pravda, September 20, 1965. Cited Hemen Roy, *Indo-Soviet Relations 1955-1971* (Bombay: Jaico, 1973), p. 142.

117. Pravda, September 20, 1965. Cited, Ray, p. 142. Report of his statement at a closed session of Senate Foreign Relations Committee, September 13, *Facts on File*, 1965, p. 325.

118. *The New York Times, International Edition* (Paris), September 14, 1965.

119. Statements of September 17 and 18. *Department of State Bulletin*, 53 (October 11, 1965), pp. 602-604.

120. Stebbins, pp. 221-22.

121. Goldberg's statement in the Security Council, September 18, 1965. See *Department of State Bulletin* 53 (October 11, 1965), p. 603.

122. S/6686, September 16, 1965. In a certain sense, U Thant's suggestions had been influenced by U.S. Senator Mike Mansfield's Senate speech that stressed the need for UN sanctions in bringing this conflict to an end, *The New York Times*, September 10, 1965).

123. The Indian allegations were largely substantiated by the subsequent UN investigation of the flare-up in Kashmir. See, Report of the UN Secretary General (U Thant), September 3, 1965, (*UN Doc. S/6651*).

124. *UN Doc. S/Res./209*, September 4, 1965; and UN doc. S/Res./210, September 6, 1965.

125. Statement by Arthur Goldberg, in the UN Security Council, September 20, 1965. *Department of State Bulletin* 53 (October 11, 1965), p. 206.

126. See Shafqat Husain Choudhry, p. 87.

127. Stebbins, p. 222.

128. Statement by Goldberg, September 20, 1965. *Department of State Bulletin* 53 (October 11, 1965), p. 605.

129. White House announcement read by Press Secretary Bill Moyers, September 22, 1965. *Public Papers of the Presidents: Lyndon B. Johnson*, p. 1010.

130. See remarks by Senators Frank Church, J. Javits, Mansfield, Gore, McGovern in U.S. Congress, Senate, 88th Cong., 1st Session, September 22, 1965. *Congressional Record*, Vol. III, pp. 24730; 24795; 24816.

131. Speech at the Board of Directors of the International Association of Lions Clubs, September 23, 1965. *Public Papers of the Presidents*, p. 1016.

132. Dean Rusk, News conference, January 21, 1966. See Department of State Bulletin 54 (February, 1966), p. 196. For text of the Tashkent Declaration see *UN Doc. S/277* (1966).

133. Address to the American Society of Newspaper Editors, Montreal, May 18, 1966. *Department of State Bulletin* 54 (June 6, 1966), p. 880.

5

The 1965-67 Crisis
and Food Aid Politics

Immediately after the Second World War, U.S. aid programs were primarily designed to reconstruct Western Europe from its wartime destruction. Subsequently, the direction of America's external assistance programs underwent several basic changes. While these changes marked a shift from Europe to the developing areas, they included new priorities for U.S. aid strategy. In Asia, unlike Europe, U.S. policymakers were faced with the task of providing the right mix of external assistance (designed to ensure political independence as well as self-sustained economic growth) to the developing, newly independent states. Their problem was clearly underlined in that many of these states had weak economic and bureaucratic infrastructures.

Among these non-Communist "front line countries"—a euphemism used by the Clay Committee report—India was one of the largest recipients of U.S. aid in Asia.[1] This is significant because it was never an ally of the U.S. in its confrontation with the Communist bloc. The U.S. extended economic assistance to India through different agencies and programs, viz., the United States Agency for International Development (AID) (from 1961), the Export-Import Bank (started in 1957) and the PL 480 (Food for Peace) program (from 1956).[2] The legislation for PL 480 was originally enacted in 1954 (Agricultural Trade Development and Assistance Act) and was re-enacted a number of times since then.

The operation of this complicated program was not tied to any specific agency. The purpose of the PL 480 program was to provide surplus agricultural commodities to developing states at concessional rates repayable in local currencies. While these surpluses were given to meet chronic food deficits or acute famines, they also supplemented developmental aid provided by the U.S. Significantly, over half of the total volume of U.S. aid to India— given as grants and loans—was repayable in Rupees under the PL 480 program. The other important component of U.S. assistance has been furnished by AID and the Export-Import Bank, repayable in dollars.

Our basic focus in this case study is the politics of the American decision to respond to the Indian appeal for emergency food assistance to meet the critical shortages of 1965-67. This decision was characterized by two different, albeit interrelated, phases. The first was President Johnson's initial decision to provide prompt emergency food relief to India (though on the condition that the latter would reorient its agricultural strategy based on "self-help" efforts.) The second relates to Johnson's famous (or infamous) "short tether" or "ship-to-mouth" supply policy. This was in response to further Indian requests for urgent relief to meet the second continuing year of drought in several parts of the country. After an overview of the food aid program, we will examine the following questions. First, what was America's basic approach to the critical food situation in India? Second, who were the actors involved in the decision to provide prompt relief to India? Third, how was the decision made and what were the basic considerations behind the decision? Finally, what were the salient features of the pattern of American response?

U.S. Food Assistance Programs

The earliest instance of food assistance to India was in August, 1950, when an amount of $4.5 million was provided as a grant to buy American food grains to meet an acute food shortage. But as shortages grew in early 1951, India requested substantial additional assistance. In response, the U.S. Congress passed the Indian Emergency Food Act of 1951 authorizing a loan of $190 million to India. It enabled India to purchase two million tons of wheat from the U.S.[3] But this was neither prompt nor adequate from the standpoint of Indian expectations. The aid request was debated for quite some time before Congress finally decided to approve the legislation. To a large extent this delay was caused by Congressional criticism of India's stand on the Korean War.[4] Though the emergency food legislation was approved at the end of fiscal year 1951, almost all financial and other commitments

stipulated under this act were made in fiscal year 1952 and amounted
to only sixty percent of the total Indian request.

Since the special wheat loan of the early 1950s, the U.S.
supplied food aid to India under the more comprehensive provisions
of Public Law 480. This comprehensive system was set up by the
Agricultural Trade Development and Assistance Act of 1954. It was
under this act that Congress had established the system of surplus
agricultural commodity aid to developing countries. In brief, the
program authorized the U.S. to sell its growing agricultural
stockpiles, largely wheat, on concessional terms to food deficit
countries through separate agreements on each transaction. But
terms of the transactions were subject to negotiation; the
concessional terms entailed sales of agricultural surpluses in
exchange for foreign currencies, reduced interest rates, and granted
a four-year grace period before the food recipients started repaying
the loans. The recipient nations had to pay shipping costs for the
food grains. Usually at least 50% of the consignments were
shipped in U.S. freighters.[5] This was later made into a requirement
under the Merchant Act of 1965.

The sale proceeds from the various transactions on PL 480
products were put into a specially created local currency account
known as the counterpart fund. In the case of India, the U.S. has
maintained this account with the Reserve Bank of India. A small
portion of the sale proceeds in India were stipulated for conversion
into dollars for certain specific uses. Excepting a small amount
earmarked for the maintenance cost of U.S. agencies in India, the
U.S. administration was not entitled to spend from this account.
Normally, this fund was designed to provide long term loans for the
purpose of developmental projects mutually determined by the U.S.
and India.[6] Counterpart funds could be made available to the
recipients—except for development grants—without congressional
appropriations.

The operational ground rules of the PL 480 program were
set up by the following titles as well as the broad objectives
stipulated in the Act of 1954 and its subsequent amendments. Title I
of this act authorized the President to sell agricultural commodities,
in foreign currencies, to nations friendly to the U.S. Title II
provided for free supplies to foreign countries to meet famine
conditions and other types of contingency situations. Title III
related agricultural surpluses for: (a) the barter exchanges of
strategic and other raw materials, and (b) donations to American
non-profit, voluntary agencies that provide help both in the U.S.
and abroad. Finally, Title-IV stipulated the sale of agricultural

surplus for dollars on a long-term basis. Instead of immediate payment, it permitted the recipients to make repayments over an extended period of forty years.[7]

Generally speaking, the broad objectives of the program related to two levels of U.S. priorities that struggled for the attention of the policymakers. At one level the basic concern was how to dispose of the postwar U.S. agricultural glut. At the other, the question was whether in light of global food deficits, its agricultural surplus could be used as an instrument of foreign policy. The introduction of the Agricultural Trade Development and Assistance Act of 1954 was symbolic of an attempt to take note of these priorities. The act sought "to increase the consumption of United States agricultural commodities in foreign countries" and "to improve the foreign relations of the United States" and for "other purposes", like helping self-supporting economic development of the recipients.[8] At its inception the act was more in terms of domestic agricultural interests than in the light of pure humanitarian or foreign policy considerations.[9]

The act stipulated a "well-insulated" program with "considerable fiscal autonomy," and thus was not amenable to instant "Congressional leverage."[10] The U.S. government subsidized domestic agriculture through an autonomous institution, the Commodity Credit Corporation (CCC)—authorized by Congress. But different groups and institutions had different expectations for the program. They inevitably viewed its performance from their respective policy perspectives—agricultural, external relations, foreign economic aid, and so forth. This meant that the program was unlikely to remain insulated from the pulls and pressures of interested actors. We will explore this later.

Even after its metamorphosis under the Kennedy administration—when it became the Food for Peace Program—the PL 480 program continued to perform a number of interrelated functions. The program implied "all things to all people", said a staff member of the Senate Committee on Agriculture.[11] Evidently, the basic concern of the major actors involved several different, but interrelated issue-areas of the food aid program.

The PL 480 program enabled the Department of Agriculture to reduce the pressure of agricultural surpluses on existing storage facilities (but, over the years, this became less important as the volume of agricultural surpluses diminished). Then, the provision for the shipment of at least 50% of the agricultural commodities on American vessels served American shipping interests. Despite its initial reservations, the State Department found in PL 480 considerable scope for political influence.[12] The program gradually emerged as a convenient tool for promoting mutual understanding with developing countries in general and India in particular. To the Department of the Treasury, the PL 480 program was tolerable so long as it did not adversely affect the U.S. balance of payments position. It was only when this became unfavorable that the Treasury wanted cash sales of food grains in currencies convertible to dollars.

Finally, Congress was involved with the PL 480 program through three sets of Senate and House committees: Agriculture, Foreign Affairs and Appropriations. Normally the Agriculture committees were most directly concerned with PL 480. They not only considered executive requests for the extension of the program but also review its operations. The Foreign Affairs committees are indirectly concerned with PL 480 insofar as it constitutes an important component of America's external assistance. The functions of the Appropriations committees relate to allocation of subsidies for the purchase of surplus agricultural commodities from the farmers.

The PL 480 program was operated by three principal actors: (a) the Department of Agriculture, which acted through its Secretary (its authority was then redelegated to the Commodity Credit Corporation); (b) the Department of State, which entrusted AID with much of its authority and responsibility to implement the goals of the program, and (c) the Director of Food for Peace—a special assistant to the President, who coordinated the various programs, after 1966 the State Department coordinated them. Though interaction among these organizational actors remained mainly informal, decision-making was formally structured within the Inter-agency Staff Committee (ISC) by a presidential directive. It did not include decisions relating to emergency food aid under Title II of PL 480. The ISC comprised representatives from the Departments of Agriculture and State, the AID, the Bureau of the Budget, the Treasury Department, the Department of Commerce, the United States Information Agency (now the International Communications Agency) and the Office of Emergency Planning. The Secretary of Agriculture's representative used to preside over the ISC meeting. The Director of Food for Peace was represented by an observer.

As vested with authority delegated by the President, the Secretary of Agriculture has been responsible for the administration of Title I. He determined the kind of agricultural commodities that were evidently in surplus. But his authority was limited by two broad qualifications. First, he was subject to presidential instructions and the continuous supervision of the Director of Food for Peace. Second, all functions under the program were subject to the Secretary of State's responsibilities pertaining to foreign policy that related to such functions.[13]

With certain exceptions, the Congressional role in the decision-making process was marked by increasing Senate and House dissatisfaction regarding the PL 480 program. Congress was particularly concerned about its inadequate stress on the originally conceived objective of developing external markets for U.S. agricultural products. Indeed, the transient character of Titles I and II permitted Congress to re-examine PL 480 whenever the question of its extension arose. One of the intensely debated questions faced by Congress was whether PL 480 should be designed to stress food aid/donations as a foreign policy instrument, or to promote the interests of domestic agriculture through concessional sales of surplus food grains.

Other key issues relating to this program result from Executive requests or Congressional scrutiny of PL 480's performance or operations. Some of these issues include the questions of: extensions of the program, desirability of Congressional supervision of the program operations as well as the accumulated counterpart funds (Title I), and the need for efficient management of the programs. It was around these major issues that the executive branch and Congress tended to interact over food aid. In many ways this conflict was symbolic of the need for reconciling Congressional domestic interests with that of the external priorities of the executive branch.[14] If to Congress it was largely a "giveaway" program, to executive branch policymakers it was beneficial to both the U.S. and the recipient nations. In view of these diverse perceptions, the program was frequently constrained by "interagency delay, bureaucratic timidity and executive branch fears of Congressional reaction."[15] This was the domestic context in which the Johnson administration had to respond to India's appeals for massive emergency food assistance in 1965-67.

India and PL 480

Though established in July 1954, the PL 480 Program was not extended to India until the financial year, 1956. PL 480 exports to India from 1956-57 to 1965-66 constituted 93.5 percent of the value of total agricultural exports to that country. By 1966 it was increased to about two-thirds of the total value of aid that India was receiving from the U.S.[16] By the end of the second plan, notwithstanding India's stress on agricultural self-sufficiency, India's dependence on agricultural imports rose quite sharply. From 5.2 percent in 1961, food imports by 1964 increased to more than 11 percent of India's total domestic food production. Incidentally, the quantum of PL 480 food assistance was increasingly becoming a major component of the total volume of food imports by 1965-66.[17]

Obviously, the PL 480 program economically benefited both the U.S. and India in a number of ways. On the one hand, the program enabled the U.S. to dispose of agricultural surplus—purchased at a subsidized rate from the farmers—thereby maintaining a commercially profitable domestic price level for the latter. On the other hand, helping India, it filled in the shortages of India's agricultural production and thereby prevented a sharp rise in food prices.[18] Second, by stabilizing food prices at a reasonable level, the program not only reduced the possibility of unmanageable political tensions, but also enhanced governmental stability. Third, because the program reduced the drainage of hard currency on food imports, it made foreign exchange available for key industrial projects. Finally, the counterpart funds generated by the sale of agricultural surplus to India helped to finance India's developmental programs.

Despite these economic benefits the program produced certain problems. It had a detrimental effect on India's food production, hindering agricultural self-sufficiency. Depressing food prices can hardly generate a farmer's incentive for increased agricultural production.[19] Some argued that India's continued dependence on food imports was caused by the United States' inability to insist on minimal "agricultural performance" as a *quid pro quo* for food aid and technical assistance.[20] Finally, the accumulated rupees in the counterpart funds had an inflationary effect on the Indian economy.

On the Indian side, there was considerable misapprehension about the implications of the counterpart funds for fear of losing foreign exchange. Yet, the more serious problem was at the political level. There was a widely prevalent view that the U.S. also used food aid to pressure India on different foreign policy issues. While there could be differences of opinion as to the basis of this allegation, one would find it difficult not to accept the conclusion that the PL 480 program was "deeply wounding to India's national pride."[21]

Food Aid and Foreign Policy

Like many other qualified commentators, former U.S. Secretary of Agriculture, Orville Freeman, conceded that the PL 480 program originally provided a "legal framework" for getting rid of surpluses. Assistance for hungry people and economic development were secondary.[22] When the PL 480 program evolved into Food for Peace under the Kennedy administration, a change was marked in its use and purpose.[23] Although these two arrangements were used interchangeably, they denote two different stages in the evolution of U.S. food aid programs. If the aims of the "original" PL 480 were "primarily domestic" and thus designed to alleviate U.S. farm surpluses, Food for Peace underlined the role of food as an instrument of American foreign policy.

The partial initiation of the Food for Peace Program under President Eisenhower, and its complete modification by the Kennedy and Johnson administrations, marked an increasing official emphasis on foreign assistance as a mechanism for pursuing foreign policy interests.[24] In a no-win military situation—resulting from the U.S.-Soviet nuclear balance—foreign aid offered a minimal risk approach to attain ends in the developing nations. The rationale behind this was to "maintain a position of influence and control" around the world, and "sustain" and support those nations which otherwise would "definitely collapse" or pass into the communist bloc."[25] This objective however, did not contradict periodic official U.S. declarations regarding the humanitarian considerations behind foreign policy. At least on one occasion, President Johnson had claimed that many of the American efforts had "moral purposes."[26]

It is inconceivable that any American administration could obtain Congressional approval only on the basis of moral purpose. In fact, both political and economic arguments frequently were put forward to secure the easy passage of foreign aid funds. A humanitarian rationale by itself is not a credible argument in convincing constituents and their Congressional representatives of the need for external assistance. Only in the case of extreme emergency situations (like drought, famine or flood) does humanitarian purpose have wide appeal and hence, permit prompt assistance.

But at the same time, the objective of acquiring friendship or goodwill had a great bearing on Congressional aid allocations.[27] Normally, foreign aid programs have been justified by the U.S. in self-interest—a flexible term capable of accommodating divergent foreign policy ends; the basic idea is to ensure prompt

Congressional endorsement of the foreign aid programs. But from a different side, the U.S. administration often has been faced with the task of dispelling the recipient nations' misapprehension regarding foreign aid strategy, by emphasizing the economic or humanitarian aspects of aid. Consequently, though "aid programs" are generally conceived as tools of U.S. foreign policy, "it may not always be clearly defined or consistently pursued," or "proclaimed loudly," said one knowledgeable observer.[28] Emphasis on foreign assistance goals has varied over time and in differing contexts, and as well in terms of the specificity of intent. In a sense, this is indicative of the diverse pulls and pressures behind U.S. aid programs generated by political, economic and humanitarian considerations. This complex process tended to produce a certain ambivalence in the decision to provide food aid to India in 1966-67, as we shall see.

Whereas in the preceding Republican administration stress was given to the domestic benefits of Public Law 480, under Johnson the program was considered in the wider context of foreign assistance. Testifying in defense of the continuation of the program in 1966, Secretary of State Dean Rusk stressed that U.S. food assistance was:

> a valuable foreign policy tool because it is directed toward positive changes—strengthening democratic governments, promoting political stability, encouraging economic stability, assisting material development.[29]

Incidentally, this is one of the most explicit statements of the role thus played by food aid in America's foreign policy.

Unlike its relatively concrete economic or humanitarian accomplishments, the successful role of food aid programs in different foreign policy areas cannot be instantly demonstrated without certain qualifications. Besides, policymakers were usually inhibited in discussing the details of possible use, if not manipulation, of the PL 480 Program for American self-interest. Presumably, any attempt to illustrate foreign policy successes in this context could produce the recipient nations' concern about the motives behind American food aid.[30] Nonetheless, in assessing the performance of the U.S. food aid program many of its critics do expect a positive demonstration of its successful role in foreign policy with more specific references.

Economic Distress and a Food Crisis

After 1964, India was again faced with a serious economic crisis. She was confronted with galloping inflation generated by a policy of deficit financing designed to support increased expenditures on both defense and industrial development. On top of this, India had to negotiate a rising demand for food as a result of population growth[31] and "increased incomes" of its population.[32] Between 1961 and 1964 certain planning pitfalls had already underlined the unsatisfactory state of the Indian economy. Notwithstanding the usual gestation period argument,[33] the fact remains that during the initial years of the ambitious Third Plan (1961-66), India's actual economic growth rate was below the projected target of over five percent a year. In part, the sluggish economic performance was caused by an increased defense outlay following the Chinese attack of October-November, 1962. A continuing threat from China had forced India to double its defense expenditure and to reorient the priorities of the Third Plan. But even before this changed situation, India's economic performance had become quite sluggish.

During the years preceding the critical food situation of 1965-67, India's economy had been under severe pressure.[34] Despite the relative increase in exports and utilization of aid, India's foreign exchange reserves had dwindled rather sharply because of the need for purchasing military hardware, machinery, raw materials and other developmental necessities. Also, industrial expansion and production had slowed down. In particular, shortages of certain imported raw materials and components put a constraint on industrial production. As a result of a strained balance of payments position, any possibility of reversing this worsening situation depended largely on the availability of more non-project aid.

While there had been some improvement in the availability of foreign aid, the servicing of past debts continued to impose a heavy burden. Debt servicing charges during 1964-65 rose to Rs 122 crores as compared with Rs 100 crores in the previous year (1963-64). In addition, an increasing proportion of the aid during the Third Plan (1961-62 to 1965-66) comprised loans relative to grants. For instance, there was a decline in grants from 36 percent of the external assistance in the first plan to three percent during the Third Plan period[35]—an additional burden to India's cumulative debt obligations.

It is conceivable this problem could have been rectified through sustained improvement in the balance of payments position;

however, the situation was hardly encouraging.[36] Though India's exports went up by more than 4 percent during the Third Plan period, there was still a decline in India's export earnings. In contrast, India's imports were very heavy in raw materials and machinery. In 1964-65, food imports were also substantially larger; the payments had to be made in foreign exchange. Despite slight changes from the previous year the 1965-66 balance of payments position continued to remain adverse.

The Indo-Pakistan war of 1965 further accentuated India's economic distress; it led to both greater expenditures and shortages. On top of this the Western nations suspended aid, expressing their displeasure over the hostilities. Its impact on the economy was that the growth of industrial production slackened due to the stoppage of imported raw materials and parts. The rupee devaluation of 1966 was the inevitable consequence of India's economic distress and the inflationary spiral in particular.[37] But the Indian rationale behind the devaluation was that it would bring massive volumes of external assistance to tide over the economic crisis. Furthermore, it would also increase exports and thereby reverse the adverse balance of trade.[38]

What was particularly disturbing, in spite of the stress on agricultural self-sufficiency under the Third Plan, was that India's production of food grains was not increasing fast enough. In fact, agricultural production remained below the annual target of 100 million tons even before the disastrous weather of 1965-67. Production of food grains rose from 54.92 million in 1950-51 to 82.02 million tons in 1960-61, and remained more or less stationary there the following year. In 1965-66 total food grains production had dropped to 72.26 million tons, the lowest since 1957-58.[39]

The worsening economic situation during the Third Plan was overshadowed by two consecutive years of catastrophic drought. Indeed, the disastrous weather of 1965-66 and 1966-67 underlined the magnitude of the critical food situation in India and thereby drew international attention to Indian needs. In many ways this critical food situation was indicative of certain emerging problems within both the agricultural sector and the broader Indian economy.

In general, Indian agricultural development has been marked by certain paradoxes. While economic planners have rightly set up higher production targets, allocated resources were too constricted to achieve the goals.[40] Nonetheless, by the end of the Second Plan period (1956-57 to 1960-61) certain perceptible changes were noticeable in the Indian agricultural sector. Irrigation and the use of fertilizers (instead of the mere expansion of unirrigated arable lands) expanded food grains production from 1960-71 onward. But again internal imbalance continued to beset the agriculture sector. While fertilizers and water were increasingly used to boost production, the use of the former was not adequate to compensate for the reduction of unirrigated arable lands. Besides, not all the farmers could afford to buy sizeable supplies of these imports.

In one important sense, however, this shift towards an expansion of output through water and fertilizers underlined the government's more direct role, which entailed the management of agricultural production through the manipulation of supply. By 1964-65, the agriculture infrastructure was overtaken by rising demand caused by the falling rate of food grain production. In many ways these "sustainable forces" hastened the onset of an "emergency"[41] over increasing farm prices, food grain imports, and increased fertilizer consumption. First, since the beginning of the Third Plan, prices of food grains had been rising quite rapidly. In a good harvest year such as 1964-65, the food grains price index rose to 149.1 (1950=100)—the highest since the beginning of the economic plans. This price rise was reinforced by the speculative tendencies of traders and the "greater holding power" of farmers in the context of growing demand—generated by continuing food shortages, rising income level, and population increase.[42] This in turn had an impact on the general price level of manufacturing products. Hence the problem was one of increasing the availability of food grains or reducing the level of consumption. Second, while production shortfalls were supplemented by growing low-cost imports, especially from the U.S., it was difficult to depend on imports because of economic and political constraints. If India was apprehensive of the U.S. administration's interference in its internal affairs, the latter was faced with growing Congressional opposition to the PL 480 program. Third, without a change in the demand for technological inputs for foodgrains production—considering the increasing use of the latest variety of crops or the expansion of irrigated acreage—the growth of fertilizer consumption could not be sustained. In short, because the introduction of technological inputs stagnated, the opportunities for maintaining higher rates of agricultural production—commensurate with growing demand—did not present themselves.

Paradoxically, the easy availability of PL 480 food grains had partially inhibited India's quest for self-sufficiency. It provided the rationale for cheap grain policies which had its impact on farmer's incentives if not initiatives. Though the Indian government underscored the need for remunerative prices and a supportive price policy, these were constrained by an insistence on cheap food grains.[43] But then this aspect should not be overstressed. In an all round inflationary situation, a continuous price rise in food grains would have further added to the economic distress of the people. For the sake of ensuring political stability, the government had to preempt unmanageable urban tension by at least providing cheap food grains. Anyway, it was the "exigencies" of the critical food situation that finally impelled the Indian government to accept, though reluctantly, the policy of remunerative prices.[44]

Slackening agricultural production in the midst of a worsening economic situation was compounded by two consecutive years (1965-66, and 1966-67) of drought. As noted earlier, in 1965-66 production of food grains slumped by 17 million tons; that meant a shortfall by about 19 percent from the previous year's bumper harvest. In 1966-67, food grain production was still below the 1964-65 level; the shortfall again by about 19 percent from the previous year. In 1966-67, food grain production was still below the 1964-65 level; the shortfall was by about 15 million tons. The overall index number of farm output in 1965-66 decreased to a level similar to that of 1959-60. According to the government report, the setback was reminiscent of the one in the 1920s.[45] Apart from the extreme distress, the crisis also caused a decline in demand for industrial goods in the wake of a fall in overall real incomes. The level of public and private investment became depressed. What was additionally disturbing was that food grain stocks had already been depleted due to the cumulative effect of the production shortfalls in the previous years. The drought and continuing anomalies within the economy led to a galloping price rise of food grains.[46] In sum, India was faced with an acute economic crisis that economists have euphemistically called "stagflation" (stagnation plus inflation).

From 1965 to 1967 adverse weather conditions prevailed over large parts of India except the South. For two consecutive years, there were serious crop failures in Bihar, U.P, M.P., Rajasthan and Gujarat. Crop damage was most extensive in Bihar and U.P. In Bihar, 30 million people were affected by the agricultural slump following the drought, and by early 1967, the Bihar state government invoked the provisions of the famine code in certain districts having a population of nearly 12.5 million people. A Ministry of Food and Agriculture report described the famine situation as a "natural calamity of a magnitude unknown in recent times." There is "hunger and distress in millions of homes," reported the Indian Prime Minister, Indira Gandhi, in a broadcast to the nation on November 16, 1966. She called for a "war on drought" and formed a Prime Minister's Drought Relief Fund. Thanks to the resolve of the Indian government and prompt international response, what could have been a major catastrophe was forestalled. A discussion of these gigantic relief operations has been told elsewhere.[47]

U.S. Perspectives, Issues, and Actors

In many ways, the severe scarcity conditions that developed in 1965-66 accentuated by continuing droughts, were the ominous signs of an impending disaster—the famine of 1966-67. While this crisis had disastrous implications in human and economic terms, it also had detrimental consequences for foreign assistance programs. It not only provided the "opportunity for external pressures" and thereby made India less willing to receive external assistance, but also generated pessimism among donors (especially the U.S.) which lessened their willingness to aid.[48] In fact, by mid-1965 there were perceptible signs of America's growing weariness with foreign aid. In the case of India, this was the result of a number of interacting developments.

First, there was a relative absence of spectacular economic results on India's part. Though some of the U.S. policymakers did appreciate the range of India's developmental constraints, they were unable to withstand the increasing Congressional opposition to foreign aid. Second, the Indian military debacle against China in 1962 signalled the end of euphoric expectations about India as an alternative mode of development to China's. Notwithstanding the supply of military and economic aid, the robust optimism of the early Kennedy years was being slowly replaced by a sober pragmatism about the extent to which the U.S. could help India's development.[49] The growing reticence soon developed into opposition against any public sector industrial project assistance, as in the case of India's Bokaro steel mill.[50]

Third, what had further accentuated American reluctance to provide aid was its impatience with India and Pakistan's inability to settle their disputes.[51] The Indo-Pakistan war of September, 1965, led to American exasperation with India, as well as the suspension of all foreign aid. Later, when economic assistance was resumed in the Spring of 1966, it continued only on a reduced scale and finally ended at the time of the Indo-Pak war of 1971. Despite the U.S. becoming disillusioned with Pakistani ties to Peking, it had not come closer to India.

President Johnson was partly responsible for the continued reduction of U.S. assistance to India. Unlike Kennedy, he did not have a special concern for India's problems or any commitment to the role of foreign assistance. His response to India's request for food supply during the grim situation of 1965-67 was marked by a considerable degree of reservation. When reports of the Indian droughts reached President Johnson around the Spring of 1965, his reactions were evidently predetermined by his overall approach to U.S. foreign aid for Indian economic development. He "did not rush the food aid impulsively and try to solve the immediate problem of ten or twenty million hungry people;" by doing this Johnson contended, the U.S. would have caused a "much more serious problem of starvation in later years." He chided India for its inefficient handling of agricultural problems and for diverting resources to the industrial sector.[52]

The following extract from his memoirs clearly brings out the basic frame of reference for response to the Indian food emergency of 1965-67:

> I understood and appreciated the reactions of my fellow Americans, including many Congressmen, who were tired of Uncle Sam carrying the main load almost everywhere by himself . . . I was irritated . . . I decided to reshape our policy to meet the changed situation in the world. We would insist that our friends make a concerted effort to help themselves before we rushed in with food, money and sympathy. As for other prosperous nations, we would insist on partnership and fair shares. The world needed a community chest effort, not just the charity of one rich uncle.[53]

Apart from its sarcastic tone, two basic postulates of Johnson's approach emerge from this statement. First, any kind of U.S. aid must be preceded by self-help efforts on the part of India. Second, the U.S. could not afford to unilaterally bear the burden of India's hunger. Instead, American contributions would constitute only part of the multilateral assistance package shared by other prosperous nations.

With these postulates President Johnson was bent upon enunciating more clearly to the Indians "what we expect or require of them."[54] Apart from any humanitarian dimension, Johnson found in the crisis an opportunity to reorient India's economic policies; he subsequently formulated the controversial "short tether" strategy in response to India's appeal for food. This entailed calculated delay in the authorization of the food transfers till a critical situation developed, and thus provided the U.S. with leverage to bring about necessary changes in Indian economic policies. However, it would be oversimplistic to view Washington's approach to India's food emergency exclusively in terms of the latter's long-run food requirements or economic development. According to knowledgeable commentators, Johnson was exasperated with the Indian stand on Vietnam and other foreign policy issues.[55] But food aid had also been considered as a tool in U.S. foreign policy in its support of friendly states, and to conduct a "Hearts and Minds" policy in many of the food deficient nations.

In Fall 1965, Johnson's initial move was to work out short run food assistance to India, in contrast to the long term provisions of the previous years. The action called for making an appreciation of India's requirements on a monthly basis. It appears from Johnson's memoirs that with food aid on a short term basis he had three purposes. First, Johnson wanted to bring about a change in India's then-current farm policy, which he felt if continued, would produce long-run adverse effects on the Indian people. Though the President did not want to bargain about food supply to hungry people, he was categorical enough to suggest that the month-by-month commitment was designed to build up pressure for agricultural policy change on the part of the Indian government and persuade other developed states to help. Second, he was trying to work toward a "balance" between quantum of food supply and population increase. Third, this action was conceived in apprehension of a possibility that the continuance of long-term commitments might jeopardize the basis of Congressional support to the program itself.

Johnson found in his Secretary of Agriculture, Orville Freeman, a confidant able to work out and implement the specifics of the evolving food strategy. Freeman not only appreciated Johnson's ideological position but also shared his belief especially in the context of India. Both of them agreed that a "strong dose of self-help" would enable the developing countries in general to reduce their "excessive dependence" on American food. But other circumstantial developments tended to underline their mutual support for action in this area. Evidently, faced with Senator Fulbright's persistent scathing criticism of his Vietnam policy and various objections about annual foreign assistance bills, Johnson was determined to lessen the Senator's control over matters of foreign policy in general.[56] Underscoring his urgency was that over the years, agricultural aid programs had been increasing rapidly, thus constituting a major segment of U.S. economic assistance—a subject under the jurisdiction of the Senate Foreign Relations Committee (chaired by Fulbright). Johnson was bent upon shifting the agricultural elements of foreign aid elsewhere. It was in this context that he looked for someone outside the State and AID, who could manage and coordinate food aid with vigor, and in accordance with the ground rules set up by the President.[57] Freeman fulfilled Johnson's requirements both because he knew domestic agricultural politics and due to his additional interest in the overseas operations of food assistance, especially in developing countries. Freeman could provide the necessary expertise in a domain hitherto monopolized by the State Department and AID.

Freeman, like any other aggressive bureaucrat in Washington, must have found the "lure" of a piece of foreign policy "action" to be powerful, especially when he had the backing of the President.[58] Thus, in no time he energetically took up the theme of "self-help" as the basis of food aid to the developing countries. While he had to transmit the message to the food recipients, an added imperative for him was to overcome the hurdles of prevailing State and AID views about the relevance of food aid in U.S. policy towards developing countries. Freeman was particularly interested in agro-economics of the developing world. His motive was evidently commercial *cum* developmental. The logic of this approach was that to the extent that PL 480 shipments injected concessional food and fiber into the developing countries and accelerated their economic growth, they also built future foreign markets for U.S. agricultural commerce in hard currency. Some USDA studies cite Japan, Taiwan, Korea and Spain as successful demonstrations of this thesis.[59]

In contrast to the USDA's perspective on the PL 480 program, the State Department had been primarily concerned with narrow diplomatic considerations, i.e. maintenance or promotion of friendly relations with the concerned recipient nations. With reference to India's food emergency, Undersecretary of State Eugene V. Rostow had pointed out: "The State Department is concerned with continued good relations with India. Food is an important element in this context as is the welfare of the hungry people at the present moment.[60] As for AID, in spite of its comprehensive developmental perspective, it was particularly concerned with industrial and technical projects. Hence, it had not been in a position to give special consideration to an agro-economic strategy for developing countries. It viewed PL 480 agricultural shipments as a necessary supplement to more urgent industrial development.

In view of their divergent goals for the PL 480 program, it was perhaps inevitable that the USDA under Freeman—with the full support and guidance of the President—would take a more active interest in India's self-help efforts in exchange for emergency food aid. Though Johnson's and Freeman's identical views on the PL 480 program and India brought the USDA to center stage, there were other factors that reinforced this process. This is not to say that the emergence of the USDA as a policy-involved department was unconstrained. Initially, through amendments to PL 480 in 1964 and 1965, Freeman was empowered to deal with the PL 480 counterpart fund. Later, by virtue of an interagency agreement (1966) his overall functions increased in regard to the technical aid programs for overseas agriculture.

These incremental changes found Freeman caught up in Washington's bureaucratic battle. In fact, it was President Johnson's intervention that saved the USDA from losing its overseas food aid programs. In 1965 when some members of the Inter-agency Staff Committee sought the transfer of responsibility for the PL 480 program to AID's "War on Hunger" office, Johnson promptly vetoed the move. Instead, the President himself became the coordinator of the PL 480 program. Further, he insisted on his personal clearance of any food aid agreements entered with the principal recipient nations (India included).[61] For reasons mentioned earlier, Johnson was not inclined to provide additional power and responsibility to the State Department or AID.

In 1966 a complete restructuring of the Food for Peace program formalized the Johnson-Freeman approach to domestic and overseas U.S. agricultural operations. It was evident since 1964 that America's great farm surpluses of the 1950s and early 1960s had come down to a normal level. The existing food aid program could not be maintained without buying non-surplus farm products from the open market which would have made it part of the foreign aid operation. In any event, diminished holdings of farm products also implied reduced economic compulsion to get rid of the surpluses. But in the light of the existing world food shortages along with reduced U.S. surpluses, the idea of "budgeting of food production" emerged.[62] This was designed to avoid serious overproduction and a resultant fall in world prices, which tend to undermine agricultural incentive in developing countries.

On February 10, 1966, some basic changes were introduced in President Johnson's message to the Congress. While structured around the original PL 480 legislation, Johnson's newly christened Food for Freedom program stressed self-help efforts on the part of the recipient nations as a condition for American food aid.[63] The program also envisaged the development and expansion of the export markets for America's agricultural commodities and thereby eliminated the surplus requirements for food aid. Like the original act, it was also designed to promote U.S. foreign policy in "other ways." What is more, the amended PL 480 program stipulated greater (though not exclusive) responsibility for the USDA with a view to promoting these goals. Though it implied USDA's increased external role, the program also stressed the need for closer cooperation between the State Department, AID, and the USDA in managing these programs.

If the amended act involved the USDA in the economic problems of developing countries, it also increased Presidential control over the program. The President was given the power to revoke any food aid agreement if he found the self-help agricultural performance of the relevant recipients unsatisfactory. Besides, through continuous adjustments and reallocations of functions among the agencies and bureaucrats, President Johnson was able to reinforce his command over the operations of the program. He had reservations even about the loyalty of his trusted aides; to him loyalty was not just "to office," but wholly personal, i.e., "first and foremost to Lyndon Johnson."[64] Even then, as noted earlier, Johnson appreciated Freeman's capabilities and his approach to the agricultural problem at home and abroad.

Johnson's program was enthusiastically supported by both Democratic and Republican members of Congress. They endorsed the view that developing countries should not expect continued food assistance. But the problem was viewed from three different sides expressed within the Congress, though largely accommodated within Johnson's program.[65] One view perceived food aid as an instrument for diffusing possible violence in the developing areas, and for preempting communist influence. Another line of thinking stressed the need for close supervision of the aid recipient countries' agricultural development as a precondition for food assistance. The third view favored an early end to food aid and wanted the existing operations to be entrusted to some world agencies. Besides, it perceived the Food for Peace Program as foreign aid in view of the end of U.S. agricultural surpluses.[66] Though the Food for Peace Program included these contrasting views, it did not fully reconcile them and thereby left room for latent conflicts in its specific operations.

In the context of the perspectives above, the U.S. responded to India's request for emergency food aid and, in many ways, predetermined the specific food aid actions vis-a-vis India. But underlining the complexity of the problem, was the Johnson administration's sensitivity about India's stand on global issues like Vietnam. U.S. food assistance to India started amidst raging controversies regarding Johnson's policies and personal predispositions. There were two different phases in the American decision to render emergency food aid to India. The first was marked by prompt, all-out response to the Indian appeal. The second phase, a controversial one, saw a policy of deliberate delay of the much needed food and thus began the famous/infamous "short tether." It is inconceivable that Johnson or Freeman really expected India's miraculous development into an attractive market for U.S. commercial sales of farm products. It would certainly have been an optimistic projection. Notwithstanding the immediate humanitarian consideration, "self-help" provisions in Johnson's India program were presumably "more an excuse" to reduce food supply and thereby end India's dependence on U.S. shipments.[67]

Stages of Response

USDA Secretary Freeman's visit to India in 1964 marked growing American concern about the lack of adequate progress on the Indian agricultural front.[68] Alternatively, it also presaged the beginning of a more direct USDA role regarding the resolution of bottlenecks in Indian agricultural development. It appears from Freeman's account that he was particularly distressed by India's "spotty" and "weak" agricultural advancement.[69] He particularly felt that in providing food and technical assistance to India, the U.S. had not insisted on minimal agricultural performance on India's part. Freeman's prescription was that a "new, bold" self-reliant approach by the Indian government, the U.S., and other donors was needed to shake Indian agriculture from its stagnant state. Apparently persuaded by Freeman's advice, the Indian government later requested the visit of a team of USDA experts to work out the details of an agricultural price-support mechanism. In January 1965, the Food Corporation of India (FCI) was established with U.S. technical assistance.[70]

While this was an example of Freeman's persuasiveness and ability to take the initiative, circumstances were not yet propitious for his emergence as an overseer of India's agricultural programs;

the USDA was still one year away from playing that role. Fundamental policy changes are seldom generated by normal conditions, and despite some difficulties, India's food situation in 1964 was still normal; this very normalcy precluded immediate Indian acquiescence to the entire range of Freeman's proposals. However, he let his offer stand and agreed to cooperate whenever the Indian government was ready. Meanwhile the idea of agricultural self-reliance was slowly gaining ground both within the Indian government and among the economists.[71] In particular, it was C. Subramaniam who (after his appointment as the Indian Food Minister) spearheaded the move towards a new agricultural policy on Freeman's lines, endorsed by U.S. Ambassador Bowles and AID.[72] Through an incentive price-level, better irrigation and credit facilities, use of high-yielding variety of seeds, application of fertilizers, etc., Subramaniam sought to modernize Indian agriculture. The result was that in FY 1964-65 India had record foodgrains production. But in light of the previous year's shortfalls and the drought of the following months, this was not to be enough to meet India's total requirements.

Washington's suspension of economic and military assistance following the 1965 war clearly underlined India's economic difficulty and the imperative of a self-reliant economic strategy. More than that, it was the grim food situation (accentuated by a severe drought) that impelled the Indian government to opt for the priority development of agriculture. Subramaniam was advised to negotiate with Freeman for an adequate food grains supply and to accept his earlier proposals on technical assistance. In the meantime, as noted earlier, President Johnson had already decided to do away with the long-run basis of U.S. food assistance to India. Henceforward, U.S. food assistance would be subject to India's economic reforms as perceived desirable by the U.S. administration.

In November 1965, Subramaniam and Freeman met in Rome and were able to work out an agricultural deal for India in light of the ground rules laid down by Johnson. Subramaniam clearly appreciated Washington's insistence on agricultural self-help efforts on India's part. He realized that India could not possibly achieve its long-run developmental goals with dependence on continued external food aid.[73] Thus with a "package of promises and penalties" he returned to New Delhi.[74] While Freeman promised further food supplies, Subramaniam had to give an understanding that India would adhere to the concept of self-help efforts in its agricultural development.[75] The logical culmination of the Rome agreement was the Indian government's announcement of a new farm policy on December 7, 1965. This brought about a sharp change in Indian developmental strategy under the fourth Five Year Plan. The highest priority for agriculture became the core of Indian planning.[76] However, the very circumstance of this change in priorities in India's developmental policy disturbed some policymakers in New Delhi.[77] Orville Freeman, who had made the Indian government accept the new American policy on food aid, had demonstrated his ability to get things done. In that process he gained Johnson's confidence, and enhanced his own power within the administration. Having seen the "first important result" of his new policy, President Johnson decided to speed up the food shipments to India. It appears from the White House press release of December 9, Freeman met Johnson and discussed India's critical food situation and its needs. To meet the immediate food crisis, Johnson authorized prompt extension of the existing PL 480 agreement with India to cover an additional 1.5 million tons of food grains. This quantity was equal to current allocations on a three month basis.[78] On the same day, Secretary of State Dean Rusk revealed in a news conference that the U.S. had also agreed to give India a substantial loan for fertilizer in order to step up its agricultural production. He declared that the U.S. would strongly urge all countries who had surplus food and shipping facilities, or had fertilizers, to make those resources available to meet the Indian food crisis.[79]

Two days later, President Johnson advised Freeman to get the wheat moving. "Consider yourself the expediter," Johnson said, "and throw your weight around as much as necessary to get the job done."[80] Armed with Johnson's instructions, the USDA Secretary set out to manage the operation.

Meanwhile the Indian Prime Minister, Lal Bahadur Shastri, died on January 10, 1966 shortly after signing the Tashkent Declaration with Pakistan President Ayub Khan. His successor, Mrs. Indira Gandhi, was confronted with a worsening food situation and a general economic slump. To meet the food crisis, she approached various countries (including the U.S.) for emergency food aid.[81] Mrs. Gandhi knew that unlike Kennedy, Johnson clearly made any form of aid subject to performance. Her attention was increasingly drawn to the conditions under which the U.S. aid was to be provided.

On February 10, 1966, as noted above, President Johnson sent a special message to the Congress, requesting it to pass his "Food for Freedom" program with emphasis on self-help efforts. The law permitted him to act on Executive authority, but he wanted

Congressional support behind his action.[82] Later in a more specific reference to India, Rusk came out with foreign policy justification of this program. He pleaded that the Food for Peace program strengthened the democratic government in India. Besides, despite specific areas of foreign policy disagreement with India, the U.S. appreciated India's adherence to democratic principles, her struggle to achieve socio-economic development, and her stand against "external communist aggression." In short, India was a deserving candidate for food aid.

After having chided India for its inefficient handling of agricultural problems, and successfully managing to bring about a change in India's developmental strategy, President Johnson sought to establish rapport with Mrs. Gandhi. If external manifestations were any indicators, her visit to the U.S. was a success. Out of his twenty-one meetings with heads of government, Johnson said later, it was the "most satisfying . . . No meeting had accomplished so much for so many."[83] President Johnson, in his meeting (March 27-April 1) promised her all possible help to "alleviate" India's food emergency.[84] Less than a few hours after Mrs. Gandhi's departure from Washington, Johnson, in a special message to Congress, asked for prompt Congressional endorsement for this "emergency action". He said: "India is a good and deserving friend. Let it never be said that bread should be so dear, and flesh and blood so cheap that we turned in indifference from her bitter need." Johnson requested the approval of an emergency shipment of 3.5 million tons of food grains in addition to 6.5 million tons provided by the U.S. for the fiscal year ending June 30, 1966, in continuation of past arrangements.[85] Later, through personal lobbying efforts, Johnson was able to persuade Congress to endorse his emergency food request in a joint resolution.[86]

In India, the government was giving "the principles underlying" new U.S. food aid plans more concrete shape. It decided to respond favorably to the World Bank's Bell Mission report.[87] In dire need of both food and foreign aid, India did not seem to have any option but to change its economic policies with a view to satisfying U.S. assistance requirements. In expectation of an increase in the flow of foreign assistance, the Indian government relaxed import and license controls in a number of industries. It also agreed to let an American oil company set up a fertilizer plant, and liberalized the internal food zone system. More significantly, the Indian government finally announced on June 5, 1966, the devaluation of the rupee. Though the U.S. in turn, reciprocated by announcing on June 15 the resumption of economic assistance (suspended earlier), the promise of massive U.S. aid did not materialize. It became quite clear to New Delhi that the State Department was not in a position to make any advance commitments of aid beyond the annual budget. Furthermore, the monsoon had failed again, making problems much worse for India. Above all, Johnson's "short tether" approach was to go into operation within a month. India seemed to have been affected by both natural disaster as well as America's actions. This led to the second stage of the U.S. response to India's food emergency.

Operation "Ship-to-Mouth"

Speaking on April 9, 1966, Mrs. Gandhi stated,

All over the world, there is considerable concern at our food shortage . . . The speedy passage which the new food bill had in the United States Congress is proof of this new awareness . . . But let me remind you that friends will help only if they are convinced that we are doing our best to help ourselves . . . We must become self-reliant. Aid and help should be a temporary phase.[88]

While this was indicative of India's awareness of the conditions imposed by the U.S. administration, it also indicated a sense of urgency. But presumably, Johnson missed the message or did not find it convincing; within three months he would be dragging his feet in working out any food shipment schedule convenient to the Indian distribution system. Initially the U.S. did respond favorably (as indicated by Mrs. Gandhi's statement) to India's new agricultural self-reliance policy; Johnson had promptly sent the first installment of the food shipments to India. But by Fall of 1966, Johnson's conditions for emergency food aid seemed to have become more exacting, just as the Indian government was faced with an impending famine. Failure to meet these conditions implied the halting of food shipments to India. The episode, called the "short-tether" approach or operation "ship-to-mouth," was the most controversial feature of America's emergency food aid to India in 1965-67. This approach was marked by delayed decisions, and once decisions were made, only short-run approval was given, and on a monthly instead of an annual or multiyear basis, (which had been the usual practice under previous PL 480 agreements).[89]

It is unclear what induced Johnson to carry out a policy of halting food supplies to India at this particular moment. It appears that apart from his insistence on India's economic reforms and resultant performance, Johnson also wanted India's silence if not acquiescence on some major world issues, especially Vietnam. An additional consideration was to fill in Congress with each of his policy decisions, to demonstrate to Congress that the Administration (in providing emergency food aid to India) was not merely guided by heart, but also by hard-headed considerations of India's agricultural development and American interests.

In analyzing Johnson's "short tether" approach some of its characteristics are worth noting. Though it constituted a new stage in American response to India's emergency appeals, it did not denote a sharp break with Johnson's overall approach. In many ways the (short tether) strategy was the logical culmination of a policy process accentuated by extra-agricultural issues.

Significantly, even in the early phase of the U.S. response, there was a perceptibly lukewarm attitude in the Johnson administration's follow-up food shipments to India. This has been clearly attested to by Chester Bowles, who was at that time the U.S. ambassador in New Delhi. It was quite evident, says Bowles, that despite Johnson's eloquent appeal to the Congress on March 20, for an urgent approval of food assistance to India, "There was little understanding at the higher levels in the White House or State Department of India's predicament.[90] As for the USDA, it seemed to have been interested in generating some instant (though not always appropriate) agricultural solutions for India.[91] President Johnson on his part, instead of expediting the food grains shipments to India, insisted to the bureaucracy: "don't be easy on them; let them get cracking and show they seriously mean business in boosting food production."[92] This was obviously a dress rehearsal for Johnson's full scale short tether operation.

Certain elements had bearing on the evolving process of the short tether policy. Normally, Public Law 480 empowered the President to act on food assistance through Executive authority. In 1965, Johnson had also assumed complete control over the food aid programs in regard to the major food recipient countries. But paradoxically, after having consolidated his direct control over the entire process of food aid programs—from authorizations to clearance of each shipment—President Johnson wanted Congress with him. "I wanted . . . it to approve," he said, "the principles of the new policy, and to accept responsibility in its execution."[93] Evidently, this idea of voluntarily sharing responsibility was in response to growing Congressional criticism over food aid. Furthermore, in his testimony on the new Food for Freedom program, Freeman, quite in consonance with Johnson's idea of short-term food aid, contended that this could save millions from famine by:

> stimulating, encouraging, and if necessary, insisting on effective self-help measures. This may mean agreements for periodic reviews of progress made toward self-reliance.[94]

Contrary to Johnson's urging, Freeman did not insist on a more exacting month by month basic food agreement.

The Gandhi-Kosygin joint communique on Vietnam issued in Moscow on July 13, 1966, seemed to have served as the necessary condition for the real beginning of Johnson's Operation "Ship-to-Mouth." Apart from calling upon the U.S. to end the bombing in Vietnam, it made some vague reference to the unlawful activities of the "imperialist powers." This communique evidently destroyed whatever goodwill and sympathy Johnson had for India. Fall, 1966, was another grim drought period for India and the Indian government requested an additional two million tons of food grains. In response President Johnson further delayed the shipments of food, thus starting his short tether operation in full swing. There was widespread suspicion about the motivation behind his deferred action; *The New York Times* wrote that "the hold-up may be partially due to President Johnson's displeasure with Prime Minister Gandhi's recent call for a halt in the bombing of North Vietnam."[95]

As anticipated, Johnson's reaction was particularly violent. Cables from Washington to the U.S. mission in New Delhi came out with sharp comments like "those ungrateful Indians"; the Johnson administration's logic seems to have been that the Indians—being poor—should "refrain from criticizing U.S. policy" or "accept the consequences."[96]

Johnson's rationale was that he anticipated difficulties with Congress in 1967, partly because he believed that the Indian government had neither sufficiently searched for alternative sources of external food aid nor introduced better distribution systems within the country.[97] Above all, food grain aid was having its domestic repercussions; it was driving up prices of wheat and cereal products and thereby creating "political difficulties."[98]

Whatever the saliency of these domestic considerations was, it is evident that Johnson's initial intention was to use food aid as a bait in times of India's acute economic distress, to induce the Indians to bring about agricultural reforms. Later, it was also apparently used to impel the Indian government to at least remain silent regarding the U.S.' role in Vietnam. In holding up the grain shipments from August to December 1966, on his personal decision, Johnson explained that this was also designed to compel other food surplus nations to bear the burden of food aid along with the U.S.[99] In the teeth of heavy official and unofficial opposition, Johnson stuck to this policy; he did what he believed was right.

In a conversation with Freeman on November 10, Johnson told him that he was not going to authorize PL 480 food aid without Congressional concurrence because the Presidential "giveaway days" were over. Around the same time Congress passed the Food for Peace Program and it was signed into law on November 12. But this was not enough for Johnson; he advised Freeman to send several USDA experts to India for a general stock-taking of the food situation. This was initially resisted by Ambassador Bowles, who was later told that this was designed to convince Congress that the administration was pragmatic in its food aid policy towards India. Perhaps Johnson felt he could not rely on the U.S. Ambassador's judgment on India's food requirements because of the latter's apparent sympathy for India. In any event, while the President did not question the U.S Embassy estimate, he considered it necessary to send two fact-finding teams; one composed of agricultural experts and the other made up of four members of Congress.[100] The Congressional delegation later suggested that the U.S. provide 1.8 million tons on an interim basis for February-April 1967. They agreed on Congressional action to back up supplementary food shipments.[101]

Even then, President Johnson was not willing to approve more than half the recommended amount, still keeping short tether. He decided to act on the remaining amount in light of Congressional action and what other nations were likely to do.

Johnson had told Freeman about his intended actions, though it is not clear whether the USDA Secretary had any voice in these decisions. Freeman was involved more as a transmitter of news of the progress of Indian self-help efforts. Freeman, because of his July (1966) trip to India, was convinced of the need of a "well-structured emergency program for the Indian agriculture."[102] He had also outlined in his discussion with President Johnson (as well as AID Administrator David Bell) what India "should do" or what the U.S. "could do" to prevent a serious food crisis in India. In light of this imperative, Freeman emphasized certain self-help measures that the U.S. should impose on India. These were later embodied in the Food for Freedom Act. The aforementioned USDA team of agricultural experts had also produced an assessment of the overall Indian food situation and their food grains distribution system. In its report to the President it clearly mentioned that perhaps the U.S. was underestimating India's food requirements.[103] But this also had no softening effect on Johnson.

Fortunately for India, it was able to get shipments of 185,000 tons of Canadian wheat and an emergency supply of 150,000 tons from Australia. The Soviet Union also committed 200,000 tons of food grains on special terms. But Johnson wanted more nations to cooperate and share the burden of food aid to India.[104] He requested that the World Bank take some initiative to bring in others. On January 15, 1967 Johnson sent Eugene V. Rostow (Undersecretary of State for Political Affairs) on a global mission to generate support for India's food requirements. This effort entailed the import of ten million tons of food grains to India in 1967, costing about $725 million. Through the efforts of Rostow and other members of the World Bank's Aid-India consortium, assistance worth about $200 million was generated for India. It anticipated the inclusion of the principle of food assistance sharing in the Food Aid Convention of the International Wheat Agreement.

Finally, by February 1967, Johnson had decided to permit a more comprehensive food shipment program for India. In his message to Congress on February 2, he insisted that each nation share India's emergency food need as an international responsibility.[105] He made an immediate allocation of two million tons of food grains to tide India over while Congress acted. Besides, he recommended an additional amount of food grains—not exceeding three million tons provided it was adequately matched by other nations. Congress responded compassionately to Johnson's proposals; on March 20, in a joint resolution the two houses approved emergency food assistance to India.[106]

On April 1, Johnson signed the joint Congressional resolution. The Indo-U.S. Food Agreement of February 20, 1967 was the first of its kind signed under the new Food for Peace program,(i.e. the amended PL 480 program). This was supplemented by three more agreements before the end of 1967, amounting to six million tons of U.S. food grains for India. Throughout the year there was a relatively steady flow of food supplies. By Fall, 1967, the food crisis in India seemed to have subsided, and due to excellent weather and improvement in agriculture techniques, India was able to reap a record harvest the following year.

Paradoxically, despite India's dependence on U.S. food imports during the drought years, there was a yawning gulf between India and the U.S. Faced with short tether treatment and pressures for economic policy changes, India sometimes went out of its way to demonstrate its independence from the U.S. The Indian government's foreign policy rhetoric about Vietnam, and Mrs. Gandhi's birthday greetings to Ho Chi Minh were symbols of India's resistance. These were also used by the government to refute its domestic critics' charges that it had allowed India to be pushed around by the U.S. Despite Johnson's reactions of strong displeasure, he did authorize, though reluctantly, the supply of six million tons of grains plus some fertilizer to India. Nonetheless, the all-round effects of Johnson's short tether approach and the persistent drive to reorient Indian development policy had traumatic effects on Indian policymakers. It also discredited many of the political technocrats, like Asoka Mehta and C. Subramaniam, who were identified with American economic policy towards India around 1965-67.

It is ironic that while the Indian government was in the midst of an acute economic predicament it was caught up in cross-pressures from both the Johnson administration and the domestic "left." One of the consequences of this situation was that the government was impelled to compensate at every step towards new agricultural or industrial reforms—as desired by the U.S.—with a corresponding posture of symbolic defiance on such international issues as Vietnam and Israel. The entire strategy was designed to dispel domestic misapprehension about the Indian government's "soft" attitude towards Washington.[107] To demonstrate its independence further, the Indian government also persuaded the U.S. to withdraw Johnson's proposed (PL 480 Rupee funded) Indo-U.S. Education Foundation.

For Lyndon Johnson and many in the U.S. administration, India's symbolic external postures produced exasperation with India's "ungratefulness." What had further exacerbated Indo-U.S. relations was President Johnson's insensitivity to the difficulties faced by the Indian government and his relative unconcern with its independence of judgement or policy priorities. He was considerably less enamored with India than his predecessor, John F. Kennedy.[108] As a consequence of his impatience with India's economic policies, his displeasure with its stand on Vietnam, and the modest contributions of other food donors, Johnson practiced a policy of food aid squeeze followed by last minute release. Instead of deriving any extra mileage out of this strategy, Johnson merely accentuated what was already a worsening economic and political relationship between India and the U.S. There can be legitimate differences as to the relative saliency of domestic and external factors in reorienting Indian developmental strategy in the mid-1960s, but it is undeniable that "as a result of pressure for agricultural and exchange-rate reform," says one recent study, "the United States reaped a harvest of Indian wrath which endured for more than a decade."[109]

Our study clearly demonstrates that the volume of an aid program by itself does not necessarily indicate the nature of the political relationship between donor and recipient. While it is easy to measure an economic relationship in terms of the rate and volume of aid and trade flow, it is altogether a different proposition to assess political payoffs by merely using the indices of resource transfers. There is a problem of conversion between two different levels—economic and political. In the 1965-67 food crisis in India, the U.S. provided about 14 million tons of food grains which was enough to feed about 90 million people. But contrary to normal expectations this aid effort did not produce better relations between India and the U.S. Instead, it generated tension between the two because of the attached conditions and "eleventh hour generosity" of the donor, coupled with the two states' divergence on certain foreign policy issues. In short, and data alone is a weak indicator of political impact, unless it is linked to the wide political context, it gives a lopsided picture of reality.

Johnson's emergency food aid to India also had certain anomalies. Because the PL 480 program had ceased to be a U.S. agricultural disposal operation and imposed conditions on the recipients, it became a subject of foreign policy—hence within the purview of Congressional foreign relations committees. But surprisingly, the program continued to remain insulated from Congressional supervision, illustrating how an insulated program can sometimes become an operational instrument in support of narrowly conceived, short-run presidential policy preferences.

Paradoxically, though the law permitted him to act on executive authority in regard to emergency food aid, Johnson wanted to take Congress with him—in anticipation of difficulties in other areas such as foreign aid and Vietnam. Congress did not give him much difficulty with regard to emergency food assistance. It debated and discussed but approved most of his proposals. In fact, at times when Congress had suggested the provision of a certain level of food supply, he deliberately withheld part of it.

Needless to say, Johnson was in complete command of the entire process, from setting up guidelines to the final release of food shipments. This disrupted normal channels of operation of the program. Sometimes neither the Indian government nor Freeman nor Rusk knew what the President was next going to do about the food shipments. This fact constrained officials from working out a supply schedule—due to uncertainty of Presidential clearance—with their Indian counterparts. He held out alone "against the urgings of all his advisors," regarding the prompt clearance of food shipments, which raises the fundamental question whether a determined President can be kept "captive" by his advisers. Johnson did not believe so, and he proudly makes that point in his memoirs.[110]

Of the relevant organizational actors, the USDA Secretary was most closely associated with the formulation of the self-help measures and other economic reforms by the recipients. As a principle of foreign aid the self-help efforts had the support of AID and the State Department, though they were not willing to see this as the USDA's instrument for putting pressure on recipient nations' agricultural development. In a certain sense, the self-help principles were more frequently used as rhetoric rather than as a specific criteria of aid determined by more concrete indicators of developmental progress. There was neither basic coordination among these agencies nor an adequate monitoring mechanism to review the implementation of self-help measures. Hence, it is correct to say that the short tether operation remained unrelated to the developmental performance or the complexity of problems of a recipient developing country like India. Thus, even when the Indian government had committed itself to self-help measures and introduced economic reforms, Johnson's "hold-up" continued. The State Department's role was to explain Johnson's erratic behavior to the Indian government in terms of its alleged failure to carry out the reforms.

Despite immense difficulties the efforts of some of the middle and lower echelon officials of the White House, the State Department, the U.S. Embassy in Delhi, and the USDA, did ensure that the supply of emergency food to India was maintained. But by then it was too late, and severe damage had been done in Indo-U.S. relations. The food aid episode produced misapprehension about American intentions regarding India, and was to determine to a great extent Indian foreign policy expectations towards Washington in subsequent years.

Notes

1. U.S. Department of State, *The Scope and Distribution of United States Military and Economic Assistance Programs*, Report to the President of the United States from the Committee to Strengthen the Security of the Free World (Washington, D.C.: U.S. Government Printing Office, March 2, 1963), p. 8 (Clay Report)

2. This was created by the Foreign Assistance Act of 1961 to bring economic aid under a unified administration. It was designed to combine the assistance programs previously managed by International Cooperation Administration (represented in India by Technical Cooperation Mission), the lending activities of the Development Loan Fund, and some aspects of the PL 480 program in regard to other countries.

3. Initially, this grant was extended under the China Area Aid Act of 1948. For a background of the emergency food aid to India, see *Department of State Bulletin*, Vol. 24, February 26, 1951, pp. 37-39; March 12, 1951, p. 424; April 9, 1951, pp. 591-92; April 23, 1951, p. 674.

4. Commenting on this episode, the then U.S. Ambassador to New Delhi, Chester Bowles, stated that "instead of generous, wholehearted cooperation," Indians became "the target of attacks and criticism, demands that if they wanted help from us, they must throw their support behind us in the Cold War." *Ambassador's Report* (New York: Harper, 1954), pp. 230-31.

5. For details about the program, see the *Annual Report on Activities Carried out under Public Law 480*, as amended, during the Period, January 1 through December 31, 1964, House Document No. 13/89/l (Washington, D.C.: Government Printing Office, March 24, 1965.) Hereafter, *Annual Report, 1964.*)

6. About 5 per cent of the counterpart fund in accordance with the Cooley Amendment provision has to be earmarked for development within the private sector.

7. This title was included in 1961.

8. *Annual Report*, 1964. Presumably, an added rationale on the part of the Administration was to circumvent Congressional opposition to foreign aid appropriations on an increasing scale.

9. For a balanced discussion on this, see Peter A. Toma, *The Politics of Food for Peace* (Tucson: The University of Arizona Press, 1967), pp. 39-42. For a more unqualified statement see, William and Paul Paddock, *Famine— 1975; America's Decision: Who Will Survive?* (Boston: Little Brown, 1967), pp. 169-75.

10. James Warner Bjorkman, "*A. Public Law 480 and the Politics of Self-help and Short-tether: Indo-American Relations, 1965-68,*" in Commission on the Organization of the Government for the Conduct of Foreign Policy, Vol. 7, Appendix V, Case Studies: II. Economic Policy (Washington, D.C.: U.S. Government Printing Press, June 1975), p. 193.

11. Unless mentioned, the following outline is largely based on Bjorkman, pp. 194-97; and also Toma, pp. 45-53.

12. In spite of periodic denials, "all foreign aid carries strings and every foreign aid relationship involves bargaining, however genteel, between the aiding and receiving parties." John P. Lewis, *Quiet Crisis in India: Economic Development and American Policy* (Bombay: Asia Publishing House 1963), p. 250.

13. By Executive Order 10900 as amended. (see *Program Assistance; Public Law 480, General,* AID Manual September 30, 1963, pp. 1-2)

14. Even in regard to foreign aid as a whole, while the executive branch has favored the program, Congress has sought to put restrictions on it. In part, this has resulted from the administration's greater contact with foreign affairs—unlike Congress, and which impels it to advocate a foreign aid program as a necessary component of foreign policy. See David A. Baldwin, *Foreign Aid and American Foreign Policy: A Documentary Study* (New York: Praeger), 1966, p. 16.

15. Statement by George McGovern (formerly Director, Food for Peace) August 19, 1964, U.S. Congress, Senate, 88th Congress, 2nd Session, *Congressional Record,* Vol. 110, pp. 20421-20422.

16. *Annual Report,* 1967, Appendix table 2.

17. For details, see *Economic Survey of India 1965-66* (New Delhi: Ministry of Finance, Government of India, 1966), Table 1:4.

18. For a cogent statement, see former ambassador to India, J. K. Galbraith's testimony on the Foreign Assistance Act of 1962. *Foreign Assistance Act of 1962.* Hearings before the House Committee on Foreign Affairs, 87th Congress, 2nd Session, March 29, 1962 (Washington, D.C.: Government Printing Press, 1962), pp. 583-584.

19. J. S. Mann, "The Impact of PL 480 Imports," *Journal of Farm Economics,* 49 (February 1967), pp. 131-46. But however, the correlation between PL 480 imports and lower levels of food production is "strong but circumstantial." Bad weather and paucity of agricultural inputs might have been more "important contributing factors." (See, Paul Streeton and Roger Hill, "Aid to India," in Paul Streeton and Michael Lipton, ed., *The Crisis of Indian Planning,* (London: Oxford University Press, 1968), p. 345.

20. Orville L. Freeman, *World Without Hunger* (New York: Frederick A. Praeger, 1968), p. 153. The author was U.S. Secretary of Agriculture in the Johnson administration.

21. P. J. Eldridge, *The Politics of Foreign Aid in India* (Delhi: Vikas Publications, 1969), pp. 116-17. See also Bowles, p. 534.

22. Freeman, p. 29.

23. The Food for Peace Program was earlier initiated by a small group of Senators headed by Hubert Humphrey. Their idea was to transform the surplus food disposal program into an instrument for the promotion of peace. While Humphrey's proposal regarding long term supply provision for the PL 480 program was partially approved, his idea about changing the title of the program to "Food for Peace" was not passed by the House. It was under Kennedy that by an executive order on January 24, 1961 the White House Office

of Food for Peace was established in conformity with the original Humphrey proposals.

24. Even earlier, in the late fifties, an MIT study submitted to the Special Senate Committee to study foreign aid, advocated the strategy of economic development aid in the developing countries for the advancement of the U.S.' national interests (Reprinted in *The Foreign Aid Program* pursuant to Senate Resolution 35 and 141, 85th Congress, Washington, D.C.: Government Printing Office, July 1957).

25. President Kennedy's speech before the Economic Club of New York, December 14, 1962. See *Public Papers of the Presidents of the United States: John F. Kennedy*, January 1, to December 31, 1962. (Washington: United States Government), pp. 875-887.

26. "America's Efforts Toward World Order," *Department of State Bulletin* (August 31, 1964), pp. 298-301.

27. Charles Wolf, Jr. *Foreign Aid: Theory and Practice in Southern Asia*, (New Jersey: Princeton University Press, 1960) pp. 264-65. There is a view that foreign aid "will not" enable the U.S. "to purchase allies and friends" Chester Bowles, *New Dimension of Peace* (New York: Harper Bros., 1955), p. 295.

28. John D. Montgomery, *The Politics of Foreign Aid* (New York: Praeger, 1962), p. 4. Also see U.S. Congress, Senate Foreign Relations Committee, *Some Issues in Foreign Aid, A report prepared by the Legislative Reference Service of the Library of Congress*, August 4, 1966, Washington, D.C.: U.S. Government Printing Press, 1966, p. 15. (Hereafter, *Issues in Foreign Aid*, 1966).

29. U.S. Congress, Senate Committee on Agriculture, *Food for Freedom Program and Commodity Reserves*, Hearings, 89th Congress, 2nd Session, 1966, p. 232.

30. Speaking at the conference on Tensions in Development in Bahia (Brazil) in August 1962, the Indian Ambassador to the U.S., B. K. Nehru, had complained: "Foreign aid is often rung out of unwilling hands with a lack of grace . . . Furthermore, it is on occasion overtly and often covertly sought to be used to ensure that recipient nations do not depart in their external political policies from the line taken by the donor country." Cited, *India News* (Embassy of India, Washington, D.C.), August 13, 1962.

31. From 1957-58 to 1963-64, India's population was growing at the annual rate of 2.3 per cent. In contrast the annual rate of growth of per capita GNP was 2.1 per cent. *Foreign Assistance, 1965*. Hearings before Senate Foreign Relations Committee, 89th Congress, 1st Session, "Washington D.C.: U.S. Government Printing Office 1965) p. 113.

32. C. Subramaniam, "India's Program for Agricultural Progress," in, *Strategy for the Conquest of Hunger, the Rockefeller Foundation*, April 1 and 2, 1968 (New York: The Rockefeller Foundation, 1968), p.16. The author was formerly Minister for Food, Government of India.

33. It denotes the gap between initial investment phase and the ultimate stage of full scale production. Edward S. Mason, Economic Development in

India and Pakistan, *Occasional Papers in International Affairs*, No. 13 (Cambridge; Harvard University, Center for International Affairs, September 1966) pp. 3-28

34. Unless mentioned, the outline of the economic situation is based on Ministry of Finance (India), *Economic Survey: India, 1964-65*, (New Delhi: Government of India, February 1965) also see *Ibid.*, 1965-66; and 1966-67.

35. See, Reserve Bank of India, *Report on Currency and Finance 1965-66*, statement 82.

36. Between 1962 and 1966, exports went up by only 14 per cent; debt servicing increased by 84 per cent. (Paul Streeten and Roger Hill, "Aid to India" in Paul Streeten and Michael Lipton, ed., *The Crisis of Indian Planning: Economic Policy in the 1960's* (London: Oxford University Press, 1968) p. 327.

37. Paradoxically, while PL 480 food aid has supplemented agricultural shortfalls, it has also been responsible for inflation. Purchase of the PL 480 food grains has impelled the government of India to take resort to deficit financing which on its part also caused price acceleration. (For a discussion on this, see "PL 480 Supplement," *Eastern Economist*, Vol. 49, No. 19 November 10, 1967).

38. Both these expectations were belied by the devaluation. It would appear by insisting on devaluation the donors were trying to initiate certain changes in India's economic policy. Various facets of this question have been handled by Harinder Shourie, *The Devaluation of the Indian Rupee in 1966: A Case Study of the World Bank and the U.S. in India*, "Unpublished paper, for the project on U.S. South Asia Policy" under Commission on the Organization of Government for the Conduct of Foreign Policy, June 1975.

39. Figures derived from *Economic Survey, 1966-67*, Table 1.4 "Agricultural Production."

40. For an analysis of this aspect see, Michael Lipton, "Strategy for Agriculture: Urban Bias and Rural Planning" in Streeten and Lipton, p. 83-88.

41. The analysis of these aspects, unless mentioned, is based on John W. Mellor, *The New Economics of Growth: A Strategy for India* (Ithaca: Cornell University Press, 1976) pp. 44-45.

42. For a discussion on food grains price behavior, see John W. Mellor and Ashok K. Dar, "Determinants and Development Implications of Foodgrains Prices in India, 1949-1964", *American Journal of Agricultural Economics*, Vol. 50 (November 1968), pp. 462-74.

43. While former Indian Minister of Food C. Subramaniam had advocated the concept of remunerative prices, he was opposed by his "colleagues" in the government. See C. Subramaniam, *India Program for Agriculture*, pp. 16-17.

44. *Ibid.*

45. Economic Survey, 1966-67, p. 10.

46. In relation to industrial prices it rose about 30 per cent from 1964-65 to 1967-68.

47. See Alan Berg, "Famine contained: notes and lessons from the Bihar experience," Swedish Foundation, *Famine: A Symposia Dealing with*

Nutrition and Relief Operations in Times of Disaster (Uppsala: Alqvist and Wiksells, 1971), pp. 113-129.

48. Mellor, pp. 46-47.

49. The U.S. seemed to have come to a point where "it would be difficult to justify continued economic assistance" without comparable contributions from other prosperous free world countries. *The Scope and Distribution of United States Military and Economic Assistance Programs*, Report to the President of the United States from the Committee to Strengthen the Security of the World, Washington, D.C.: Department of State, March 20, 1963). More commonly referred to as the Clay Committee Report.

50. This happened largely because of the Clay Committee recommendations (*Ibid.*, p. 5) and Congressional opposition. For details about the Bokaro aid controversy, see B. Maheshwari, "The Politics of American Aid," *International Studies*, Vol. 10 (July-October 1968) pp. 163-80.

51. Chairman Morgan (House Committee on Foreign Affairs), captured the mood of the Congress in this regard: "I think our position ought to be firm that they are able to live with each other or we shouldn't make the investment" (*Foreign Assistance Act of 1964*, Hearings before House Foreign Affairs Committee, 88th Congress, 2nd Session, April 8, 1964, Washington: U.S. Government Printing Office, 1964, pp. 238-239).

52. Lyndon B. Johnson, *The Vantage Point: Perspectives of the Presidency 1963-1969* (New York: Holt, Rinehart and Winston, 1971), p. 224. The irony of Johnson's approach was that like the proverbial life-saver, he was lecturing a drowning man about the virtue of learning to swim.

53. *Ibid.*, p. 223.

54. Four years earlier Johnson had suggested this to Kennedy in a report of his visit to Asian countries.

55. See, John W. Finney, "Stopgap U.S. Wheat Aid is Annoying New Delhi," *The New York Times*, September 29, 1965; also J. Anthony Lukas, "U.S.-Indian Discord: New Delhi Believes Stand on Food has a Concealed Johnson Motive," *The New York Times*, January 26, 1967. This is also confirmed through personal interviews. See also Daniel Green, *The Politics of Food* (London: Gordon Cremonesi Ltd., 1975) p. 84.

56. Bjorkman, p. 199.

57. Complimenting Freeman, Johnson wrote in his memoir: "Freeman did a magnificent job. More than any other man he was responsible for turning my policy into actions that worked." (Johnson, p. 226).

58. This insight is derived from I. M. Destler, *Presidents, Bureaucrats, and Foreign Policy: The Politics of Organizational Reform* (Princeton, N. J.: Princeton University Press, 1972), p. 162.

59. Secretary of Agriculture, Orville Freeman's letter to the House Speaker, John W. McCormack, February 18, 1964. (See *Report on the Extension and Amendment of Public Law 480*, 88th Congress, 2nd Session, Report No. 1767, August 11, 1964) 1966, p. 36.

60. Undersecretary of State, Eugene V. Rostow's Communication in response to House Representative John R. Rarick's written questions, March 3, 1967. (See *Congressional Record*, Vol. 113, Part 6, 1967, p. 6907).

61. For details of this episode, see Bjorkman, p. 200.

62. Freeman contends that these surpluses were due to "misguided policies" in the 1950s, Freeman, p. 43-44.

63. For the text of the message, see *Department of State Bulletin* 54 (February 28, 1966), pp. 336-41. Despite Johnson's intention, however, due to Congressional opposition the old name "Food for Peace" was retained. It was signed on November 12, 1966 as "The Food for Peace Act 1966." (PL 89-108).

64. David Halberstam, *The Best and the Brightest* (New York: Random House, 1972) p. 433.

65. For a perceptive treatment of this aspect, see Toma, p. 137-39.

66. As represented respectively by Senators McGovern, Ellender and Fulbright. See Senator McGovern's speech, June 17, 1965. *Congressional Record*, Vol. III, pp. 13998; Senator Ellender's speech, August 29, 1965, *Ibid.*, Part 112, Part 116, pp. 21102-21104; Senator Fulbright's remarks, August 29, 1966, p. 21104.

67. Bjorkman, p. 203.

68. One of the earliest beginnings of a direct U.S. effort in this regard can be related to a very significant study by the Ford Foundation. This study projected a serious food crisis in 1966 unless the Indian government adopts a more vigorous agricultural policy on modern lines. *Ford Foundation Report on India's Food Crisis and the Steps to Meet It*, (New Delhi: Issued by Ministry of Food and Agriculture, Government of India) April 1959.

69. Orville L. Freeman, *World Without Hunger* (New York: Frederick A. Praeger, 1968) especially, Chapter 9, "The Food Crisis in India."

70. The FCI was designed to deal with the vital problems of procurement, distribution, storage and movement of foodgrains. The FCI was expected to compete with private traders in purchases on the open market by offering attractive prices to producers.

71. The Meaning of Self-reliance, collection of articles from *Yojana* (New Delhi: Publications Divisions, Ministry of Information and Broadcasting, Government of India, 1965); also, Gyan Chand, "Food and Self-reliance", *Mainstream*, December 4, 1965, pp. 9-11; V.K.R.V. Rao, "Agricultural Production," *Yojana*, October 24, 1965, at a later date the theme of self-reliance was further spelled out by K. N. Raj, "Food, Fertilizer and Foreign Aid," *Mainstream*, April 30, 1966, pp. 10-12; and, V. M. Dandekar, "Food and Freedom" (an article in two parts), *Mainstream*, March 25 and April 1, 1965.

72. Most U.S. policymakers who came to know Subramaniam were impressed by his extraordinary ability (Bowles, *Ambassador's Report*, p. 509; Johnson, p. 226).

73. Freeman, p. 159.

74. Bjorkman, p. 204.

75. The Rome meeting took place on November 25, 1965. Significantly, no sooner did President Johnson peruse Freeman's report of these

talks than he urged (December 1, 1965) on the release of a loan of $60 million (from the frozen Aid India Fund) in support of India's fertilizer requirements for the next wheat crop. See *Indian Recorder & Digest* (New Delhi), January 1966, p. 16.

76. See *Fourth Five-year Plan: A Draft Outline* (New Delhi; Planning Commission, Government of India, 1966), p. 30.

77. Initially Subramaniam found it difficult to convince his colleagues of the merits of this new agricultural policy. (Subramaniam, *India's Program for Agriculture,* p. 17)

78. Press Secretary, Bill Moyers' announcement, December 9, 1965 (See *Department of State Bulletin*, Vol. 53 (December 27, 1965) p. 1009 n.

79. *Ibid.*, p. 1009.

80. Johnson, p. 226.

81. In response to Mrs. Gandhi's request, a joint UN-FAO appeal issued on February 11 called on the World Community to provide all possible aid to India in facing its grave food emergency.

82. Statement by Rusk, House Committee on Agriculture, February 25, 1966. See *Department of State Bulletin*, Vol. 54 (March 28, 1966) p. 497.

83. *The Times of India*, April 4, 1966.

84. Johnson-Gandhi Joint Communique, March 29, 1966. For text, see, *Department of State Bulletin* 54 (April 18, 1966), pp. 603-5.

85. Message to the Congress, March 30, 1966, *Ibid.*, p. 606.

86. H. J. Resolution 997, *Congressional Record*, Vol. 112, April 4, 1966, p. 7498.

87. Report prepared by David Bell, Administrator, AID. The report is secret; according to informal reports in New Delhi, it recommended relaxation of import restrictions, liberalization of excessive economic controls, agricultural priorities and devaluation. Eldridge, p. 219, f.n. 30.

88. From Speech at a conference of State Chief Ministers and Agriculture Ministers, New Delhi, April 9, 1966. See *Selected Speeches of Indira Gandhi, January 1966-August 1969*, (New Delhi: Publications Division, Government of India) 1971, p. 137.

89. Alan Berg, pp. 121-22, f.n. 4.

90. See Bowles, p. 524.

91. Often these were diverted by the U.S. Embassy in India. *Ibid.*

92. Cited in Bjorkman, p. 205.

93. Johnson, pp. 224-225.

94. In March, 1966.

95. *The New York Times*, November 29, 1966.

96. Bowles, p. 526. When Bowles explained that Mrs. Gandhi was only saying what U Thant and the Pope had repeatedly said, he was told by one official "the Pope and U Thant do not need our food." (*Ibid.*, p. 526).

97. See Alan Berg, p. 121. Also see, Johnson, p. 228.

98. The President was faced with the task of deciding about food aid to India at a time when women in America were picketing against price-hikes near supermarkets. Alan Berg, *Ibid.*

99. Johnson, p. 229. This explanation was clearly in contrast to his initial rationale behind the "short tether" approach.

100. These four members were Congressmen Robert Poage (D-Texas), Chairman of the House Agriculture Committee; Robert Dole (R-Kansas), member of the House Agriculture Committee; Senator Gale McGee (D-Wyoming); and Senator Jack Miller (R-Iowa), member of the Senate Agriculture Committee.

101. On February 6, 1967, Congressmen Poage and Dole introduced legislation in the House to assure the food grains supply to India.

102. Freeman, pp. 154-55.

103. Bowles, p. 529.

104. India had to purchase 200,000 tons of these grain imports with her own scarce foreign exchange. Derived from President Johnson's message to the Congress, February 2, 1967. See *Congressional Record*, Vol. 113, Part 15, February 28, 1967, pp. 918-20.

105. *Ibid.*, p. 300.

106. *Department of State Bulletin*, Vol. 56 (May 1, 1967) p. 700.

107. This was reflected in the left journal, *Mainstream*, Republic Day Special Issue, January 26, 1967. About the same time the Soviet Union was also particularly concerned about India's foreign policy changes. See Hemen Ray, *Indo-Soviet Relations 1955-1971* (Bombay: Jaico Publishing House, 1973) pp. 152-pp. 159.

108. According to Bowles, Johnson "mistrusted anyone who pleaded India's case, on the grounds that he must be prejudiced in India's favor" (Bowles, p. 535).

109. Lawrence A. Veit, India's Second Revolution: *The Dimension of Development* (New York: Council for Foreign Relations, 1976); p. 144.

110. Johnson, p. 225.

6

The 1971 Indo-Pakistan War and U.S. Foreign Policy

The Indo-Pakistan war of 1971 was the outgrowth of civil strife in the geographically divided state of Pakistan. This domestic conflict developed because of the failure of the governing class "to create a sense of political participation, partnership and economic justice amongst the Bengalis of East Pakistan."[1] Indeed, the Pakistan Army's crackdown of March 25, 1971, marks the climactic ending to the story of Pakistan's failure in national integration between its two wings.

A disastrous consequence of the military crackdown was the evolution of a domestic political crisis into a major regional conflict as a result of the movement of millions of Bengali refugees into India. With India and Pakistan entangled, the United States also became involved further internationalizing the crisis, when the Nixon administration decided to support Pakistan because of certain extra-regional considerations.[2] This chapter will examine the various facets of the making and operation of America's South Asia policy during the 1971 war.

Origins of a Crisis

The Indo-Pakistan joint declaration at Tashkent (January 10, 1966) is a useful starting point in surveying the course of Pakistan's dismemberment. After the signing of the declaration, Pakistan was torn by political turmoil at two different levels—a struggle for greater democratic participation in West Pakistan and the demand for greater regional autonomy by East Pakistan. This dual struggle unleashed forces which Ayub Khan and his basic democratic system could not cope with it.

The Tashkent Declaration came as a shock to many Pakistanis. This declaration formalized the military stalemate between India and Pakistan following the 1965 war, and thus shattered the prevailing aura of Pakistani invincibility. To many Pakistanis (especially in the West Wing) Tashkent was a "Yalta": what Pakistan had gained on the battlefield had been lost at the conference table. Hence, the ceasefire, withdrawal and settlement was looked upon as a "betrayal of the nation."[3] In East Pakistan the 1965 war was viewed differently. The military argument that the East Wing could be defended from the West Wing had raised serious doubts in East Pakistan about the importance of their part of the country.[4] The idea immediately gained currency—in the context of continuous political and economic dissatisfaction—that East Pakistan was an inconsequential element in the State of Pakistan. During the entire period of this conflict, East Pakistan remained not only cut off from the world outside (including the West Wing) but also virtually undefended, though there was no fighting in that Wing. The fact that India did not attack in the east, whether because of its own calculations or because of Chinese protection of East Pakistan (as claimed by Foreign Minister Bhutto) was hardly satisfactory to the East Pakistani Bengalis. Additionally, the stoppage of Indo-Pakistani trade had hurt them more than the West Pakistanis.[5] It was this anomalous situation that gave rise to the East Pakistani demand for full autonomy in external as well as defense affairs. This was later used by the major East Wing political party, the Awami League, as a basis of their famous six-points.[6] As expected this demand was denounced by the Ayub regime.

By 1968, Ayub Khan's power base in West Pakistan had become shaky. There was widespread civil disorder and violence, with demands for the restoration of civil rights and political participation. A shaken and ill Ayub was compelled to resign in March, 1969. He was succeeded by General Yahya Khan as President and Chief Martial Law Administrator. The new President announced the legal framework of a federal parliamentary system, and the prospect of a general election based on universal franchise. The authority for constitution-making was delegated to the newly elected Constituent Assembly—which had to complete its task within 120 days.[7] Meanwhile, relations between the East and West wings had been strained by the Federal government's inept handling of relief operations in the aftermath of a great cyclone that struck East Pakistan in November, 1970.

The elections finally took place in December 1970. The Awami League was skillfully led by Sheikh Mujibur Rahman and fought the election on the issue of East Pakistani political autonomy. It won 291 seats, an absolute majority in the National Assembly. In the West Wing Bhutto's People's Party had swept the polls and Bhutto had firmly declared that his party would not permit anyone to "chisel us out" of power and responsibility.[8]

This electoral outcome was not to what General Yahya Khan's military regime had anticipated. Former U.S. Secretary of State Henry Kissinger records Yahya's reply to his query about the fate of presidential powers in Pakistan after the elections, Yahya stated that he expected:

> . . . a multiplicity of parties to emerge both in West and East Pakistan, which would continually fight each other in each wing of the country and between the two wings; the President would therefore remain the arbiter of Pakistan's politics."[9]

Obviously, the military regime had failed to understand the mood of the people or the extent of popular support of the Awami League and Pakistan People's Party. The margin of error in the election forecast was greater in the West than in the East Wing.[10]

Bhutto had made full use of his tactical advantage and insisted on political consensus about the outline of the constitution before convening the National Assembly. But Mujib was not willing to accommodate Bhutto's demand; there were serious differences between them on the question of Pakistan's new constitution. After its first free election, Pakistan had emerged politically split.

Pakistan was drifting towards a disaster. After their initial displeasure with Bhutto prior to the elections, the military regime's attitude towards him underwent drastic transformation, primarily because of his electoral success and their shared misgivings about the Awami League's six-point program. Hence, the army was not unhappy when Bhutto also claimed his share in power. But they started acting in collusion once they failed to reach an agreement with Mujib. In an important sense therefore, the subsequent civil strife stemmed as much from Bhutto's 'obduracy' as from the army's manoeuvres—in the context of deep-seated interwing mutual suspicion.

Thus as the question of East Pakistan autonomy came up in the dialogue between Mujib and Yahya Khan, the increasingly important issue was whether the Awami League's six-point plan could be reconciled with the continued existence of a united Pakistan. It is interesting that after one of those dialogues with Mujib in Dacca around mid-January 1971, President Yahya Khan called the East Pakistan leader the Prime Minister of Pakistan.[11] But the meeting of the National Assembly was still not announced. Finally, Yahya Khan moved on Bhutto's threat of a general strike and the pressure of the West Pakistan dominated civil-military bureaucracy. On March 1, 1971, Yahya Khan announced the postponement of the National Assembly.[12] The stage was thus ready for a conflict between East and West Pakistan. When Mujib gave a call for a civil disobedience movement, the Bengalis responded. There were widespread demonstrations and strikes followed by police firings. Faced with this desperate situation Yahya Khan announced fresh dates for convening the National Assembly (first on March 6 and then on March 25, 1971). In light of subsequent developments however, it would appear that the army was trying to gain time so it could send reinforcements to the East Wing. Meanwhile, because of the hijacking of an Indian aircraft to Pakistan, India had suspended inter-wing flight over Indian territory; that meant men and material had to be hauled via longer sea or air routes.

Thus with the failure of the initial tripartite Mujib-Yahya-Bhutto talks and the eventual collapse of the Dacca dialogues, Pakistan plunged into a civil war on March 25, 1971.[13] Moving in strength, the Pakistan Army had started its "Operation Flashlight"— a crackdown against the local police, offices of opposition newspapers, Awami League members and various political activists. On the same day Mujib was arrested and later taken to West Pakistan. The Pakistan Army also began to disarm Bengal elements of the military and paramilitary forces. On March 26, Yahya Khan banned the Awami League and suspended all political activity.[14] But on the same day a clandestine radio broadcast proclaimed the independent People's Republic of Bangladesh.

Thousands of people were killed in the Pakistan Army's crackdown. To escape from the reign of terror let loose by the army, people started pouring into neighboring India. By April 2, 1971, the exodus numbered more than a quarter million refugees. About 90 per cent of them were non-Muslims from Pakistan's minority Hindu community.

It is not definitively known what or who had actually prompted Yahya Khan to unleash the "reign of terror" on March 25. Henry Kissinger suggests that "sometimes the nerves of the public figures snap." He goes on to add that, "Incapable of abiding events, they seek to force the pace and lose their balance."[15] There is a good deal of truth in this. It is indeed amazing, with 40,000 troops, Yahya Khan decided to establish West Pakistani control over 75 million people living in a territory thousands of miles away. There are reasons to believe that the general was exhausted by the intractability of the complex political issue confronting the military regime. There was also an element of ad hocism in Yahya's approach to the problem. While on March 4, he agreed to visit Dacca for resolving the crisis, the same night he changed his mind. Yahya cancelled his visit because he was "convinced that it won't bring me anywhere near the solution." By March 6, he telephoned Mujib, counseling for restraint and then set the date for a National Assembly meeting on March 25 at Dacca. Later on March 15, he would be visiting Dacca as if it was a matter of routine. It was after his fruitless talks with Mujib on March 17 that Yahya gave his go-ahead signal for military action. His immediate rationale was that Mujib was "not behaving."[16]

The military crackdown in the East Wing had in fact turned Pakistan's domestic political problem into a major international crisis. The refugees pouring into India, followed by India's denunciation of the Pakistan Army's brutalities and its support to the Bangladesh struggle, inevitably transformed Pakistan's civil war into a problem of Indo-Pakistan relations.[17] It was evident that without political normalcy and conditions guaranteeing personal safety and security inside East Pakistan, it was unlikely that these huge masses of people would return to Bangladesh. Furthermore, a Bangladesh government-in-exile was established in the areas bordering India, with Tajuddin Ahmad as the acting Prime Minister. Pakistan was indeed on the brink of disaster.

The second phase of the civil war was marked by intensification of guerrilla activities inside East Bengal—with direct and indirect support from India. Though India was not yet prepared to recognize the government-in-exile set up on its own territory, in the subsequent months it gave "moral, political and material support" to the Bangladesh liberation movement.[18] Faced with the burden of the refugee influx India appealed to the international community for relief assistance and for pressure on Pakistan to give credible guarantees for the safe return of the refugees. India had declared that "if the world does not take heed, we shall be constrained to take all measures as may be necessary to assure our own security."[19] Relations between India and Pakistan further deteriorated as a result of sporadic armed clashes on the Indo-East Pakistan border.

Despite the worsening situation in East Bengal, the world community failed to fully respond to the problem. While there was widespread international sympathy for the human suffering in East Bengal, there was official hesitation to address the political roots of the problem and formulate the basis of a political settlement. The chain of events that had begun with the army crackdown had entrapped India and Pakistan in a situation from which they could withdraw. War broke out on December 3, 1971,[20] and the Pakistan Army in East Bengal was defeated by the combined forces of India and the Bengali Mukti Bahini (Liberation Force). This led to the establishment of an independent state of Bangladesh in East Pakistan.

Although our main interest is in the process of U.S. decision-making during this final phase—the war—we are also concerned with U.S. decisions during the first two phases. In analyzing the pattern of response we will focus on the U.S. approach to the unfolding crisis, the specific actions taken by the Nixon administration, the basic considerations behind these actions, and the locus of the policy decisions.

The U.S. Approaches the Crisis

Writing after the Indo-Pakistan war of 1971, one noted American expert commented that "few if any postwar American policy ventures have brought forth as immediate and widespread opposition as the Nixon administration's policy toward the Indian Subcontinent during 1971."[21] In a certain sense, this opposition was generated by ambivalence. The administration had to decide whether the U.S. should treat South Asia on its own terms outside the context of the superpowers or whether it should approach the region from the perspective of superpower considerations. This dilemma had always given America's South Asia policy a characteristic "oscillation."[22] But while Nixon's administration had inherited this problem, its task was complicated by the need for an early rapprochement with China. That implied a reversal of the Johnson administration's assumption concerning Chinese intentions in South Asia.

It was not easy to pull down the structure of a U.S. policy that had sought for so long to bolster South Asian capabilities against a possible Chinese threat. What is more, it was conceivable that Sino-American rapport would have an impact on New Delhi because of the latter's continuing conflict with China. While the Nixon administration sought to delink the two levels (regional and global), the linkage in this context was too strong to permit an easy way out. An additional complication was that having found the Warsaw connection inconvenient for initiating a high-level dialogue with Peking, Nixon's choice fell on President Yahya Khan of Pakistan. As the "indispensable middleman" helping the secret exchange of communications between Washington and Peking, Yahya Khan was in the scheme from the outset. His "discretion and cooperation" were important considerations in the Nixon 'tilt' towards Pakistan in the Indo-Pakistan war of December 1971.[23] Since communications were being transmitted through Islamabad in the midst of Pakistan's civil war, the Nixon administration did not want to openly criticize the military crackdown in East Pakistan. From the standpoint of a prospective Sino-American detente, the South Asian events at that point—even if tragic—were considered inconsequential to the reality of the great powers relationship. Thus while the Sino-Pakistan entente was a major irritant in the Johnson administration's policy towards Pakistan, under Nixon it became an important tool for establishing high-level contacts with Peking.

In making this point, we are not characterizing Pakistan as a prime factor in the evolving American approach to the 1971 conflict. In a certain sense, Pakistan's importance in the emerging U.S. power calculations was incidental rather than fundamental. But then, it would be wide of the mark to suggest that the U.S. relations with Pakistan were marked by a "superficial friendliness" and devoid of "concrete contents."[24] In any event, during Nixon's first term South Asia was not expected to move to the top of America's foreign policy agenda, except in terms of contingency relief. The priority before the Nixon administration lay elsewhere. It urgently needed to work out a rapprochement with Peking to achieve a greater bargaining position vis-a-vis the Soviet Union. In their quest for a diplomatic coup, Nixon and Kissinger found Pakistan—for obvious physical and technical reasons—a convenient channel to Peking. In anticipation of this vital service, President Nixon was to approve a military package amounting to more than $50 million for Pakistan, as a "one-time exception" to the U.S. arms policy of 1966-67. It would be oversimplistic to suggest that Pakistan would have been willing to play middleman merely in exchange for Nixon's "somewhat warmer tone"—without any concrete gesture.[25]

It appears in the absence of anything more substantive, Pakistan initially emerged as a mutually acceptable contact between the U.S. and China. It may be recalled that since the Sino-Indian war of 1962, a closer cooperative relationship had developed between Pakistan and China. Under the Johnson administration this was considered contrary to U.S. interests because of the hostile Sino-U.S. relationship. In contrast, the Nixon administration in its search for a major diplomatic breakthrough, found the Sino-Pakistan detente not only acceptable but also convenient for opening a dialogue with China. Besides, Pakistan was technically an alliance partner. Thus, from a point of conflicting interest, Pakistan emerged as a joint Sino-U.S. concern.[26]

This Sino-American rapprochement had a direct bearing on India. Even if one assumes that the Sino-U.S. detente was basically designed to affect Soviet global policy, it is inconceivable that its spillover effect on the Subcontinent could have been prevented—because of closer Indo-Soviet ties and the ongoing hostile relationship between India and China. The subsequent signing of the Indo-Soviet treaty (August 9, 1971) was symbolic of the attempts to "supplement each other's efforts to combat competing forces and thereby promote the national interests," recorded one informed Indian analyst.[27]

Normalizing relations with Peking and retaining Pakistani goodwill determined the Nixon administration's approach to the 1971 Subcontinental conflict. The task precluded any heavy pressure on the Pakistani military regime. However, there were obvious contradictions. While the administration more or less accepted the inevitability of an "independent Bengal State," and occasionally gave the impression in private that America was interested in East Pakistani autonomy, it did not take any initiative to defuse the civil war. This inaction was presented as giving "political evolution a chance." But by Fall, 1971, the U.S. groping had ended; Kissinger "began to display an unmistakable pro-Pakistan bias."[28]

There were also certain strategic and personal factors that determined overall American approaches and their response pattern. President Nixon had a personal disdain for Mrs. Gandhi. He found her cold-blooded and particularly difficult to understand. In contrast, "bluff, direct military chiefs of Pakistan," were more agreeable to Nixon.[29] A former senior State Department official (of the Nixon administration) observes that Nixon's reaction to South Asia was largely "influenced by his long-standing dislike for India" and "his warm feeling toward Pakistan." In fact these "contrasting feelings undoubtedly colored his judgments in 1971."[30] Aside from these personal predispositions, perception of the shifting Asian power balance seems to have had a bearing on the U.S. South Asia policy stance. Evidently, the Nixon-Kissinger team recognized that long-range interests in this region could be ensured by countering the "budding" Indo-Soviet "alliance" with an "informal Pakistan-China-American hook up." Their major concern was that if Pakistan were to disintegrate under Indian pressure, it would not only imply India's regional predominance but also boost Soviet influence in the area to the detriment of the strategic balance (and thus cause a major war). What probably concerned the U.S. administration more was that the "Chinese would become alarmed," in the process.[31]

President Nixon's second annual foreign policy report to Congress in early 1971 is revealing. Nixon called China to come out of its self-imposed isolation and then signalled:

> We are prepared to establish a dialogue with Peking. We cannot accept its ideological precepts, or the notion that Communist China must exercise hegemony over Asia. But neither do we wish to impose on China an international position that denies its legitimate national interests.[32]

With hindsight, it is clear that the orchestration of a diplomatic breakthrough with Peking had already started. It was also unlikely that Nixon would have liked to see his efforts derailed because of the considerations of a non-priority area, such as South Asia.

Reflecting on South Asia in the same report, Nixon said that since the Chinese attack of 1962, India has been following a policy of non-alignment of a different cast. "These policy changes", Nixon added:

> by definition, affect the intimacy of our relationship with the countries of South Asia. We have no desire to try to press upon them a closer relationship than their own interests lead them to desire.[33]

The message was that it was up to India to decide whether it should seek a closer relationship with the U.S. Nixon also reported China's major effort to develop a "strong relationship with Pakistan," which the United States had no intent to jeopardize.[34] Evidently, in Nixon's international system, even a relegated Third World country had importance to the extent that it had a "special relationship" with one of the major power centers.

In contrast to his reference to closer Sino-Pakistan relations, Nixon had no comments on Indo-Soviet relationships. Though he noted the Soviet attempts to create a "compatible" area of stability on its southern borders, he had declared that no external power had a claim to "predominant influence" in the Subcontinent.[35] The Nixon administration wanted to delink the affairs of the region from its diplomatic initiative with Peking. But as often happens, ambitions were overtaken by events shaped by others.

The Sequence of Response

The American response to this crisis varied greatly. But as it unfolded into a full scale war between India and Pakistan in December 1971, the Nixon administration tried to take a position designed to reinforce the Sino-U.S. detente. The response was marked by three different though interrelated phases: calculated reticence, relief assistance and reduced arms aid, and physical intervention on Pakistan's behalf.

Military Crackdown:
Calculated Reticence and After

On March 25, the Pakistan Army started its brutal crackdown on Awami League supporters, intellectuals, students, and Bengali detachments of the Pakistani military and paramilitary forces. In the absence of authentic sources there are no reliable figures as to the magnitude of the killings. The figures vary between Bhutto's estimate of 30,000/40,000 to Mujib's three million.[36] Whatever the real figures, the fact remains that the gruesome killings had taken place along with the widespread destruction of property and the raping of women. Even after the crackdown, people arrested under suspicion were summarily executed without trial.[37] In any event, while the Pakistan armed forces had won the first round, their control was largely confined to the principal towns and key communication centers. Pakistan's governmental authority had collapsed in the countryside; most Bengali middle-ranking officials had fled to India or joined the guerrillas.

The international community was shocked by the tragic events in East Bengal and during the following months Pakistan came under tremendous international criticism. India's first reaction was to abide by "proper international norms"; but it expressed its profound sympathy and support for the people in East Bengal in their struggle for a "democratic way of life."[38] Britain seemed to have been the first major power to express its view and to have taken the plea of Pakistan's internal affairs into account in reacting to the military crackdown.[39] The Soviet President (Podgorny) told the Pakistan President to solve the problem politically, without use of force or continued "bloodshed".[40] There was no direct Chinese reaction until April 13, when Premier Chou En-lai (in a letter to the Pakistan President) supported Yahya's attempts to uphold the unity of Pakistan.[41]

In contrast, the U.S. was rather halting in expressing its view. A decision seemed to have been taken in favor of a low key position and to "downplay the seriousness of the action" and avoid commenting on the killings.[42] This was ironic, given the general outrage at the atrocities within the U.S. administration—especially by middle-level State Department and AID officials and at the U.S. Consulate-General's office in Dacca.[43] However, this did not have much effect on policy; Nixon was reluctant to issue any statement of condemnation. In fact, there was reluctance to offend Yahya Khan in any manner.

In defense of this posture, Kissinger later explained in his memoir that the Nixon administration "faced a dilemma" in regard to the East Pakistan crisis. While he submits that the "United States could not condone a brutal military repression," he goes on to add that "Pakistan was our sole channel to China; once it was closed off it would take months to make alternative arrangements." A low profile posture was the only option available to the United States.[44]

In any event, in a statement on April 5 the United States government expressed grave concern about the reported use of U.S. arms against the Bengali demand for autonomy. However, it did not support any party[45] to the conflict. On April 7, the State Department also expressed concern about the loss of life and offered sympathy for the victims. The statement emphasized that "we continue to believe it important that every feasible step be taken to end the conflict and achieve a peaceful accommodation."[46]

From the outset, Kissinger submits the consensus within the U.S. administration was "to avoid precipitate action even among those who knew nothing of our China initiative." He claims further that from the earliest phase he had reiterated the possibility of East Pakistan's "civil war leading to independence fairly quickly." The point is that President Nixon did not want to take initiative in the matter. He did not want to be in a position where he could be "accused of having encouraged the split-up of Pakistan." It is rather surprising that while Nixon concedes, "we knew that Yahya Khan eventually would have to yield to East Pakistan's demand for independence and urged him to take a more moderate and conciliatory line,"[47] he does not spell out the methodology of this eventual development. Hence, the whole idea on Nixon's part was to avoid a very active policy regarding East Pakistan.[48]

Thus, the U.S. administration was not unaware of the violent repression following the military crackdown. In fact, the U.S. Consul-General (Archer Blood) at Dacca had promptly intimated to Washington the "imposed conditions" that impelled thousands of Bengali refugees (especially Hindus) to flee to India.[49] This was taking place at a time when the Pakistan government had declared that things had normalized in East Bengal.[50] Paradoxically, the Dacca Consulate General's reports were treated as being "partial" and hence disregarded by the U.S. Embassy in Islamabad.

The Administration's view was that the refugee influx was caused by continuous fighting between the Pakistan armed forces and the guerrillas, as well as the distressing economic conditions, and was thus an internal Pakistani matter. The internal affair argument was an important element in the American position. Commenting on this, the U.S. Ambassador to India stated on April 15 that "the phrase, internal affair, is overdone and this is not certainly a case of internal affairs." The statement was immediately disputed by the State Department. It reiterated its earlier stand indicating that the U.S. ambassador had no authority to issue such statements.[51]

The State Department also refused to comply with the request of the Senate Foreign Relations Committee Chairman (Senator J. W. Fulbright) for a copy of the communication sent by the Consulate General in Dacca. Disclosing this refusal, Fulbright noted that the administration was playing down the serious situation in East Bengal on the grounds that "stability and support for the status quo is more to our interest than any upheaval."[52] Blood's report was found inconvenient by the State Department. Later he was removed from Dacca—more than a year before his term was scheduled to end—when he sent a Consulate staff petition to Washington critical of the Administration's policy.[53]

It is significant that despite the excessive control of the Nixon-Kissinger system and its apparent bias in the crisis, the contents of the (in-country) Mission communications were usually not influenced by this consideration.[54] Incidentally, even later during the Indo-Pakistan war, Blood's successor (Spivack) was able to send a report along with UN Assistant Secretary General Paul Marc Henry regarding Pakistani complicity in a bombing incident in Dacca.[55]

Although the White House policy prevailed, concern was expressed by legislators, intellectuals and the general public about the upheaval in East Bengal. As early as April 1, 1971 speaking in the U.S. Senate, Senator Edward Kennedy expressed his anguish about "indiscriminate killing, the execution of political leaders and students, and thousands of civilians suffering and dying every hour of the day."[56] Later he described the army action as genocide. There were indications that even by military standards of violence, the situation was far worse than the U.S. Administration had stated. There were extensive newspaper accounts describing the Pakistan military action as one of "genocide."[57] But until the middle of 1971, there was no direct public reference to this even by legislators who were critical of the administration's reluctance to condemn Pakistani action. Reflecting on this, Senator Kennedy stated in a report that "our national leadership has yet to express one word that would suggest that we do not approve of the genocidal consequences" of the Pakistan government's policy of violence and repression.[58]

In any event, the first phase ended without any official U.S. condemnation. But at the same time, embarrassed by public criticism, the administration decided to take symbolic if not substantive action. The basic motivation was probably to allay public suspicions that the Administration had acquiesced to Pakistan's repressive actions. Thus in a WSAG meeting on March 26, Kissinger projected the possibility of a "civil war leading to independence fairly quickly." At the same time, he told his colleagues that Nixon's: "inclination is the same as anybody else's. He doesn't want to do anything. He doesn't want to be in a position where he can be accused of having encouraged the split-up of Pakistan." In short, Kissinger added, Nixon did not favor a very active policy.[59]

Relief Assistance
and Reduced Arms Aid

On April 23, 1971, UN Secretary General U Thant, in a letter to President Yahya Khan, offered UN emergency assistance to Pakistan. The purpose was to relieve "widespread" misery, hardships and suffering" which had befallen the people of East

Bengal "as a result of recent events". U Thant had proposed the
relief operation through the UN's specialized agencies. Yahya's
reply was that there was "no cause for concern," and that reports
about misery and widespread destruction were highly exaggerated.
However, he pointed out that Pakistan was making assessments of
present as well as future international relief assistance. At the same
time he made it clear that international relief assistance, if and when
required, would be administered by Pakistani relief agencies.[60]
Until May 24 no specific request for relief assistance had come from
Pakistan.

There was growing Congressional concern about the plight
of people in East Bengal and the flight of refugees to India.
Congress stressed the need for necessary steps on at least four
fronts. The first step entailed "stronger" efforts by individual
governments and the UN to encourage and facilitate political
accommodation between the Pakistan government and the relevant
forces within East Pakistan. The purpose was to stop the flow of
refugees to India and to ensure the return of others who had left the
country. The second step called for attaching emergency relief
operations in East Bengal as a condition for any normalization of
U.S. economic aid to Pakistan. Third, Congress wanted the
Administration to take the initiative in reducing the "escalating
tensions" between India and Pakistan, and thereby preventing a
Great Power confrontation in that area. Finally, it wanted the
Administration to respond (on a "bilateral basis") to an Indian appeal
for refugee relief assistance—in the light of continuing UN
immobilization.[61] But what is more, Congress recommended in
early April to suspend all aid to Pakistan during the period of the
civil strife. Incidentally, the World Bank made similar
recommendations in a report in June, 1971. It recommended to the
Aid to Pakistan consortium not to extend any new aid to Pakistan
until the East Pakistan crisis was settled amicably.[62]

Meanwhile, on April 23, India appealed to the UN for
immediate international assistance to meet the burden of the
continuing flood of refugees. But the UN failed to respond. The
U.S. Administration ruled out UN intervention because of the
"political aspects" of the East Bengal situation. But at the same
time, it called for UN participation in humanitarian relief efforts in
both India and East Pakistan thereby promoting "peace and
conciliation in the area."[63]

There were three basic elements in U.S. policy towards the
refugee situation and the turmoil in East Pakistan from which it
stemmed. First, the administration fully supported international

relief efforts. Second, it contended that since the situation had potential for an Indo-Pakistan conflict "we are relying on diplomatic efforts to relieve tension." Third, the U.S. Administration seemed to have taken the position that normalcy should be restored through "peaceful political accommodation."[64]

In contrast to the Administration's position, Congress wanted to concentrate more on refugee relief operations in India than for the people in East Bengal. Its apprehension was that in the absence of any guarantee, this aid to East Bengal would be diverted for Pakistani military purposes. By the middle of 1971, the U.S. administration seemed to have agreed that unless the flow of refugees was reversed it might lead to a greater burden on India, and thereby enhance the possibility of an overt aggressive Indian reaction. Thus, when the Indian Foreign Minister, Swaran Singh, visited Washington he was told about the two-pronged U.S. plan: (i) additional refugee relief assistance to India and (ii) appropriate measures to reverse the flow of refugees from East Bengal.

However, it is not clear what concrete steps were taken— aside from relief measures—to create proper conditions in East Bengal as a prerequisite for the return of the refugees. While relief assistance could have resolved the immediate problem of starvation there, this by itself was not adequate to ensure the return of the refugees. The creation of a peaceful political situation was imperative for inhibiting the outflow of the refugees and ensuring their return from India. But the U.S. Administration was reluctant to clarify its plan of political accommodation in East Bengal. It appears that the middle-echelon members of the State Department had a very limited brief on the problem and Nixon and Kissinger were more concerned about the China "breakthrough" in July 1971.[65] It is now clear that if Yahya Khan's help had to be taken to make the China connection possible, there would be only a passing reference to the question of political accommodation in East Bengal.

The amount of U.S. relief aid was attacked as a "self-serving public relations effort".[66] It has been estimated by the World Bank that the total cost of refugee relief to India came to about $700 million by March, 1972. Of this amount, India was bearing $3 million a day, and the rest of the world was providing 30% of the total—half of which was the U.S. share. That means India was providing 70% of the cost of relief operations. As for the authorized sum of $276.7 million for American aid to East Pakistan relief operations, 73% of this amount was not spent.[67] Congress did try to take a major initiative in the refugee relief efforts—

notwithstanding an initial underplaying of the issue by the Administration.

An important American policy decision involved the reduction of arms transfers to Pakistan. The Administration took a decision around April, 1970, to hold back the supply of military sales and to stop the issuance of any new licenses for arms. In a letter to Senator Kennedy, Assistant Secretary of State for Congressional Relations, David Abshire, confirmed that "since the outbreak of fighting" in East Bengal on March 25-26, the Administration had not provided to Pakistan any "lethal end-items of military equipment."[68]

Despite the ban on the delivery of lethal weapons to Pakistan, the Administration had in fact supplied these items by taking advantage of a technical loophole. It was explained that any contract of arms supply entered with the Pakistan Government before the military crackdown was deemed delivered prior to the cutback announcement. The story of this confirmed supply was leaked to *The New York Times*. The newspaper reported on June 21, 1971, that according to the "status report" of the spare aircraft parts supplies to Pakistan, the latter had delivered a cheque of $404,116.49 in May, 1971, for the additional sales. The leak came at a time when Indian Foreign Minister Swaran Singh was returning home from Washington with assurances that the U.S. had suspended the supply of arms to Pakistan. This must have caused misapprehension in New Delhi and had a certain bearing on the subsequent decision to escalate the crisis. According to John P. Lewis, what in fact happened was that:

> The White House and the Department of State really believed in April [1971] that they were telling the truth that the arms flow had been halted . . . But officials in the middle echelons of the Pentagon interpreted their instructions to mean that the United States would cancel all new commitments of arms to Pakistan but would continue to supply military equipment under the terms of the contracts made, but not implemented.[69]

There was an anomaly in America's entire handling of the arms supply to Pakistan. While Frank Kellogg, Special Assistant to the Secretary of State, denied the report of arms shipments to Pakistan when he was in India, about the same time a Defense Department spokesman reiterated that arms were being legally supplied to Pakistan.[70] Later a State Department spokesman clarified the position and confirmed on June 24 that "military cargo will be loaded on four or five other Pakistani ships within the next month or two."[71] Commenting later on the arms supply episode, President Nixon contended:

> Immediately, in early April, we ceased issuing and renewing licenses for military shipments to Pakistan, we put a hold on arms that had been committed the year before, and we ceased new commitments for economic developmental plans.[72]

Yet Nixon's contention is contradicted by the investigation made by Senator Kennedy's Judiciary Subcommittee on Refugees. It is evident from this that the Administration had made new offers to provide additional military supplies to Pakistan as late as mid-June.[73] The mid-June decision was understandable in the context of Kissinger's impending secret visit to Peking through Islamabad. If President Nixon had really decided to revoke arms supplies to Pakistan at that stage, Yahya Khan could have jeopardized the mission by disclosing the secret. In any event, it was not until November 8th, that the State Department could revoke all outstanding arms licenses worth $3.6 million and thereby end the flow of arms supplies to Pakistan. Before that, for obvious reasons, the U.S. government did not feel that it should revoke the licenses that had been issued. Interestingly, in his memoir Kissinger suggests in contradiction, that the State Department had been moving in a contrary direction. He reveals: "Ignorant of the China initiative, heavily influenced by its traditional Indian bias, in early April—without clearance with the White House—the Department moved towards a new arms embargo on Pakistan." Furthermore, according to his National Security Council staff expert, Harold Saunders, the State Department was moving from a posture of "detachment" to one of dissociation from the Pakistan military regime.[74]

Physical Intervention

In June 1971, on his way to Peking (via Pakistan), Kissinger had also visited New Delhi. On this visit he was reported to have raised the possibility of Chinese involvement on Pakistan's behalf in the event of Indian intervention on Pakistan's East Wing.[75] Some of the Indian analysts and government leaders who met him seemed to have done some plain talking. When the issue of supplies to Pakistan came up in the course of these discussions, Kissinger explained it away as one of "bureaucratic muddle."[76] Significantly, some of the specialists in India with whom Kissinger had discussed the problem of East Bengal, had also broached the subject of the Sino-U.S. connection and its bearing on Indo-U.S. relations. The Presidential aide had reportedly given an evasive reply.[77]

The dramatic announcement about Kissinger's trip to Peking and the upcoming Presidential visit to China disturbed New Delhi. The Indian Government saw in this development, the formation of an axis that could lean heavily on India. Meanwhile the Indian Ambassador in Washington, L. K. Jha was reportedly told by the American Secretary of State, Rogers: "you can rule us out even if you attack Tibet."[78] America's perception of China as a hostile state had undergone a drastic transformation. Hence, the Nixon administration would not be supportive of any hypothetical anti-China action on the part of a third State (even if friendly to the United States). India would have to look for a counterposition to this new triangular relationship in regard to the crisis in East Bengal. From Washington's perspective, the "global priorities" were this time in "maximum contradiction with regard to India and in maximum harmony with regard to Pakistan".[79]

Having sensed danger inherent in changing U.S. priorities, the Indian government sent D. P. Dhar to Moscow to "revive" the Indo-Soviet Treaty of Friendship proposal that had been offered to India as early as 1969. The entire operation was kept secret by Prime Minister Indira Gandhi; only when the draft was finalized did she inform her two senior colleagues. On August 9, the treaty was announced. The important operational clause of the Indo-Soviet treaty was that in the event of "an attack or threat thereof," the two parties will "immediately enter into mutual consultations in order to remove such threat and to take appropriate effective measures."[80] The signing of this treaty meant more vigorous moral and material Soviet assistance to India. In addition, it emboldened India to more vigorous action in regard to East Bengal.

Incidentally, by July, 1971, there was growing consensus among Indian strategic experts that a "war would be economically less burdensome" than the continued care of millions of refugees. It was also believed that India would be in a position to carry out the liberation of Bangladesh, notwithstanding the major powers' opposition.[81] By the end of Autumn this idea gained ground because of the Indo-Soviet treaty and the ineffectiveness of guerrilla warfare in Bangladesh. The Pakistan Army had apparently established control over key production centers and communications points, which posed a dilemma to the Indian government: would the emigre Awami League leadership hold on together, or should it take greater initiative in the confrontation between the Pakistan Army and the guerrilla forces? However, this does not imply that New Delhi was already bothered about decisive action on this issue. One U.S. official has remarked subsequent to his retirement that there is no firm evidence that "India by mid-summer had made a definite decision to go to war or that the Soviets wanted war."[82]

By early August the Nixon administration had decided to persuade Yahya Khan to restore normal conditions in East Bengal. The new policy called for sizeable American aid for the improvement of general political and economic conditions. The Administration however, ruled out any overt pressure for security, Yahya's compliance to the release of Mujib, or the possible working out of a political settlement in East Bengal. Speaking at a news conference on August 4, 1971, President Nixon stated:

> We do not favor the idea that the United States should cut off economic assistance to Pakistan . . . We believe that the most constructive role we can play is to continue our economic assistance to West Pakistan and thereby be able to influence the course of events in a way that will deal with the problem of hunger in East Pakistan, which would reduce the refugee flow into India and which will, we trust, in the future look toward a viable political settlement. We are not going to engage in public pressure on the Government of West Pakistan . . . These are matters that we will discuss only in private channels.[83]

Nixon meanwhile had asked Secretary of State Rogers to discuss with U Thant the conditions in East Bengal. It is not clear whether the U.S. President was seriously thinking about a political settlement there; the above extract suggests that his basic thrust was to generate peaceful conditions rather than a political settlement.

As early as April, Nixon had endorsed a course of action that entailed the use of economic aid as a carrot to induce political concessions by Yahya, but at the same time insisted, "Don't squeeze Yahya at this time". For obvious reasons, the White House had realized that if the U.S. failed to show support to Pakistan, "China would be lost."[84]

Though even earlier in his letter to Mrs. Gandhi and Yahya Khan, Nixon had stressed the need for "political settlement",[85] no reference was made in regard to its structure. According to Kissinger, from August to October eight contacts were made with the leaders of the emigre Bangladesh government. These contacts were presumed to be negotiations between Yahya's regime and the Bangladesh government-in-exile representatives. But the negotiations remained a non-starter; the U.S. was not involved in "substance". It was also claimed that the U.S. Administration had Pakistan's approval to establish contact with Sheikh Mujibur Rahman.[86] A contrary view has been that of Mrs. Gandhi; in a letter to President Nixon she had complained that "there was not even a whisper that anyone from the outside world had tried to have contact with Mujibur Rahman."[87]

Kissinger claims in his memoir that American efforts to initiate secret talks with the Bangladesh government-in-exile representatives was aborted because of Indian obstructions. According to him, it was on the Indian Ambassador to the U.S., L. K. Jha's suggestion that contacts had been established with the exiles in Calcutta. This led to what he called a three month long search for "political accommodation." Using hindsight, Kissinger declared that this process could have been completed if India and Bangladesh had not hindered it.

Kissinger makes another claim without any basis, that Yahya Khan had favorably reacted to such secret talks. He, however, concedes that Yahya wanted to go along with such efforts without any preconditions—such as Mujib's release, etc. At the same time, he takes a paradoxical position that the U.S. did not insist that East Bengal remain part of Pakistan. In this context, Kissinger contends that he had told a WSAG meeting on one occasion, that should India accept this "evolutionary process" and agree to "cooperate with us we could work with them on 90 percent of their problems, like releasing Mujib or attaining some degree of autonomy for Bangladesh, and these steps would lead eventually to their getting it all."[88]

Nowhere does Kissinger spell out the methodology of this approach. Evidently, the entire exercise was designed to buy time for the successful establishment of the U.S.-China connection. In fact, other informed sources suggest that there were only "vague stories and rumors" about secret American "contacts and negotiations" in 1971. Despite Kissinger's reference to these secret talks, details about this episode are not precisely known. There is evidence to suggest that the Nixon administration did make attempts to establish contacts with a faction of the Bangladesh government with a view to split the independence movement.[89] Furthermore,

President Nixon admits in his 1972 Foreign Policy report—presumably drafted by Henry Kissinger—that the "United States cannot be certain that the steps it proposed would have brought about a negotiation, or that such a negotiation would have produced a settlement."[90] This is endorsed by some of the participants in the process. Since neither the U.S. nor Yahya were agreeable to the idea of an independent Bangladesh, the Bengali exiles backed off from such talks. Also, "it is highly unlikely that Yahya's timetable for political evolution would have succeeded." Indeed, according to Kissinger, it would have taken a longer time to bring about a political evolution "than the Indian capacity to withstand the pressures generated by the refugees."[91]

Despite this, President Nixon later stated (in his 1972 state of the world message) that the United States had informed India that she was "prepared to promote discussions of an explicit timetable for East Pakistan's autonomy." In a similar vein Henry Kissinger submits that the Nixon administration had told the Indian Ambassador (L. K. Jha) about its willingness to talk on the precise time for establishing "political autonomy" in East Bengal.[92] Yet, the American Ambassador to New Delhi (Keating) denied that he was aware that Pakistan and the U.S. were prepared to work out the timetable.[93] For all practical purposes, negotiations were a fruitless exercise. Still, President Nixon complained later that even though India was fully informed of these developments, she "indicated little interest." Then he adds: "Meanwhile, India expanded its support of the guerrillas and hostilities along the eastern border."[94]

After the outbreak of war, the U.S. Administration tried to give the impression that India was responsible for escalating the conflict. The U.S. sought to demonstrate that it was aware of the seriousness of the East Bengal problem and hence tried to take the initiative to release Mujib, direct contacts between the Pakistan government and the emigre Bangladesh political leadership, and even make efforts towards political autonomy for East Bengal. But in reality these were distortions; it takes time to prepare such initiatives. Till July, Nixon and Kissinger were more interested in working out the China connection. It was not until late October that Kissinger could devote time to the East Bengal crisis.[95] Keating's revelations do not indicate that Pakistan had authorized contacts with Mujib (on Washington's persuasion). However, it would be quite reasonable to say that if the U.S. really had made some efforts for political settlement, these must have been rather belated and failed to stop the Indo-Pakistan conflict in December.

Despite public pronouncements by the U.S. Administration, there were definite indications by November 12 that the Indo-Pakistan war was "imminent".[96] Earlier, the U.S. tried to make some concerted moves (along with other major powers) to develop a package of assistance, political pressure and restricted arms supply that would defuse the crisis. But this attempt failed partly because of India's diplomatic success in Moscow and the Soviet's refusal to "compromise" on the Indo-Soviet treaty. This meant that the U.S. had to "drop a policy of 'restraint' and develop a policy of action."[97] The U.S. was the only great power in 1971 that had close ties with both India and Pakistan, and hence it was in a position to provide a "political alternative" to a "military solution."[98] This put the burden on the Nixon administration, but without great power unanimity, having ties with two contestants was not enough to manage a crisis.

War Breaks Out

Bangladesh declared its independence on April 17, 1971 at a place called Mujibnagar just inside the border of East Bengal. By Fall, sporadic guerrilla activities had escalated all along the borders inside East Bengal. But it soon became apparent that without Indian military intervention, hit-and-run tactics would not be able to dislodge the Pakistan forces from Bangladesh. While the Indian government wanted the return of the refugees to East Bengal, it also wanted to have a friendly Bangladesh; this was an opportunity to break hostile Pakistan's power once and for all. India presumably calculated that a divided Pakistan would find it difficult to maintain a credible military capability against India, because of the loss of foreign exchange from the breakaway East Wing.

By the time India made its move around the end of Autumn, there were about 100,000 guerrillas (more popularly called Mukti Bahini) operating inside East Bengal.[99] Meanwhile, around the third week of October, amidst the accelerating deterioration in India-Pakistan relations, a final round of diplomatic activity had started. Indira Gandhi started three weeks of diplomatic visits to major western capitals. After her visit with Nixon on November 8, it was stated that the U.S. and India had reached a better understanding about each other's positions. On the same day the U.S. announced the Pakistan-U.S. agreement on the cancellation of licenses for $3.6 million worth of military hardware.[100] Washington was to later argue that there was an understanding that Mrs. Gandhi would again try for a negotiated settlement between the Yahya regime and the Bengalis.[101]

Earlier on October 27, a joint Indo-Soviet statement was issued under Article 9 of the Treaty of Friendship. It declared that the parties agreed that Pakistan was soon going to start an aggressive war in South Asia. The statement was apparently issued as a warning-regarding India's intentions—on the eve of Mrs. Gandhi's departure for Washington. The Soviet counter to any U.S. reactions seemed to have been worked out.[102] The Soviets had evidently come a long way from the days of superpower unanimity over the 1965 conflict.

Throughout the month of November tension built along the Indo-Pakistan border with the deployment of regular army units and continuous skirmishes that marked the outbreak of a war. The United States appealed directly to the two governments to defuse the crisis. On November 10, Assistant Secretary of State Joseph Sisco summoned the ambassadors of India and Pakistan to receive the appeal.[103] Later speaking on November 12, Secretary of State Rogers declared: "diplomatically, we are going to do all that we can to prevent a war from breaking out . . . we have no intention of getting into another war".[104] Later he personally pressed the Pakistani Ambassador and the Indian *charge d'affaire* for military disengagement and the mutual withdrawal of both countries' forces from the border.[105] On November 30 the State Department welcomed Pakistan President Yahya's call for a UN observer force to be sent to East Bengal. However, the war finally began on December 3 after a preemptive Pakistan airstrike on six Indian airstrips in northwestern India. On December 4, India launched a combined ground, air and naval offensive in East Bengal. Linked up with the Mukti Bahini, the Indian armed forces entered East Bengal from five directions and India announced its recognition of the provisional Bangladesh government. In retaliation, Pakistan broke off diplomatic relations with India. By December 15 the Indian forces closed in on Dacca from all sides and in the same day Pakistani military commander General Niazi sent a communication to General Manekshaw through the U.S. Consulate in Dacca and the U.S. Embassy in New Delhi offering cessation of fighting. In his reply General Manekshaw insisted on an unconditional surrender. By December 16 the Pakistan garrison had surrendered and by the next day (following India's announcement of a unilateral ceasefire) the war ended on the West Pakistan border.[106]

Meanwhile, in response to India's military intervention, the Nixon administration tried to force a ceasefire. On December 6,

1971, a State Department official announced the suspension of $87.six million worth of economic aid to India. It was also stated that the U.S. "was not going to make a short-term contribution to the Indian economy to make it easier for the Indian government to sustain its military efforts."[107]   Indian intervention must have angered President Nixon; evidently he felt that India had not given him sufficient time for a political solution. The major efforts of his administration were now directed towards containing this conflict. But this did not mean that the U.S. would be evenhanded in its response. Thus, from diplomatic activities in the UN to direct crisis management initiative, the Nixon administration made it a point to "tilt" in favor of Pakistan. On December 4, on the request of the U.S., an urgent session of the UN Security Council was called; it voted ll to 2 for an immediate ceasefire and withdrawal of foreign forces. The U.S. draft resolution failed adoption as a result of the Soviet Union's negative vote.[108] A second resolution was again vetoed by them. On December 7 the matter was taken to the General Assembly under the Uniting for Peace Resolution. The General Assembly, in a resolution passed by 104 to ll (with ten abstentions), called upon India and Pakistan to cease firing.[109] As anticipated, the Soviet Union had supported India to the hilt.

The secret Washington Special Action Group (WSAG) met four hours after the outbreak of the war. The minutes (revealed by columnist Jack Anderson) indicate that no WSAG member believed that India would agree to a ceasefire until it had achieved its goal of an independent Bangladesh.[110] When the news of the war came, CIA Director Richard Helms was in confusion. He said "there are conflicting reports from both sides and the only common ground is the Pak attacks on the Amritsar, Pathankot and Srinagar airports". Kissinger knew what his mentor wanted; President Nixon was not interested at that point in the relative faults of the contestants. Kissinger made this point clear:

> I am getting hell every half hour from the President that we are not being tough enough to India. He has just called me again. He does not believe we are carrying out his wishes. He wants to tilt in favor of Pakistan. He feels everything we do comes out otherwise.[111]

In any event, the primary task of WSAG was, as it appears from the minutes, to prevent the possible Indian offensive against West Pakistan and Azad Kashmir.

Reporting on this later, Nixon stated that during the week of December 6:

> We received convincing evidence that India was seriously contemplating the seizure of Pakistan-held portions of Kashmir and the destruction of Pakistan's military forces in the West. We could not ignore this evidence. Nor could we ignore the fact that when we repeatedly asked India and its supporters for clear assurances to the contrary we did not receive them.[112]

He added in his report that unless the U.S. had taken a stand against the war, "it would have been prolonged" and there would have been a "greater likelihood", of an attack on West Pakistan. Hence, he concluded, "the war had to be brought to a halt."[113] Needless to say, his preferences had been well taken earlier by his aides.

President Nixon submits in his memoir that he felt that it was important to discourage both "Indian Aggression and Soviet Adventurism." In this context he agreed with Kissinger's recommendations that "we should demonstrate our displeasure with India and our support for Pakistan." His basic rationale was that if the U.S. failed to remain absolutely steadfast behind Pakistan or provide it necessary help, then Iran or any other country within the reach of the Soviet Union might begin to question the credibility of American assistance.[114] Nixon, however, ignored the point that such a preventive action regarding a regional issue involved rather high-risk decisions—almost out of proportion—for the United States. One informed American observer noted that the Nixon-Kissinger geopolitical approach" suffered from certain pitfalls. In fact, in seeking to resolve essentially regional geopolitics, the Nixon administration exaggerated the role and influence of the major external powers in the Subcontinent. Furthermore, both Nixon and Kissinger had been convinced—maybe through their conversations with the Pakistani leaders—that India was determined to destroy Pakistan. But whatever the reasons, "the 'dismemberment' thesis became a fixed idea for both Nixon and Kissinger."[115] In many ways, the U.S. response to the Bangladesh war was a self-fulfilling prophecy.

By December 6, an evacuation crisis had emerged in Dacca. There were reports of an abortive attempt to bring out foreign nationals stranded in the beleaguered city. The U.S. Administration used this as a pretext for putting an eight-ship naval Task Force (headed by an attack carrier, the *Enterprise*) on a holding position near Singapore.[116] While the secret orders to the Task Force mentioned the problem of evacuation, it was also entrusted with the task of negotiating any contingency situation having a bearing on the U.S. interests in the area.[117] While the war as well as the evacuation problem were almost over in Dacca, the naval Task Force was still cruising ahead to the Bengal coast, in search of a mission.

This decision was rationalized by both Nixon and Kissinger in terms of the American government's resolve "to preserve West Pakistan as an independent state." They comprehended that the real Indian aim was to bring about West Pakistan's destruction. The Bangladesh war was considered by the White House as a ruthless power play by New Delhi with alleged Soviet encouragement. Hence, the Nixon administration decided to undertake a high-risk naval intervention.

But in terms of global politics, an additional reason for the Nixon administration was an evident desire to demolish the myth of the Soviet's ability to underwrite decisive actions in crisis situations. Spelling out the rationale behind this naval venture, Kissinger states in his memoir:

> The assault on Pakistan was in our view a most dangerous precedent for Soviet behavior, which had to be resisted if we were not to tempt escalating upheavals. Had we acquiesced in such a power play we would have sent a wrong signal to Moscow and unnerved all our allies, China and the forces for restraint in other volatile areas of the world. This was, indeed, why the Soviets had made the Indian assault on Pakistan possible in the first place.[118]

In a similar vein, Nixon asserts that he wanted to let the Soviets know that the U.S. would strongly oppose the dismemberment of Pakistan by a "Soviet ally using Soviet arms."[119] In light of subsequent developments, it is quite apparent that the Nixon administration had not only misjudged Indian and Soviet intentions, but had also wrongly anticipated a strong Chinese physical reaction on Pakistan's behalf. China played a cautious role during this episode.

According to the Anderson report, the planning of the naval operation was worked out in Kissinger's basement command post.[120] As hindsight suggests, the timing of the Enterprise's move towards the Bay of Bengal might have been determined by strategic rather than tactical considerations. First, it sought to signal to India and the Soviets that the U.S. could not allow an ally to be destroyed. Rightly or wrongly, the Nixon-Kissinger team was fearful that India would deliberately force the disintegration of Pakistan.[121]

The second purpose was to demonstrate to the Chinese that the U.S. was capable of taking a stand against any Soviet-supported strategic changes on China's periphery.[122] Third, it was a naval demonstration to match the possible Soviet naval presence in South Asia. This "demonstration" was, in some ways, inherent in the strategic relationship between the U.S. and the Soviet Union. Finally, it is not impossible in view of Pakistan's role in the bridge-building efforts to Peking, that there was also an attempt on the Nixon's part to demonstrate American credibility as an alliance partner, even if at a symbolic level. Thus, while Indian intentions were used as a rationale for naval demonstrations, in reality it was a reminder to the Soviets that a tactical victory should not be converted into a strategic advantage. Paradoxically, though the Administration was not eager to enact a Cuban missile drama on the Bay of Bengal, seems to have inadvertently overcommitted itself.

In any event, with the fall of Dacca followed by India's announcement of a unilateral ceasefire on December 16, the *Enterprise* episode came to an end. This unilateral ceasefire was later interpreted to be the result of the naval demonstration. Kissinger claims that by moving the naval Task Force, the United States had created precisely the "margin of uncertainty" necessary for compelling New Delhi and Moscow to agree to a ceasefire in the West.[123] There is, however, no substantive evidence to suggest that the American fleet movement had a bearing on Soviet decision-making. In fact, a Brookings study of this episode tends to confirm that "Soviet and Indian support for a ceasefire was not the result of U.S. military pressures generated by Task Force 74." Aside from long-term impact on U.S. interests, the *Enterprise* deployment did not have much immediate political or military bearing on South Asian developments.[124]

The Policy Process

The U.S. policy process in regard to the Indo-Pakistan war of 1971 was highly centralized—a characteristic feature of the Nixon administration. The three principal decisions were: a) avoidance of overt comments on the military crackdown in East Bengal; b) the question of refugee relief assistance and the cutback of arms sales to Pakistan; c) a threat of physical intervention. In making these decisions the administration kept things under excessive control. (It should be noted that the WSAG leak was one of the events that led Nixon to establish the "Plumbers" of Watergate fame, which ultimately led to his own resignation.) While one could argue that this was a salient feature of the Nixon-Kissinger system, there were operational reasons stemming from the U.S.' pursuit of China. Paradoxically, Nixon, a one time cold warrior, had developed a less doctrinaire approach towards international relations when he became President. Though like Kennedy and Johnson his system was also based on close consultation with aides, there was one basic difference: he believed in a more structured format of consultation rather than the weekly informal lunch-group meetings of his two predecessors. Kissinger provided the policy memorandum on each foreign policy issue which deserved Presidential attention. Everything followed according to plan. While this system has its merits, it was too rigid to respond effectively to a rapidly changing situation, or absorb new information. In a certain sense this is what happened to the Nixon administration in handling the South Asian crisis of 1971: the policy mechanism designed to implement a global strategy was inadequate to handle the complexity of a distant and unfamiliar regional problem.

Presumably, the Nixon administration's slow response to the 1971 South Asian crisis was also produced by the low status of the area. One scholar has perceptively observed that a problem in a low priority area such as South Asia "has to be more serious before it reaches the crisis level."[125] This factor complemented the American interest in achieving a diplomatic breakthrough with China.

Because of its excessive centralization and secrecy, U.S. policy towards the 1971 Indo-Pakistan war was marked by certain distortions. Since every small policy decision had to be fitted into Kissinger's grand strategy, it underplayed the reality of even obvious humanitarian issues, e.g. refugee relief aid, mass killings, etc. But at the same time, deceptions were used to hide the U.S. administration's real intentions regarding the problem. There was a lack of policy coordination between the White House and the State Department. From the outset the State Department tended to perceive the East Pakistan crisis less alarmingly than the Nixon-Kissinger team. It believed India had only a limited aim in East Pakistan and no designs on West Pakistan. It also reasoned that there was only the smallest risk of Soviet or Chinese intervention in this matter. Hence, it advocated a policy of wait and see. President Nixon disagreed with this, what he calls a "bland assessment." This led to a White House-centered, closed decision-making system that was not equipped to deal with a multifaceted regional crisis—not especially a part of the White House agenda.[126]

In several ways, Nixon's pique with India had contributed to the tilt towards Pakistan. In this context, in "imposing" this policy Kissinger also exhibited an anti-India bias.[127] Perhaps, the Nixon administration was willing to pay the price for Yahya's role as an intermediary in the Washington-Peking connection, and earn Indian enmity because the two key decision-makers cared little for India's respect?

As for some of the other decision-makers, the U.S. Congress also influenced certain aspects of U.S. policy during the crisis. Of the various Congressional Committees, Senator Kennedy's Senate Judiciary Subcommittee on refugees played a significant role in highlighting the tragic events in the Subcontinent. Surprisingly on an issue such as this, the Foreign Relations committees of the Senate and House did not take any direct initiative. However, Congressional members in general did put pressure on the Administration to suspend arms and economic aid to Pakistan.

Thus, so far as the decisions were concerned, the entire crisis had been handled by Kissinger and the WSAG team under the supervision of the President himself. In analyzing the minutes of its meetings, one gets the impression that there was a "group think" prevailing which inevitably seemed to have produced the *"Enterprise* episode."[128] First, there was consensus in the meeting—despite Sisco's initial reservations—that India was all set to drive through West Pakistan and Azad Kashmir to destroy Pakistan's armor and the military machine. Second, most members had apparently acquiesced in the idea that at least strategically, it was counterproductive to follow an evenhanded policy via-a-vis India and Pakistan. But the point is, that Nixon's "tilt" towards Pakistan preceded and did not follow the considerations of these basic issues produced by the Indo-Pakistan conflict. From this standpoint, the WSAG members merely reinforced Nixon's policies and perceptions, they did not influence them.

Notes

1. Hasan Askari Rizvi, *Internal Strife and External Intervention* (Lahore: Progressive Publishers, 1981), pp. 62-84. This is a careful account by a Pakistani scholar. For a Bangladeshi study of the failure of national

integration in Pakistan, see Rounaq Jahan, *Pakistan: Failure in National Integration* (New York: Columbia University Press, 1972).

2. For a broader study of the sources and pattern of the American foreign policy response to the evolving South Asian crisis of 1971, see Dan Haendel, *The Process of Priority Formulation: U.S. Foreign Policy in the Indo-Pakistan War of 1971* (Boulder, Colorado: Westview Press, 1977).

3. In the subsequent period, the entire episode in retrospect was seen as a "defeat without surrender" because of Pakistani inability to reactivate the Kashmir issue even after triggering the armed conflict with India in 1965. This in turn generated a myth that there was a deeply-laid conspiracy to oust Ayub Khan by getting him discredited. For different Pakistani viewpoints, see, "1965 War: Was it a Conspiracy," *Defence Journal* (Karachi), IV (Nos. 9-10, 1978). The entire issue is devoted to this problem.

4. Brig. A. R. Siddiqi (Retd.), "1971: Causes and Conduct," *Ibid.*, 2 (No. 12, 1976), pp. 1-11.

5. See, G. W. Chaudhury, *The Last Days of United Pakistan* (Bloomington: Indiana University Press, 1974), p. 8; also see S. M. Burke, *Mainsprings of Indian and Pakistani Foreign Policies* (Minneapolis: University of Minnesota, 1974), p. 191.

6. These six points were: (1) a federal basis of the state; (2) center shall deal only with Defense and Foreign Affairs; (3) two separate currencies for the two wings; (4) power of taxation and revenue collection to the federating units; (5) two separate accounts for foreign exchange; (6) setting up of a militia or a para-military force for East Pakistan.

7. For a detailed account of the political turmoil in Pakistan, see H. Feldman, *From Crisis to Crisis 1962-1969* (London: Oxford University Press, 1972).

8. *Dawn*, December 28, 1970. It appears from an informed participant observer's account that Mujib had assured Yahya that he would modify his six-point autonomy plan. Cited, G. W. Chaudhury, n. 7, p. 128.

9. Cited, Henry Kissinger, *White House Years* (Boston: Little Brown, 1979), p. 850.

10. While most analysts expected the Awami League to win the elections in East Pakistan with a convincing margin, not many of them were prepared to make firm electoral forecasts about West Pakistan. Writing in *The Observer* (London) Gavin Young predicted at least 130 seats out of 162 seats for the Awami League. But AFP, the French News Agency made a projection of 70 per cent of these seats for the Awami League (cited, Dilip Mukerjee, *Zulfiqar Ali Bhutto: Quest for Power* (New Delhi: Vikas, 1972), p. 69. In contrast, Werner Adam of the *Far Eastern Economic Review* (Hong Kong), December 5, 1970, expected not more than 20 per cent of the People's Party candidates to win in the West Wing.

11. *Bangladesh Documents*, Vol. I (New Delhi: Ministry of External Affairs, no year), p. 213.

12. Contrary to the normal practice, the announcement was read out on his behalf. There was speculation that Yahya had to make this decision against

his will. Bhutto seemed to have worked with other senior army generals to derail the move towards any arrangement based on autonomy of the units. For details see, G. W. Chaudhury, *The Last Days of United Pakistan*, pp. 146-47; also see Kuldip Nayar, *Distant Neighbors*, pp. 146-50.

13. For an inside view of these talks and dialogue see, Chaudhury, pp. 132-79.

14. For text of the "Operation Searchlight" plan see Siddiq Saliq, *Witness to Surrender* (Karachi: Oxford University Press, 1978), Appendix III, pp. 229-234.

15. Henry Kissinger, *White House Years*, p. 852. "The miscalculation on which" this "murderous campaign" was based "is beyond understanding" of even informed observers. See Chaudhury, p. 181.

16. Based on Siddiq Saliq, pp. 49-62. A public relations officer in the Pakistan Army, Saliq was on a tour of duty in Bangladesh (then East Pakistan) from January 1970 to December 16, 1971. It appears from his account that it was in disapproval of this "policy of deliberate crisis and consequent repression" that Lieutenant General Yaqub Khan had earlier resigned from the position of East Pakistan's governor. (He was succeeded by Lieutenant General Tikka Khan on March 7.)

17. A resolution in support and sympathy for the East Bengal people was moved by the Indian Prime Minister Indira Gandhi on March 21, 1971. It declared "the House wishes to assure them that their struggle and sacrifice will receive the whole-hearted sympathy of the people of India." For text, see *Bangladesh Documents*, p. 672.

18. It seems Prime Minister Gandhi was requested by Foreign Secretary T. N. Kaul for Indian recognition of the emigre Bangladesh government. Her position was that unless the Bangladesh government was able to establish effective territorial control, Indian action could create global misapprehension that India was trying to set up a puppet regime in Bangladesh. Her plea was "when the time comes, we will do it." cited T. N. Kaul, *Diplomacy in Peace and War* (New Delhi: Vikas, 1979), pp. 181-82.

19. *Bangladesh Documents*, Vol. I, p. 674.

20. For an Indian account, see Pran Chopra, *India's Second Liberation* (Cambridge Mass.: The MIT Press, 1974); also see D. D. Khanna, *India-Pakistan Conflict 1971: Causes and Conflict* (Allahabad: Department for Defence Studies, University of Allahabad, 1981). For the Pakistan side of the story see Fazal Muqueem Khan, *Pakistan's Crisis in Leadership* (Lahore: National Book Foundation, 1973).

21. William Barnds, "India, Pakistan and American Real politik," Christianity and Crisis (June 12, 1972). Cited G. W. Choudhury, *India, Pakistan, Bangladesh and the Major Power: Politics of a Divided Subcontinent*, (New York: The Free Press, 1975), p. 207.

22. Stephen P. Cohen, "South Asia and U.S. Military Policy", *Commission on the Organization of the Government for the Conduct of Foreign Policy*, June 1975 (Washington: U.S. Government Printing Press, 1975), Vol. VII, p. 149.

23. Marvin Kalb and Bernard Kalb, *Kissinger* (Boston: Little Brown, 1974), pp. 243-244.

24. Kissinger, p. 849. While he submits that because of "hardheaded reasons" the U.S. attached priority to its relations with India, he finds the 1965 American "evenhandedness" in suspending military supply to both India and Pakistan as being "deceptive." He reveals that even President Johnson was aware of this "one-sidedness of his action"—considering India's greater potential and alternative supply sources. Johnson had promised to rectify this distortion by supplying tanks through a third party such as Turkey. (*Ibid.*, pp. 846-849).

25. The 1966-67 policy stipulated the sale of "non-lethal" arms to India and Pakistan on a case by case basis. This one-time exception was publicly justified as a "symbolic offset to Pakistan's growing dependence on Chinese arms." cited Stephen P. Cohen, South Asia Policy and U.S. Military Policy," in *Commission on the Organization of the Government for the Conduct of Foreign Policy*, Vol. VII, Appendix V, June 1975, Washington, D.C. p. 155. Kissinger admits that the one time exception had been part of the price for securing Yahya Khan's service for playing middleman between Peking and Washington. (Kissinger, pp. 32-33).

26. For an analysis of this aspect, see Shivaji Ganguly, *Pakistan-China Relations: A Study in Interaction* (Urbana: Center for Asian Studies, University of Illinois, 1971), pp. 32-33.

27. Sisir Gupta, "The Soviet-Indian Treaty", *Survival* (November, 1971), p. 377.

28. Marvin Kalb and Bernard Kalb, *Kissinger* (Boston: Little Brown, 1974), pp.258-264.

29. Kissinger, p. 848-849.

30. Christopher Van Hollen, "The Tilt Revisited: Nixon-Kissinger Geopolitics and South Asia", *Asian Survey*, Vol. XX, No. 4 (April 1985), p. 341 (The author was Deputy Assistant Secretary of State for Near Eastern and South Asian Affairs). Nixon was reported to have assured Yahya Khan in October 1980 "nobody has occupied the White House who is friendlier to Pakistan." G. W. Chaudhury, "Reflections on Sino-Pakistan Relations," *Pacific Community*, 7 (2) January, 1976, p. 266.

31. Kalb and Kalb, p. 258.

32. Second Annual Report to the Congress on U.S. foreign policy, February 25, 1971. See, U.S. President, *Public Papers of the Presidents of the United States* (Washington D.C.: Office of the Federal Register, National Archives and Records Service, 1969-74), Richard Nixon, 1971, p. 277.

33. *Ibid.*, p. 280.

34. *Ibid.*, p. 281. "Do not forget the bridge which you crossed in coming here," the Chinese Premier had reminded Henry Kissinger in Peking. Cited, Zulfikar Ali Bhutto, *Bilateralism: New Directions* (Islamabad: Ministry of Information and Broadcasting, Government of Pakistan, No Year), p. 22.

35. *Ibid.*, p. 281.

36. Kuldip Nayar's interview with Bhutto and Mujib. Cited, Nayar, *Distant Neighbors* (New Delhi: Vikas, 1972), p. 152.

37. For a Bengali view expressed by a former West Pakistan based journalist, see A. Mascarenhas, *The Rape of Bangladesh*(Delhi: Vikas, 1971), pp. 10-120. For a Pakistani view, see L. Rushbrook Williams, *The East Pakistan Tragedy* (London: Tom Stacey, 1972), pp. 66-76.

38. Prime Minister Indira Gandhi's statement in the Indian Parliament, March 27, 1971; also, resolution passed by the Indian Parliament, March 31, 1971. See, *Bangladesh Documents*, Vol. I., pp. 670-672.

39. Statement by British Prime Minister, Edward Heath March 27, 1971. Cited, *Pakistan Horizon* 24 (No. 2, 1971), pp. 141-42.

40. President Podgorny's message to President Yahya Khan, April 2, 1971 see *Soviet Review*, (USSR Embassy, New Delhi), 9 (January 18, 1972), supplement, pp. 16-17.

41. For text, see *Pakistan Horizon* XXIV, pp. 153-4.

42. Philip Oldenburg, "The Breakup of Pakistan," in, *Organization of the Government*, Vol. 7, (referred to earlier in Chapter 1), p. 169.

43. Hollen, p. 342. He was one of these officials. In a rare act of collective dissent the officials led by Consul-General (Dacca) Archer Blood sent a joint cable entitled, "Dissent From U.S. Policy Towards East Pakistan" to the State Department. This was also supported by the State Department's South Asia area specialists. The cable charged the Nixon Administration with "bending backwards to placate the West Pak dominated government." For text of this cable and further reactions within the State, see Appendices to Part II: A. The Carnegie Papers, in Lawrence Lifschultz, *Bangladesh: The Unfinished Revolution*(London: Zed Press, 1979), pp. 155-68, the U.S. Ambassador to New Delhi, Kenneth Keating, had also reported to Washington that he was "deeply shocked at the massacre." He urged the American Administration not only for public condemnation of "this brutality" but also abrogation of the "one-time exception," regarding arms supply to Pakistan. Cited, Kissinger, p. 853.

44. Kissinger, p. 854. Some informed observers suggest that a U.S. statement of disapproval would not have made Yahya Khan back out as a contact point between Peking and Washington. Besides, there were alternative channels of communication available to the U.S. Administration.

45. See, *Facts on File*, 1971, p. 243.

46. See, *Department of State Bulletin*, Vol. LXIV, No. 1661, April 26, 1971, p. 554.

47. Kissinger, p. 853.

48. Richard Nixon, *Memoirs* (London: Sidgwick and Jackson, 1978), p. 525.

49. See Consul General Archer Blood's testimony, June 28, 1971, U.S. Congress, *Senate Judiciary Subcommittee to Investigate Problems of Refugees and Escapees, Relief Problem in East Pakistan and India*, Hearings, 92nd Congress, 1st Session, 1971, p. 46. (Hereafter, *Senate Judiciary Subcommittee Hearings*.)

50. Statement by General Tikka Khan (in charge of Pakistan military operations in East Bengal), cited, *The New York Times*, May 7, 1971.

51. Speaking at a press conference in Bombay, April 15, 1971. *Times of India*, April 16, 1971.

52. Cited, J. K. Ray, "The United States and Bangladesh," *The Institute for Defence Studies and Analyses Journal*, 4 (April 1972), p. 499.

53. He was transferred in early June, 1971. Laurence Stern, "Diplomacy in the Face of Holocaust," *The Guardian* (Manchester), January 7, 1972.

54. Oldenburg, p. 170. But no one who disagreed with the Administration's stand on the crisis resigned.

55. Jack Anderson, with George Clifford, *The Anderson Papers* (New York: Random House, 1973), pp. 242-45.

56. Senate Judiciary Subcommittee, *Hearings*, p. 87.

57. About the outbreak of the crisis and the killings see, Peggy Durdin, "The Political Tidal Wave That Struck East Pakistan," *New York Times Magazine*, May 2, 1971.

58. U.S. Congress, *Senate Judiciary Subcommittee to Investigate Problems of Refugees and Escapees, Crisis in South Asia, a report submitted by Senator Edward Kennedy* (November 1, 1971), p. 55. (Hereafter *Crisis in South Asia*).

59. Kissinger, p. 853.

60. For the text of the communications, see *Pakistan Horizon* 24 (No. 2, 1971), pp. 140-41.

61. Letter from Senator Edward Kennedy (Chairman Subcommittee on Refugees) to Secretary of State William Rogers, May 27, 1971. See Senate Judiciary Committee Hearings, pp. 84-85.

62. For the text of this report see, Senate Judiciary Subcommittee *Hearings*, pp. 211-26.

63. Secretary of State, Rogers' letter to Chairman, Senate Judiciary Subcommittee on Refugees, Senator Kennedy, June 15, 1971. *Ibid.*, pp. 85-86.

64. Testimony by Deputy Assistant Secretary of State for Northeast and South Asia, in Senate Appropriations Subcommittee on Foreign Operations, July 14, 1971. See, *Department of State Bulletin* LXV (August 23), 1971, p. 206.

65. U.S. Statement released by Charles Bray, Director, Office of Press Relations (Department of State) June 17, 1971. See, *Department of State Bulletin* LXV (July 12), 1971, p. 41.

66. Oldenburg, p. 172.

67. Cited, *Ibid.*, for the reference about the Indian cost of refugee relief, see, statement by Samar Sen, Indian Representative to the U.N., Security Council, December 4, 1971. *Bangladesh Documents*, Vol. 1, p. 428.

68. Letter dated April 20, 1971. See, Senate Judiciary Subcommittee *Hearings*, p. 82.

69. Bulletin of the American Academy of Arts and Sciences. Summer (1973). See, U.S. Congress, Senate Judiciary Subcommittee on Refugees, Relief Problems in Bangladesh, *Hearings*, 92nd Congress, 2nd Session, February 2, 1972, Appendix III, pp. 85-92. Testimony by Christopher Van Hollen,

Deputy Assistant Secretary of State for Near Eastern and South Asian Affairs, Department of State, October 4, 1971. *See Senate Judiciary Subcommittee on Refugees, 1971*, p. 376.

70. *International Herald Tribune*, June 23, 1971, cited, J. K. Ray, p. 504.

71. *Statesman*, June 30, 1971. *Ibid.*, p. 505.

72. See State of the World message in, *U.S. Foreign Policy for the 1970's: The Emerging Structure of Peace, a report to the Congress by Richard Nixon, President of the United States*, February 9, 1972, p. 142.

73. *Senate Judiciary Subcommittee on Refugees*, 1971, p. 356. Senator Frank Church said on June 22, 1971, that the arms shipment to Pakistan was "one more instance of our Government saying one thing and then Congress and then the American public hearing later that the facts are contrary".

74. Kissinger, p. 854. Van Hollen, in a subsequent article on the Bangladesh episode, claims that during the crisis there was lack of Presidential leadership and "coherent policy direction." See Van Hollen p. 345.

75. Pran Chopra, *India's Second Liberation* (New Delhi: Vikas, 1973), p. 84.

76. *Times of India*, July 8, 1971.

77. Based on personal research in New Delhi.

78. Cited, Kuldip Nayar, *Distant Neighbors*, p. 163.

79. Wayne Wilcox, *The Emergence of Bangladesh* (Washington, D.C.: American Enterprise Institute for Public Policy Research, 1973), pp. 33-34.

80. For a background to the making of the treaty see Kuldip Nayar, *Distant Neighbors*, pp. 163-164. For text of the treaty see *Foreign Affairs Reports* (New Delhi), Vol. XX (September 1971), p. 1.

81. On July 3, 1971 there was a close-door conference of Indian Journalists, academicians, retired army officials and some government officials at the Indian Council of World Affairs, New Delhi. Some of the presentations were later published in *Foreign Affairs Reports*, 21 (January 1972), pp. 1-25.

82. Cited in Van Hollen, p. 364. In fact he reveals that "contrary assessments" were made by CIA Director Richard Helms and Assistant Secretary of State Joseph Sisco. This is contrary to commonly held notions. Kissinger claims in his memoir that in May, 1971, it was learned from "reliable" sources that Mrs. Gandhi had "ordered plans for a lightning 'Israeli-type' attack to take over East Pakistan" see Kissinger, p. 856.

83. *Public Papers of the Presidents of the United States. Richard Nixon*, p. 851.

84. Cited, Kissinger, p. 856. Also derived from the Carnegie Study on the conduct of U.S. government policy during the Bangladesh crisis cited by Lawrence Lifschultz, *Bangladesh: The Unfinished Revolution* (London: Zed, 1979), p. 162.

85. *The Emerging Structure of Peace*, p. 143.

86. "India-Pakistan: Background Briefing with Henry A. Kissinger", printed in *Congressional Record*, December 9, 1971, p. S21014. (Hereafter Background).

87. Letter dated December 16, 1971. For text see, *Bangladesh Documents*, Vol. II, pp. 302-304.

88. For details, see Henry Kissinger, pp. 842-918. President Nixon also claims confidently in his memoirs, "We knew that Yahya Khan eventually would have to yield to East Pakistan's demand for independence and we urged him to take a more moderate and conciliatory line.", *The Memoirs of Richard Nixon*, (London: Sidgwick and Jackson, 1978, p. 525.)

89. See "The Carnegie Papers," cited in Lawrence Lifschultz, *Bangladesh: The Unfinished Revolution*, (London: Zed, 1979), Appendices to Part II, p. 155.

90. *The Emerging Structure of Peace*, p. 145.

91. Kissinger's statement to the press in December 1971. Cited Van Hollen, p. 349.

92. For Nixon's submission see, *The Emerging Structure of Peace*, for Kissinger's remarks see Background, p. S. 21013 (Also see his memoir, Chapter XXI.

93. Cited, Anderson, p. 238.

94. *The Emerging Structure of Peace*, p. 145.

95. Kalb and Kalb, p. 295.

96. Intelligence report from Islamabad and New Delhi, D1A1B, 219-71, referred in Keating's secret cable to White House. See Anderson, p. 238.

97. Wilcox, p. 43.

98. Nixon's foreign policy report, 1972, See,*The Emerging Structure of Peace*, p. 143.

99. For details see Louis Dupree, Bangladesh: Indian Intervention Wins Bangladesh its Independence, Part II, *Fieldstaff Reports* 16 (No. 6, 1972).

100. Statement by Department of State Spokesman Charles Bray, November 9, 1971. For text see, *Pakistan Horizon* 24 (No. 4, 1971), p. 172.

101. Background Briefing.

102. *The Times* (London), October 28, 1971. Wilcox, p. 45.

103. Statement by State Department Spokesman, November 11, 1971. Text in *Pakistan Horizon* 24 (No. 4, 1971), p. 173.

104. *Ibid.*

105. Statement by Department of State spokesman, November 25, 1971. Text, *Ibid.*, pp. 174-75.

106. For an account of the war see, Robert Jackson, pp. 106-45.

107. For an analysis of the decision to suspend economic aid to India, see Joan Hochman "The Suspension of Economic Assistance to India" in *Organization of the Government for the Conduct of Foreign Policy*, p. 105

108. *S/10416* (1971).

109. *U. N. Doc. A/RES/2793* (xxvi).

110. Texts of Secret Documents on Top-Level U.S. Discussions of Indian-Pakistani War. (1971), *Minutes of Washington Special Action Group* (Hereafter *WSAG Minutes*).

111. *Ibid.*

112. *The Emerging Structure of Peace*, pp. 147-48.

113. *Ibid.*
114. See Nixon, p. 526.
115. Christopher Van Hollen, p. 355.
116. Dispatch by Craig Whitney, *The New York Times*, December 13, 1971.
117. J. M. McConnell, "Super-Power Naval Diplomacy" *Survival*, 15 (November-December 1973), pp. 289-290.
118. Kissinger, pp. 886, 913-14.
119. Nixon, p. 527.
120. Anderson, p. 263.
121. WSAG minutes. December 8, 1971. This was what Kissinger had expressed in that meeting. In his recent television interview with David Frost, the former President insisted that but for the U.S. naval demonstration, West Pakistan might have been destroyed by India. See, excerpts of interviews, *The New York Times*, May 25, 1977.
122. Based on personal interviews.
123. Kissinger, pp. 912-13. Nixon recalls in his memoir that in a letter to Brezhnev he had urged him in the strongest terms to restrain India. Then he goes on to claim that by using "behind-the-scene pressure" the U.S. government was able "to save West Pakistan from the imminent threat of Indian aggression and domination." See Nixon, p. 530.
124. Barry M. Blechman and Stephen S. Kaplan, *Force Without War* (Washington: The Brookings Institution, 1978), p. 200; also Christopher Van Hollen, p. 356.
125. Oldenburg.
126. Nixon, p. 527. Kissinger contends that it was because of his deteriorating relations with Secretary of State Rogers that their policy differences had been exacerbated—which in the process "endangered coherent policy." Kissinger, p. 887. Also see Christopher Van Hollen, p. 357.
127. Dan Haendal, *The Process of Priority Formulation: U.S. Foreign Policy in the Indo-Pakistan War of 1971* (Boulder: Westview Press, 1977), pp. 297-301.
128. See *WSAG Minutes*, especially the meeting of December 6, 1971.

7

Conclusion

When considered together our case studies of the American response to crisis in South Asia reveal a number of important points about the American foreign policy process in general and its relationship to a region that was marginal to America's larger strategic interests. Two points seem to be overriding.

First, no single description or theory of the American foreign policy process explains U.S. behavior over all four cases. This suggests extreme caution in absorbing and applying the "lessons" drawn from either single-case studies or sweeping surveys of American foreign policy that extend over decades. The U.S. behaves not only like a great power, with a full complement of planning staffs, departments, strategists, and doctrine, but also as a power new to the world with a changing and volatile domestic politics that often impinges on foreign policy, even where not intended. While particular policies have been pursued by the U.S. with persistence over a long period of time, the U.S. is no more (and perhaps a lot less) consistent than most other major powers.

Second, the characteristic American pattern of involvement in South Asia has been intervention and withdrawal—or "in and "out"—or, perhaps a systolic and diastolic alternation of engagement and disengagement, steered largely by broader, non-regional strategic interests. This may well be the pattern for other "marginal" areas as well. Since most decision-making studies of U.S. foreign policy dwell on superpower-superpower relations (and the memoir literature is dominated by such relations) America can be rather parochial and uninformed about important regions of the world that are not central to its own immediate interests. Many scholars and policy makers have pointed out over the years that the U.S. has tended to make serious mistakes in "marginal" regions, especially in Asia; our case studies seem to bear this out.[1]

It remains in this chapter to further explore these and other conclusions and speculate briefly about the future. For, in foreign affairs as in all politics, past patterns may influence the future, but new developments do occur. Indeed, we have seen that throughout America's intermittent engagement in South Asia there *have* been region-based American interests at stake. It is particularly important to note where these have grown in importance, even during the recent Carter and Reagan administrations.

The Policy Process: Essential Unpredictability

This book has been based on the assumption that a better understanding of the U.S. foreign policy process in a region marginal to vital American interests could be obtained by studying intensively a number of cases.

To recapitulate, these studies were guided by five organizing propositions:

—First, superpowers do act purposively towards even a relatively marginal region and have in mind some conception as to how the latter should be managed or structured;

—Second, any major nation tends to behave adaptively when responding to an emerging situation. It may also reveal a degree of ambivalence, because of the simultaneous and conflicting pressures of global, regional, and bilateral relationships;

—Third, foreign policy is the resultant of a multi-causal process determined by the interaction of systemic and institutional forces, operating within the context of a perceived "national role" in the particular international environment;

—Fourth, the U.S. policy making process is marked by a high degree of Presidential involvement, even in a low priority area such as South Asia;

—Finally, decisions—whether concerning a conflictual or non-conflictual situation—tend to remain within the executive branch, except for cases calling for sizeable and rapid transfer of economic or military resources, or requiring (as they increasingly have, under recent intrusive legislation) Congressional endorsement.

Our study of the Sino-Indian war is supportive of the first proposition. Here U.S. interests in the Subcontinent coincided with a major goal of its wider Asian policy—containment of Chinese power. As such, U.S. policy during the crisis was based on a clear conception of the issues at stake and the posture that should be adopted.

The second case study (on food aid) again lends support to our first proposition. But certain caveats need to be entered here. Despite the fact that the grant of food aid was linked to humanitarian considerations as well as the need to underwrite the stability of the major South Asian state, the "eleventh hour generosity" generated a considerable amount of Indian resentment.

In the 1965 Indo-Pakistan war the U.S. maintained a low profile and worked chiefly through the medium of the United Nations. Clearly, the basic intent was to prevent the further conflagration of the crisis. This policy was facilitated by a similar Soviet position.

In the final case study, the absence of a similar Soviet position effectively blocked the U.S. desire to diffuse the conflict. Certain aspects of American policy during the crisis (for example, the dispatch of the *Enterprise*) were related not only to U.S. interests in South Asia but to Washington's relations with Peking and Moscow as well. There was a need to lend substance to the newly found China connection by demonstrating to China that the U.S. was capable of responding to the attempts of the Soviet Union to attain predominant position through proxy. Each of these case studies demonstrate that the U.S. had a clear conception of its interests in each instance. However, episodes such as the Bangladesh crisis and intervening factors prevented a complete realization of these interests.

As far as the second proposition is concerned, only the Bangladesh case study reveals American ambivalence toward the situation. While the Nixon administration could not remain impervious to the humanitarian question, it also realized that Indian ambitions vis-a-vis Pakistan had to be curtailed and the scope and level of Soviet involvement kept within bounds. The ambivalent approach toward humanitarian issues was determined by the operation of these cross-pressures. The impact of cross-pressures was less significant in the case of the 1962 Sino-Indian war, the Food Crisis and the 1965 Indo-Pakistan war.

In the case of the third proposition, all the case studies are corroborative. In each case there was a clear conception of what the U.S. role should be and where its interests lay. As the proposition suggests, several different factors determine the decisions that were taken. In the case of food aid, humanitarian consideration played a role in spite of Johnson's "holding action" on the food shipments. In regard to the other cases strategic considerations were important.

As for the fourth proposition, which deals with the degree of Presidential involvement, in the case studies on U.S. food aid and the naval demonstration in the 1971 Bangladesh crisis, the decisions were marked by considerable Presidential involvement. On the other hand, in the case of the Sino-Indian war and the Indo-Pakistan war of 1965, the evidence does not indicate that the involvement of the President was conspicuous. There was far greater delegation of authority than in the other two case studies. In the Sino-Indian war, the U.S. Ambassador in New Delhi (John Kenneth Galbraith) and in regard to the 1965 Indo-Pakistan war, the U.S. Representative in the U.N.(Arthur Goldberg) played critical roles in the formulation of U.S. policies.

The fifth proposition, in regard to legislative endorsement, is applicable only to a limited degree in the present study. While in the case of food aid President Johnson consulted the Congress—in apprehension of growing Congressional concern about foreign aid—in the other case studies legislative involvement appears to have been routine rather than critical. A partial exception was the decision to suspend arms transfers to the sub-continent during the 1965 Indo-Pak war. Here, however, the initiative came from the Administration, with the Congress playing a complementary role.

If one adopts the decision-making approach in foreign policy studies, this necessarily entails paying relatively more attention to a decisional setting. A clear case in point is the bureaucratic politics model which seeks to disentangle the interplay of competing perspectives on a given issue. While this aspect is undoubtedly of importance to any decisional outcome, a more complete picture is obtained by looking at another aspect of the question—the pertinent features of the issue-area itself and the way in which the major decisionmakers assess them. For example, in an issue area such as the 1962 India-China war, our understanding is enhanced by focussing on the features of the particular issue. The relevant factors here are: the nature of the issue area (whether it is conflictual or non-conflictual), the approach it entails, the form of action taken toward the situation, and the rationale provided for the consequent action. The table on the following page classifies each of the issue areas in terms of the criteria just mentioned.

Our case studies demonstrate that no single approach is adequate to explain the complexity of the foreign policy process—in terms of decision-making and the consequent patterns of response. This pattern changed markedly from administration to administration, and this suggests the inadequacy of the bureaucratic politics model, or, indeed, any other single model. Our basic assumption has been that while the study of a single foreign policy decision highlights the mechanics of deciding about a certain action at a given time, it does not provide a systematic understanding of the salient features of the entire process over a period of time. Our strategy of enquiry permitted the integration of our findings on a superpower's external behavior at the specific regional as well as the wider global level. While some of the case-studies—especially the food crisis—do stress autonomous developments within South Asia and the U.S. response to the situation, they also noted the impact of these issues on global power relationships.

Issues, Process and Policy: Summary Table

Event/ Issue	Situational Variable	Decision or Action	Nature of Approach	Rationale
Sino-Indian war, 1962	Conflictual	Arms Aid	Cooperative Interaction	Limited strategic consideration: to ensure regional peace and stability by underwriting Indian defense capabilities
Indo-Pak war, 1965	Conflictual	Stoppage of military and economic aid	Tactical non-interference (backed by limited pressure)	Conflict resolution through persuasion *cum* restrained pressure to prevent third power intervention (China)
Indian food crisis, 1965-67	Non-conflictual	Emergency food aid	Intervention through controlled flow of food supply	Humanitarian and economic needs
Indo Pak war, 1971	Conflictual	Military display *cum* economic pressure against India	Intervention	Strategic/global: to demonstrate credibility of U.S. power against USSR and regional: to prevent destruction of Pakistan

The interrelatedness of regional and global policies is underlined by the fact that the U.S. response to South Asian problems has been shaped by its own changing relationship with the Soviet Union and China. Specifically, the U.S. actions in 1962, 1965 and 1971 were strongly influenced—if not dominated—first by its hostile relationship with Beijing, then by its coincidence of interest with Moscow, and then by the developing, warmer relationship with China. In the first instance American policy took the form of arms aid to India. In the second, the U.S. assumed a low profile, seeking to defuse the crisis by resorting to the UN, and ultimately, encouraging the Soviets to serve as the regional balancer. In the final instance, with its new relationship with Beijing on the line (or so American policy makers thought), the U.S. engaged in a major display of naval power and provided Pakistan with high-level diplomatic support—although not with any effective military assistance.

It is necessary to underscore the fact that South Asia itself has acquired a degree of autonomous influence on U.S. policy. Though of marginal importance, one obvious lesson is that it has attracted U.S. attention over the years (no more so than recently, following the Soviet intervention into Afghanistan, which we shall discuss below). For a marginal region, South Asia has attracted a considerable degree of U.S. attention and military and economic assistance.

Finally, it is important to note that within the U.S. itself, these periodic regional involvements—both conflictual and non-conflictual—have generated considerable conflict within the U.S. administration, and sometimes between the administration and Congress. The Food Aid and 1971 Bangladesh case studies reveal a high degree of presidential involvement in decision-making, while the 1962 Sino-Indian war study showed the broader executive branch predominating, but in all three there was considerable disagreement and conflict within the executive, and, in 1971, both within the executive and between it and Congress. Only in 1965, when the issue was essentially transferred to the UN, was there a degree of consensus within the decision-making process—and that largely because all parties had become tired with South Asia, and were in the process of leading America into a major involvement in Southeast Asia. It was only in the Johnson Presidency that we find that Congress was most directly involved in the making of South Asian foreign policy—especially the issues of emergency food aid (1965-7) and the earlier suspension of military and economic aid (1965). Neither Kennedy nor Nixon were constrained to consult the Congress regularly in making South Asian policy; the difference may well have been Johnson's own predilection to anticipate objections from and work with the institution he had known so well.

Interlude: American Policy Under Carter

It is not yet possible to construct detailed case studies of America's recent South Asia policy. The memoir literature is not particularly strong, and key documents and policy papers remain classified. Further, the major South Asian "crisis" of this period—the Soviet invasion of Afghanistan—has been extensively studied as a function of U.S.-Soviet relations, although not as a facet of Washington's South Asia policy.[2] We will here merely summarize some key events and decisions, and note how they compare with the other important turning points in America's regional policy.

Carter and the Bomb

After 1972—until the Soviet invasion of Afghanistan in December, 1979—global strategic issues were not uppermost in shaping American policy towards South Asia. In one sense, the U.S. again "forgot" about South Asia (as it had, strategically, after the 1965 Indo-Pakistan war). Henry Kissinger went so far as to state in a speech in New Delhi that the U.S. accepted India's preeminent position in South Asia, and even endorsed New Delhi's policy of non-alignment.[3] The initial American response to India's nuclear test in 1974 was apathy, as was (despite a few words of concern) Washington's response to the declaration of a State of Emergency by Indira Gandhi in June 1975.

American policy quickly reversed itself on both of these issues under Jimmy Carter, but he did not change the overall strategic approach to the region. Carter, whose mother had been a Peace Corps volunteer in India, praised the restoration of democracy under the Janata Government (in 1977), and made a highly publicized trip to India (but not Pakistan) in early 1978. However, his administration was obsessed with an issue that had only been lightly touched upon by his predecessors—nuclear proliferation—and this came to dominate U.S.-Indian and U.S.-Pakistan relations until the day the Soviets invaded Afghanistan.

As for India, even though the new Prime Minister (Morarji Desai) had gone out of his way to assure the United States that he had no intention to go nuclear, or even to stage another test (and Desai's anti-nuclear attitudes were widely known), the Carter administration pressed India to the point where relations were very deeply strained. Carter not only urged New Delhi to sign the NPT, but the new (1978) Nuclear Non-Proliferation Act passed by Congress—with administration encouragement—threatened what slim ties had been built up since 1972. It took a great deal of presidential pressure on Congress to get the release of two shipments of enriched uranium to India to keep the U.S.-supplied Tarapur atomic power station running (later, it took a great deal of complicated diplomacy by the Reagan administration to get the French to assume the resupply of Tarapur before the issue subsided).

U.S.-Pakistan relations were much worse. Despite evidence of a communist coup in Afghanistan, the fall of the Shah, growing Soviet regional ambitions, and the weak position of the American-trained General Zia ul-Haq in Islamabad, the Carter administration cut off all military and almost all economic assistance to Pakistan. The feeling was reciprocated—enraged Pakistani mobs burnt down the U.S. embassy in Islamabad and a number of American cultural centers on the basis of a false rumor concerning the Israeli occupation of the Great Mosque in Jerusalem. Ironically, Carter's rapid reversal of policy after the Soviet invasion (expressed by the imposition of a grain embargo on the Soviets, the boycott of the Moscow Olympics, the creation of the Rapid Deployment Force, and an offer in 1980—subsequently refused—of about $400 million in military aid to Pakistan) created new strains in Indo-U.S. relations.

Again, the U.S. found itself between two "friends," both of which it had recently alienated. And, again, as in 1962 (when it aided India) and 1971 (when it appeared to be aiding Pakistan), assistance to one was seen as a threat by the other. In this case, as was the case with Pakistan in 1962 and India in 1971, the country that was not offered assistance (India) not only felt that such assistance was a direct threat to its own security but that the cause of that assistance, the Soviet invasion, was being exaggerated by both the U.S. and Pakistan, and some Indian observers went so far as to claim that it was merely a pretext for the revival of a U.S.-China-Pakistan axis aimed at New Delhi.

The Carter administration ended its term with a South Asian policy in shambles. It had abandoned its own emphasis on nuclear proliferation and human rights, yet its failure to anticipate and counter-act the Soviet invasion was a major strategic embarrassment. It wound up with the worst of all worlds.

The Foreign Policy Process Under Carter

As we have noted,there was more congressional activism in American South Asian policy under Carter than previous administrations. This was largely confined to the areas of human rights and nuclear proliferation—where there were many activists within the administration itself. However, there was no "India" lobby or "Pakistan" lobby in Congress, nor were there organized private groups attempting to influence American policy towards the Subcontinent.

The earlier pro-Pakistani "lobby" of conservatives and the military had faded away after 1971, although it was weak even then. The "India lobby" was itself in shambles. Consisting largely of liberals and intellectuals, these groups were alienated first by the Indian nuclear test of 1974 and then the declaration of the State of Emergency in 1977. Many of those who had supported political and economic assistance for India in earlier years were disillusioned, others had turned to the recently 'opened' China. Jimmy Carter was enthusiastic over renewing ties with India, but not at the price of his human rights and non-proliferation policies.

Free of any pressure from such interest groups the administration could pursue its own policies towards South Asia, albeit under severe Congressional restraint (some of which it had itself encouraged). Thus, South Asian *policy* was largely made within the executive, although there was not much policy to make, given the overriding concern with proliferation and human rights. Perhaps the only significant new regional American initiative was the promotion of a regional river and water development project between Eastern India, Bangladesh, and Nepal. This initiative had begun in the National Security Council staff and although eventually backed by State, it was eventually lost in the rush of more dramatic events, and has not been revived.

The Reagan Administration: Renewed Aid to Pakistan

With the election of Ronald Reagan as president, American policy towards South Asia was again shaped predominantly by a perception of global strategic interests. Unlike Carter, who came late and apologetically to such concerns, Reagan and his principle advisers *began* with a consideration of strategic (i.e. Soviet and Chinese-related) issues. Pakistan was quickly identified and labeled as a "frontline" state, and offered a comprehensive $3.2 billion five-year package of military and economic aid. The Reagan administration also agreed to meet Pakistan's request for forty F-16 fighter planes, among the best in America's inventory. This package was renewed in 1987, with a slight increase.

The new arms package was justified to Congress on two broad policy grounds. The first was that the aid was necessary to allow Pakistan to defend itself against pressure from the Soviet Union and its Afghan ally. Implicitly, this aid would enable Pakistan to let the Mujahedin continue to use its territory and to channel weapons to these groups. In this sense, the aid package was a revival of the anti-communist assistance program of the 1950s and early 1960s, first Pakistan in 1954, and then to India in 1962. Interestingly, the latter relationship was also linked to cooperation between the U.S. and India in support of Tibetan guerillas operating in the People's Republic of China.

The second justification was, however, a departure from past American policy in two ways. First, it tried to address Congress' non-proliferation concerns. Administration spokesmen argued in 1981 that Pakistan had to feel "secure" in its conventional capabilities A conventionally secure Pakistan would have less incentive to pursue a covert nuclear weapons program. This policy had only limited success—later public revelations about the Pakistani nuclear program indicate that Islamabad continued to work on a nuclear weapon after 1981.[4]

The policy of contributing to Pakistan's sense of security by providing it with advanced conventional weapons was also a departure from previous American policy in that it implied that India was a threat to Pakistan, and that U.S. aid to Pakistan could be used against India. As we have seen, a bitter public dispute arose between the U.S. and India (and privately, between the U.S. and Pakistan) about Pakistan's use of American weapons against India in the 1965 war. Subsequent ad hoc arms sales to both India and Pakistan reduced or eliminated restrictions on use, but the 1981 sale was the first major break with the (unsuccessful) effort to provide weapons to Pakistan for use only against a communist threat.

The administration put heavy pressure on Congress to approve this aid package, arguing that Pakistan's strategic needs were so great that its nuclear weapons' activities and doubtful human rights record had to be excused. For its part, Congress went along with large annual appropriations for Pakistan from 1981 to 1988—i.e., as long as Islamabad was under direct Soviet pressure. While the Indian government early mounted an extensive public relations and diplomatic campaign against the Pakistan aid package it had no effect on Congress, and in part served to antagonize the conservative Reagan administration.

The Rediscovery of India

Interestingly (perhaps because it was in power for eight years and had time to adjust to regional military and strategic realities) the Reagan administration evolved its policy towards South Asia, and has constructed a shaky but possibly durable relationship with India, even while continuing to arm Pakistan.

For more than thirty years, India has very much resented what it sees as an American search for fostering a "balance of power" between Islamabad and New Delhi despite large differences in size and potential.[5] In an important sense therefore, barring the short-run exception of the Indo-U.S. honeymoon in the India-China war (1962), and sustained developmental assistance to New Delhi (although by 1988 the levels of direct bilateral assistance have fallen to about $10 million per year), the relationship between the two countries has been erratic. Initially, the Indo-American relationship had been constrained by controversial issues such as the concept of non-alignment, building military alliances, the Kashmir problem and other explosive global issues of the time. But, starting with the 1961 Goa episode, followed by divergencies over the Vietnam crisis and the accumulated pressure of Johnson's "short-tether" food aid policy, Indo-American differences reached an all-time low during the Bangladesh war (1971). It is also important to bear in mind—as our case studies have shown—that the periodic deterioration in relations between these two countries had been accelerated by their rather high and exaggerated mutual expectations.

Perhaps because expectations were so low by 1983-4 (India had refused to join the anti-Soviet chorus on Afghanistan, and the American government had succeeded in pushing through a major arms and economic assistance package for Pakistan) there was no place but up for Indo-U.S. relations to go. Both sides had come to realize that they needed each other, indirectly, on the Afghan-Soviet issue, but both had also come to an awareness of a whole range of new, non-strategic ties that were of value in their own right without neglecting Pakistan.

Since 1982 the U.S.-Indian relationship has been stabilized to some degree by making it more autonomous, i.e. by emphasizing growing bilateral issues and contacts. For example, major Indian migration to the U.S. following changes in the latter's immigration act in 1968 has created a large body of Indo-Americans with economic and cultural ties to both countries. This population is expected to reach one million by the end of this century. There are other important areas of cooperation: the sharing of advanced technology, joint anti-narcotics and anti-terrorist operations, and high-tech economic ties (India is one of the world's leading producers of software, some of it being exported via satellite back to the U.S.).

Thus, beginning hesitantly during Indira Gandhi's visit to the U.S. in 1982, but moving quickly after Rajiv Gandhi's successful visit in June 1985, both countries began to explore new areas of bilateral cooperation, while reserving the right to disagree on such issues as American aid to Pakistan, and India's continuing ties to the Soviet Union. Indeed, it was certainly a calculation on both sides that the new, non-strategic relationship might yield benefits on these strategic issues.[6] Surprisingly, these new ties were viewed favorably by President Zia of Pakistan, who had himself launched a "peace" campaign towards New Delhi. The Soviets raised no objection either and demonstrated their continued support for India by several very large sales of advanced weapons, including the lease of a nuclear powered attack submarine in 1988.

Policy and Process in the Reagan Administration

There is, as yet, little reliable evidence as to how the Reagan administration developed its policy towards a marginal region such as South Asia.[7] Certainly, there was little direct presidential interest in the area (Reagan never visited South Asia in eight years), and the higher levels of his administration saw the region largely in anti-Soviet, strategic terms. However, many middle-level bureaucrats and political appointees had extensive regional experience, and after 1983-4 began, without neglecting Pakistan, to subtly reshape American policy. This group was scattered throughout the Departments of State and Defense and their views were shared by a number of Congressmen. They conceived of and supported the "opening" to India; some were looking ahead to a post-Afghanistan period when the center of regional influence would shift eastward to New Delhi, others saw India as a legitimate, democratic counterpart to communist China, and still others saw India as the key to the proliferation problem.

However, American politics remains fragmented, nowhere more so than in the foreign policy process, which still lacks a consensus on many major (let alone relatively minor, regional) issues. Given the historic lack of continuity from administration to administration and the major changes now underway in South Asia itself it is unlikely that any issue coalition will survive into the next American administration, and if it does, whether it will pursue the same policies. We are in the pages above merely reiterating in a specific case the general conclusion of this book: there are no models and few general insights to guide us in our search for an understanding of the American foreign policy process over an extended period of time.

Notes

1. See two books in particular: Selig S. Harrison, *America and Asian Nationalism* (New York: The Free Press, 1978), and Jonathan Kwitny, *Endless Enemies* (New York: Viking Penguin, 1984).

2. For the former see Henry S. Bradsher, *Afghanistan and the Soviet Union* (Durham, N.C.: Duke Press Policy Studies, 1983), Zbigniew Brzezinski, *Game Plan* (Boston: Atlantic Monthly Press, 1986), and Selig S. Harrison, *In Afghanistan's Shadow: Baluch Nationalism and Soviet Temptations* (Washington, D.C.: Carnegie Endowment for International Peace, 1981).

3. See Secretary of State Henry Kissinger's speech to the Indian Council of World Affairs, New Delhi, on October 28, 1974.

4. For a survey see the various volumes by Leonard S. Spector: *Nuclear Proliferation Today* (New York: Vintage, 1984), *The New Nuclear Nations* (New York: Vintage, 1985), and *Going Nuclear* (Cambridge, Mass.: Ballinger, 1987).

5. Derived from John W. Mellor and Philip Oldenburg, "India and the United States," in John W. Mellor, ed., *India: A Middle Power* (Boulder: Westview Press, 1979), p. 4.

6. There are longstanding areas of conflict, of course. Bilaterally, these include the U.S. reluctance to aid India's nuclear program until India signs the NPT. Multilaterally, as we have noted, the continuing American aid relationship with Pakistan (projected even after the withdrawal of Soviet troops from Afghanistan), and American tolerance of Pakistan's nuclear program have been major irritants. On the other hand, the public American support given to India's peacekeeping mission in Sri Lanka in July 1987 showed that the U.S. had come to take seriously its long-standing proclamation that it regarded India as the region's preeminent power. But both sides have learned to cooperate around these obstacles.

7. For a brief statement by a former official see Stephen P. Cohen, "The Reagan Administration and India: Right for the Right Reasons?," *India International Centre Quarterly*, May, 1988.

Index

DATE DUE

HIGHSMITH #45230

Printed
In USA